Law and Democracy

Contemporary Questions

Law and Democracy

Contemporary Questions

Edited by Glenn Patmore and Kim Rubenstein

Australian
National
University

PRESS

ANU PRESS

Published by ANU Press
The Australian National University
Canberra ACT 0200, Australia
Email: anupress@anu.edu.au
This title is also available online at http://press.anu.edu.au

---

National Library of Australia Cataloguing-in-Publication entry

Title:	Law and democracy : contemporary questions / editors: Glenn Patmore, Kim Rubenstein.
ISBN:	9781925022018 (paperback) 9781925022063 (ebook)
Subjects:	Democracy--Australia
	Constitutional law--Australia.
	State, The.
	Political science--Australia
	Australia--Politics and government.

Other Creators/Contributors:
Patmore, G. A. (Glenn Anthony), 1961- editor.
Rubenstein, Kim, editor.

Dewey Number: 320.994

Cover design and layout by ANU Press

Contents

I. ASSUMPTIONS AND SCOPE OF CONSTITUTIONAL DEMOCRACY

II. ACCOUNTABILITY AND RESPONSIBLE GOVERNMENT

III. DEMOCRACY, LAW AND CULTURE

Preface

This book has evolved from ANU College of Law, Centre for International and Public Law's Seventeenth Annual Public Law weekend, held at The Australian National University from 20–22 September 2012.

The idea for the conference theme, 'Law's Challenge to Democracy/Democracy's Challenge to Law' was formulated through our discussions with Kim's ANU colleague, Dr Katharine Young, who assisted us in the work associated with organising the conference. We thank her for her enthusiastic intellectual contribution to the foundations for this book.

In addition to the contributors to this collection, there were other speakers who presented at the conference, who we would also like to acknowledge. They include, in the order they presented, Michael Kirby, Simon Butt, Phillip Tahmindjis, Moeen Cheema, Darren O'Donovan, Rosalind Dixon, Carlos Bernal, Svetlana Tyulkina, Louise Parrott, Brendan Lim, Claudia Geiringer, Robyn Holder, Paul Kildea, Ron Levy, Tim Gartrell, Shireen Morris, Rowan Mcrae, Elizabeth Bowes, Mark Jennings, Tania Voon, and Tom Smyth.

We are grateful for the support of ANU College of Law, including the College Outreach and Administrative Support Team (COAST). In addition to organising the logistics of the conference, they supported the organisation around the Annual Sawer lecture, presented by Professor Adrienne Stone, and the Annual Kirby Lecture in International Law, presented by Judge Christopher Weeramantry, both held around the 2012 Public Law weekend.

Following the conference, we felt there were valuable ideas that were worth developing into a substantial research contribution. We thank each of the contributors in this volume for responding to our call of 'expression of interest' and for taking on this work. We thank Professor Don Anton, Chair of the ANU Press Law Editorial Board, for shepherding the publication process, and Duncan Beard, who worked as our copy editor to ensure we met ANU Press's requirements.

Finally, we thank each of our families for the love and support they provide us in all that we do.

Glenn Patmore, University of Melbourne

Kim Rubenstein, The Australian National University

September 2014

1. Law and Democracy: Contemporary Questions

Glenn Patmore[1] and Kim Rubenstein[2]

Constitutional democracy is a contested concept. Caselaw since the early 1990s has recognised implied principles of representative and responsible government that go well beyond the mere text of the Australian Constitution, providing for a 'direct choice' of representatives by 'the people', and for electoral democracy.[3] These judicial implications remain contentious to the present day. Moreover, the constitutional conventions that provide accountability for responsible government are evolving and subject to challenge. In addition, law's regulation of political and popular culture is becoming increasingly important due to changing social circumstances and technological developments. These changes create challenges, which this book responds to by asking a number of fundamental questions:

- How should the meaning of 'the people' in the Australian Constitution be defined by the High Court of Australia?
- How do developing judicial conceptions of democracy define citizenship?
- What is the legal right to participate in the political community?
- Should political advisors to Ministers be subject to legal accountability mechanisms?
- What challenges do applied law schemes pose to notions of responsible government and how can they be best addressed?
- How can the study of the ritual of electoral politics in Australia and other common law countries supplement the standard account?
- How might the ritual of the pledge of Australian citizenship limit or enhance democratic participation?
- What is the conflict between legal restrictions of freedom of expression and democracy, and the role of social media?

---

1   g.patmore@unimelb.edu.au; Glenn Patmore wishes to thank for their assistance, Mr Tom Appleby, Ms Candice Parr and Ms Anna Seddon who read material to him and provided research assistance. Their work was much appreciated. Special thanks must also be given to the Melbourne Law Research Service.
2   kim.rubenstein@anu.edu.au.
3   Australian Constitution s 7: 'The Senate shall be composed of senators for each State, directly chosen by the people of the State, voting, until the Parliament otherwise provides, as one electorate'; s 24: 'The House of Representatives shall be composed of members directly chosen by the people of the Commonwealth, and the number of such members shall be, as nearly as practicable, twice the number of the senators.'

Examining the regulation of democracy this book brings together emerging and established scholars and practitioners with expertise in public law. It enriches public law scholarship, deepening and challenging the current conceptions of law's regulation of popular participation and legal representation. This volume is divided into three parts to identify the complexity and nuance of law and democracy in its contemporary doctrinal, conventional and socio-legal context.

These are:

- Assumptions and scope of constitutional democracy;
- The frontiers of accountability and responsible government; and
- Democracy, law and culture.

The purpose of the book is threefold. First, it raises and addresses a number of novel questions regarding law's regulation of democracy. Second, it aims to deepen our understanding of doctrinal scholarship by exploring its assumptions and its scope. Third, the book goes beyond doctrinal scholarship to consider important socio-legal questions about law's regulation of politics and culture. By considering a diverse range of topics pertaining to law's engagement with democracy in Australia and elsewhere, we believe the contemporary function of law will be better understood in its constitutional, political and cultural contexts.

Assumptions and scope of constitutional democracy

The modern conception of democracy is representative.[4] The Australian Constitution establishes representative government by requiring that senators and members be 'directly chosen by the people'.[5] In other words, the Parliament is regarded as representative since the citizens directly choose members of Parliament in regular elections.[6] However, very little about the electoral system is spelt out in the Australian Constitution.[7] The design and function of the electoral system was left to Parliament and the political process.[8] Moreover,

---

4   See Nicholas Aroney, 'Towards the "best explanation" of the Constitution: Text, Structure, History and Principle in Roach v Electoral Commissioner' (2011) 30(1) *University of Queensland Law Journal* 145. Anne Twomey, 'Rowe v Electoral Commissioner: Evolution or Creationism?' (2012) 31(2) *University of Queensland Law Journal*, 181–202; Jennifer Clarke, Patrick Keyzer and James Stellios, *Australian Constitutional Law Materials and Commentary* (Lexisnexis, 9th ed, 2013) 1210–16.

5   See Stephen J in *Ex rel McKinlay v The Commonwealth* (1975) 135 CLR 1 [20].

6   Suri Ratnapala and Jonathan Crowe, *Australian Constitutional Law: Foundations and Theory* (Oxford University Press, 3rd ed, 2012) 33.

7   David Clark, David Bamford and Judith Bannister, *Principles of Australian Public Law* (LexisNexis, 3rd ed, 2010) 175; Cheryl Saunders, *The Constitution of Australia: A Contextual Analysis* (Hart Publishing, 2011) 110.

8   ibid.

key democratic concepts are not defined in the Australian Constitution, such as 'the people', 'citizenship' and 'political participation'. While the representative principle remains strong, there are uncertainties that exist, due to the sparse provisions for the establishment of democracy in the Australian Constitution.[9] This uncertainty is reflected in High Court jurisprudence.

Elisa Arcioni addresses the meaning of the term 'the people' in the Constitution, highlighting the High Court's murky and complex treatment of the term. She considers cases on the meaning of the terms 'representative government' and 'alien', focusing respectively on who is included in, and who is excluded from the term 'the people'. The High Court has resolved the tensions in these definitional issues by identifying 'the people' through legislative developments, which has constitutionalised that membership. Arcioni concludes that whether we prefer deferral to the parliamentary choices over time recognised in legislative developments, as a new form of constitutional construction, or the judicial application of standards seen in other legal sources, depends not on an absolute rule regarding constitutional interpretation but rather on classic differences of viewpoint regarding the role of judicial review.

Kim Rubenstein and Niamh Lenagh-Maguire explain that there is no expressly defined concept of citizenship in the Australian Constitution. Citizenship is defined by Commonwealth legislation and in its relationship with the concept of representative government. After explaining the significance of citizenship in Australia's democratic structure, they examine the important case of *Re MIMIA; ex parte Ame*, which tied citizenship to voting rights, a 'thin' conception of citizenship. They argue for the adoption of a 'thicker' or broader conception of citizenship focusing on rights, political participation and identity. This offers the potential for a deeper understanding of citizenship to inform judicial development and popular views.

Glenn Patmore examines the right to participate in democratic decision making. The modern conception of democracy recognises a right of citizens to elect representatives to make legislative and executive decisions on their behalf. While this is a relatively limited conception of participation, his chapter illustrates how it can usefully define the scope and structure of contemporary constitutional democracy. He examines how this right to participate in collective decisions is authorised in the Constitution, legislation, and constitutional conventions. Patmore also enlarges upon the more limited understanding of the constitutional protection of the right to vote or to participate in the political life of the community referred to by members of the High Court in recent decisions. Like others, Patmore argues that the constitutional protection of the right to vote

---

9   Suri Ratnapala and Jonathan Crowe, *Australian Constitutional Law: Foundations and Theory* (Oxford University Press, 3rd ed, 2012).

may act to entrench democratic rights like the secret ballot that have hitherto only been recognised in legislation. He also posits that there is a permeability between the norms of the Constitution and legislation in order to help better understand the nature and scope of this right. Thus, he conceives the right to participate to include the making of legislative and executive decisions, not just voting in elections.

Accountability and responsible government

The grand difficulty in politics is how to make the few accountable to the many. In Australia, formal accountability is provided through the principle of representative and responsible government. Representative democracy means that representatives are accountable to electors and responsible government means that Ministers must be members of Parliament, and accountable to it. Responsible government has been described as a chain of command or responsibility. According to the 'chain' metaphor, the Queen and Governor-General are accountable to Ministers, who are accountable to the Parliament, which is in turn accountable to the people. Thus, officials are either responsible for or subject to the control of others. Only a few of the essential links in this chain are expressly recognised in the Constitution, for instance the requirement that Ministers must be members of Parliament and heads of government departments. Other conditions are to be found in the constitutional conventions of responsible government. According to constitutional convention, public servants are accountable to Ministers, who are accountable to the Parliament.

Two chapters address contemporary challenges to effective accountability provided by the system of responsible government. Yee-Fui Ng examines the responsibility of ministerial advisers. According to the principle of responsible government, Ministers receive advice from ministerial advisers, and are answerable for the implementation of that advice. Unlike public servants, ministerial advisors are not subject to public accountability mechanisms. However, Yee-Fui Ng argues that ministerial advisers are increasingly exercising executive power beyond what is allowed in the Statement of Standards for Ministerial Staff, and should therefore be subject to legal accountability mechanisms. These include appearing before parliamentary committees, as part of the concept of responsible government and judicial review under section 75(v) of the Constitution. She concludes that such measures would generate a more nuanced and multi-faceted notion of accountability. While Yee-Fui Ng examines the accountability of ministerial advisers, Joe Edwards examines accountability under intergovernmental agreements and their effects on the efficacy of responsible government. Edwards explains that applied law schemes are intergovernmental agreements, in which the various interested jurisdictions

— either the Commonwealth and the States and Territories, or just the States and Territories — agree that a particular area requires regulatory uniformity through the adoption of a model law. These schemes can be administered by the Commonwealth, by States, by both, or by an independent authority. Edwards asks whether applied law schemes might undermine the accountability provided by responsible government. This doctrine assumes the voters have sufficient information to hold the government to account through elections at the ballot box. Given the complexity of applied law schemes, it appears that the chains of accountability become blurred and difficult to ascertain for citizens and legal advisors. Edwards concludes that while applied law schemes challenge traditional conceptions of accountability, ultimately they should be retained given they are capable of balancing the aim of regulatory uniformity with the requirement of responsible government.

Democracy, law and culture

The laws and institutions we adopt necessarily shape political participation. According to participatory theorists of democracy, citizens, through participation in democratic practices and institutions, can develop a 'public-spirited type of character' or may become a 'community-minded individual'. This is regarded as the 'educative effect' of democracy, which occurs through participation, not necessarily formal education. While this might be regarded as an idealised version of democracy, it challenges us to consider how participation in democratic institutions can promote self-development. Enhancing self-development provides an important rationale for contemporary representative democracy. Laws may provide opportunities for enhanced development such as through participation in voting, jury service and in small-scale organisations such as workplaces and community organisations.

The function of political participation and law is analysed by three contributors, taking us beyond the traditional educative function of democracy, with its focus on participation in political decision-making. These chapters examine popular forms of civic participation and democratic culture and its impact on the individual.

Two contributors address the role of ritual in politics that are authorised by the law. Graeme Orr examines the ritual dimensions of electoral law, explaining that the way the law structures an election creates a shared experience, patterned by norms. Political participation in Election Day creates a communal event — a ritual of diverse shared experiences: for some, a chore, a public duty or a confessional moment. However, as Orr explains, 'the ritual is primarily built up in the patterned behaviour — what transpires in the internal reflections of different individuals is another matter'. One important pattern is based around the legal obligation to vote, which occurs on the one day that our secular society congregates to renew the mandate of representatives. Appreciating this enables us to better understand the social power of Australian electoral law. Orr also compares the ritual element of electoral law in Australia with the United States and the United Kingdom.

Anne Macduff examines the ritual of the citizenship pledge, and explains how it gives meaning to the state's conception of the ideal citizen. The pledge states:

> From this time forward [under God]
>
> I pledge my loyalty to Australia and its people
>
> Whose democratic rights and liberties I respect, and
>
> Whose laws I will uphold and obey.

While the citizenship applicant has the choice not to affirm with the words 'under God', they must make the pledge publicly at a citizenship ceremony. Macduff is critical of the public performance of the pledge and its content. She makes two key criticisms:

- The ritual situates the Australian ideal citizen as being obedient, compliant and law-abiding; and
- Although the pledge includes words such as 'democratic beliefs', 'rights' and 'freedoms, these words of the pledge do not clearly convey the active agency of Australian citizenship.

By active citizenship, she means 'more than political participation within the existing framework of laws and institutions, and includes critical protests that question the founding framework'. However, she notes that once a migrant becomes a citizen, 'they are legally free to engage in Australian democracy as they choose and to benefit from the democratic freedoms that other Australian citizens have'. Interestingly, while these rights and freedoms are referred to in the words of the pledge, she sees the ritual of the pledge as potentially adversely influencing future citizens' active engagement in democratic politics. She argues that the submission to legal authority embodied in the ritual of the pledge has the capacity to 'influence the behavior of candidates after they become citizens'.

Stephen Tully examines the political participation of citizens in democratic culture through social media. While Orr adopts a socio-legal approach, and Macduff adopts a critical legal studies perspective, Tully's analysis is grounded in respect of liberal rights. First, he considers how social media may enhance and limit democratic participation. Not only does he consider its opportunities and limits but, like Orr and Macduff, his work highlights the importance of the experience of democratic participation, in this case through social media. Tully provides examples of its use in countries like Egypt and Tunisia, where he examines social media's ability to shape democratic culture. Secondly, he highlights how legal restrictions can curtail democratic opportunities. While democratic states acknowledge the importance of freedom of expression through social media, they have justified some limits to protect national security and law enforcement. While some limits are legitimate, others are not. Tully argues that, '[s]tated at its highest, the use by governments of blocking or filtering technology violates the obligation of States to guarantee freedom of expression'. The freedom to participate through social media is also threatened in non-democratic countries. This includes by removing internet-content and by sometimes banning social media altogether. Tully's analysis highlights the tension between the new opportunities provided by social media for democratic participation, and resistance by the state through law. Social media can be perceived as a threat to the safety and stability of the state or, more contentiously, when it challenges the socio-political status quo.

Conclusion

While constitutional democracy has existed for over a century in Australia, key concepts in the field continue to be contested and developed. Some of these concepts have not been questioned and examined in sufficient detail. The contributions in this volume identify the value of rethinking the assumptions and scope of this field. Some contributors argue that the current constitutional assumptions need to be broadened in light of contemporary theories of democracy. Others propose reforms to accountability mechanisms for responsible government. Some others contend that the discipline needs to respond to new cultural and social realities. Thus, this book does not aim to provide a single answer; after all the law of democracy is multi-faceted and complex. Rather, this book offers a rich selection of new ways of thinking and provides us with new approaches to interpreting existing laws as well as understanding law in its broader social context.

I. Assumptions and Scope of Constitutional Democracy

2. Democracy and the Constitution: The People Deciding the Identity of 'the people'

Elisa Arcioni[1]

Introduction

The phrase 'the people' appears at the beginning of the preamble to the Australian Constitution, where the people of the colonies are recognised as 'the people' who 'agreed to unite in one indissoluble federal Commonwealth'. That agreement is a reference to the referenda held in each colony to accept the draft Constitution, which had been drafted by predominantly elected delegates to the constitutional conventions in the late 1890s.[2] Those conventions resulted in a *Constitution Bill* which was taken to the United Kingdom by the Australian delegation and, with one significant alteration,[3] was passed by the Imperial Parliament.

There had been an earlier attempt, in 1891, to adopt a Constitution. However, due to a lack of political will in NSW and a depression, it did not progress through the colonial Parliaments as had been planned.[4] The second attempt involved 'the people' both in the political movement for federation, as well as in the drafting and acceptance of the *Constitution Bill*. 'The people' played a big role in the final successful push for a Constitution.[5]

---

1   elisa.arcioni@sydney.edu.au.
2   For the history of the two conventions and the various referenda see John M Williams, *The Australian Constitution: A Documentary History* (Melbourne University Press, 2005). Western Australia is not mentioned in the preamble, as its people did not vote in a referendum to accept the draft until after the draft was taken to the United Kingdom for passage through the Imperial Parliament. Covering clause 3 refers to the possibility of Western Australia being joined in the Commonwealth if the people of Western Australia agreed to the Bill. They did so through referendum on 31 July 1900 and the Constitution came into effect from 1 January 1901.
3   Section 74 was amended to retain some appeals to the Privy Council. See J A La Nauze, *The Making of the Australian Constitution* (Melbourne University Press, 1972) ch 16. In addition, covering clause 2 was amended to remove the statement that 'This Act shall bind the Crown' and covering clause 6 was amended to remove the definition of 'colony'.
4   For details on this period, see John M Williams, *The Australian Constitution: A Documentary History* (Melbourne University Press, 2005).
5   See Helen Irving, *To Constitute a Nation: A Cultural History of Australia's Constitution* (Cambridge University Press, revised ed, 1999) ch 8 'The People'. It is particularly interesting to note, for the argument later developed, that not all women were fully part of 'the people' in terms of voting rights at the time of the

The phrase 'the people' appears in sections 7 and 24 of the Constitution. Section 7 requires that senators be directly chosen by the 'people of the States' and s 24 requires that members of the House of Representatives be directly chosen by 'the people of the Commonwealth'. Those choices occur by election.[6] Section 128 provides for the electors in the States and Territories to vote in referenda, which is the process by which the text of the Constitution can be changed.[7] There are also a number of other references to 'the people' in the Constitution,[8] or to other categories of persons.[9]

Read together, these sections reflect the fact that 'the people' were involved in the making of the Constitution, are involved in making amendments to the constitutional text, and are the ones who choose members of Federal Parliament. Who are these people? For the purpose of this chapter,[10] I begin with the premise that what connects the different manifestations of 'the people' in the Constitution is an idea of the constitutional community. 'The people' is a reference to that community, which has both legal and symbolic implications. The constitutional community is a concept which reflects the fact that every Constitution governs a community of people, which exists separate from the document, but whose *constitutional* identity is affected by the Constitution itself. This draws on the work of scholars such as Michel Rosenfeld.[11]

In the Australian context, an understanding of who is included or excluded from the constitutional community informs not only the categories of membership,

---

'final successful push for a Constitution'. See Kim Rubenstein and Deborah Cass, 'Representation/s of Women in the Australian Constitutional System' (1995) 17 *Adelaide Law Review* 3 and Helen Irving (ed) *A Woman's Constitution?: Gender and History in the Australian Commonwealth* (Hale & Iremonger, 1996).

6   See for example the textual indication of this in s 7 'voting', ss 8 and 30 'qualification of electors'.

7   The process also necessarily involves the Parliament and the Governor-General.

8   For example, reference to 'the people' in s 53.

9   For example, reference to 'subjects of the Queen' in s 117.

10   For other work regarding the identity of the constitutional 'people', see Elisa Arcioni, 'Identity at the Edge of Constitutional Membership' in K Rubenstein, M Nolan and F Jenkins (eds), *Allegiance and Identity in a Globalised World* (Cambridge University Press, forthcoming) addressing the status of the people of the Territories; Elisa Arcioni, 'Excluding Indigenous Australians from "the people": A Reconsideration of Sections 25 and 127 of the Constitution' (2012) 40(3) *Federal Law Review* 287; as well as a preliminary overview in Elisa Arcioni, 'That Vague but Powerful Abstraction: The Concept of "the people" in the Australian Constitution' (Paper presented at Gilbert + Tobin Constitutional Law Conference, Sydney, 20 February 2009) http://www.gtcentre.unsw.edu.au/sites/gtcentre.unsw.edu.au/files/mdocs/469_ElisaArcioni.pdf.

11   See Michel Rosenfeld, *The Identity of the Constitutional Subject: Selfhood, Citizenship, Culture, and Community* (Routledge, 2010) as developed in Symposium, 'Comments on Michel Rosenfeld's The Identity of the Constitutional Subject' (2012) 33(5) *Cardozo Law Review* 1839. I acknowledge that there is a debate regarding the identity and role of the constituent people before a Constitution is formed. It is sufficient for the purposes of this chapter to note that there is a theory that the constituent power, which has the authority to create the Constitution, becomes the constituted people upon enactment of the Constitution. This raises difficult questions regarding precisely who was the constituent authority and on what basis, to what extent membership of the constituent authority automatically translates into membership of the constituted people, and how to address changes in the composition of the constituted people over time. See, for example, Ulrich K Preuss, 'Constitutional Powermaking of the New Polity: Some Deliberations on the Relations Between Constituent Power and the Constitution' in Michel Rosenfeld (ed), *Constitutionalism, Identity, Difference, and Legitimacy: Theoretical perspectives* (Duke University Press, 1994) 143.

but also the nature of the constitutional community. However, simply re-naming 'the people' as the community under the Australian Constitution does not get us very far in understanding who those people are. Thus I arrive at the focus of this chapter. Here I look at the method adopted by the Australian High Court in trying to grapple with the meaning of this phrase, 'the people'.

The jurisprudence of the Court regarding the phrase 'the people' is addressed in this chapter through an examination of two groups of cases. The first is a series of cases concerned with representative government, and most recently focusing on the exercise of the federal franchise. The second is a series of cases about migration or deportation, centred on the constitutional concept of 'alien'.

By looking to the text of the Constitution, it is obvious why the phrase 'the people' is of concern in cases relating to the system of representative government. Representative government is centred on what has been referred to as the bedrock of 'choice by the people',[12] in the sections to which I have already referred — ss 7 and 24 — whereby the people of the States and Commonwealth directly choose the members of Federal Parliament. In the representative government cases, especially the most recent ones, a majority of the High Court has given great weight to that phrase 'chosen by the people', to the extent of invalidating legislation because the legislation was inconsistent with that mandate.[13] Not only is there a series of cases referring to 'the people', from which to extract patterns regarding how we can understand that category, but those cases also show how jurisprudentially significant that phrase can be.

The second series of cases, relating to migration or deportation, is not as obviously connected to the phrase 'the people'. As Gleeson CJ stated in the case of *Singh v Commonwealth*: 'Sometimes the problem of meaning lies, not in understanding the concept that a particular word or expression signifies, but in understanding the relationship between a number of concepts referred to in the Constitution.'[14] That is true of the migration cases, in which a number of categories intersect to inform the meaning of 'the people'.

The migration cases are relevant to understanding the meaning of 'the people' because they assist in determining boundaries of membership. The cases all turn on the status of 'alien', referred to in s 51(xix) of the Constitution, which grants the Federal Parliament power to make laws with respect to aliens.[15] Aliens are individuals who fall outside the constitutional community. By understanding who is considered to be outside the constitutional community, we get some

---

12 *Rowe v Electoral Commissioner* (2010) 243 CLR 1, 12 [1] (French CJ), referring to *Roach v Electoral Commissioner* (2007) 233 CLR 162, 198 [82] (Gummow, Kirby and Crennan JJ).

13 ibid.

14 *Singh v Commonwealth* (2004) 222 CLR 322, 334 [15].

15 It also grants power regarding naturalisation. This aspect becomes relevant in underpinning at least aspects of citizenship legislation which affect the reasoning in the second group of cases, addressed below.

guidance as to the outer limits of that community, an idea of what line forms the boundary. Such an understanding assists in determining who falls on the right side of the boundary, and therefore within the constitutional 'people'.

These two groups of cases, regarding representative government and 'aliens', help us to understand who the constitutional 'people' are. The connection I make between those groups of cases is a reflection on the method of reasoning adopted by a majority of the Court. That connection is in the use of legislative indications of membership in determining the meaning of constitutional terms.

My argument in this chapter is that when the Court tries to work out these questions, concerning who is included as amongst 'the people', or who is excluded by being an 'alien', a majority of the Court defers to, or uses in some form, *legislative* indications of membership in order to determine the content of the *constitutional* concepts. While the Court starts and ends with a constitutional expression, the way it fills the constitutional expression with meaning is to see what the legislature has done in the areas of law affected by that phrase, in order to decide what the constitutional limits might be. This indicates broader issues regarding constitutional interpretation. In the next section, I outline how this method of reasoning operates in both groups of cases. I then indicate some of the implications of this pattern and how this approach can be understood as the Court's deferring to the people's indication of their own identity.

The reasoning in the representative government cases

Over a series of cases from the 1970s,[16] the High Court confirmed that there is a system of representative government contained within the Constitution. After some changes in approach, the current view is that the constitutional elements of that system are those required by the text and structure of the Constitution,[17] not freestanding principles of democracy or politics more generally.

What is a common element amongst these cases is the requirement of choice by 'the people' as the heart of the system of government, and that constitutional implications may arise from that phrase. The most significant implication is

---

16   There were earlier mentions of elements of representative government, for example *Judd v McKeon* (1926) 38 CLR 380 where the notion of 'choice' was at issue.

17   See especially the unanimous statement in *Lange v Australian Broadcasting Corporation* (1997) 189 CLR 520.

the implied freedom of political communication.[18] That implied freedom was deemed to be necessary in order for the people to make an informed choice as required by ss 7, 24 and 128 of the Constitution.

Two of the most recent cases addressing the system of representative government under the Constitution are the cases which are the focus here — *Roach v Electoral Commissioner*[19] and *Rowe v Electoral Commissioner.*[20] *Roach* was a challenge to the blanket disenfranchisement of prisoners from the federal franchise, on the basis that it breached ss 7 and 24 of the Constitution. The majority struck down the legislation. The majority reasoned that the power of the Parliament to determine the franchise was restricted by the requirement of ss 7 and 24 that parliamentarians be 'directly chosen by the people'. Limited disenfranchisement was allowed, but to disenfranchise *all* prisoners went beyond the justifiable limits on the federal franchise.

Rowe was a case which challenged the timing of the closing of the electoral rolls prior to the 2010 federal election. Parliament had passed legislation which reduced the amount of time within which eligible persons could enrol to vote following the calling of an election. The Court, again by majority, struck down the legislation as being inconsistent with the constitutional mandate of choice by 'the people'. The detriment caused by the legislation outweighed any potential benefits of the early closing of the rolls.

In those two cases, a majority of the Court used the notion of choice by 'the people' to invalidate the laws in question. In examining the meaning of that phrase, and determining who 'the people' are, the majority started from the position that a universal adult franchise is now protected by the Constitution. That is, that all capable adult citizens should have the right to vote. This was the baseline against which the Court in *Roach* determined whether it was justifiable to disenfranchise all prisoners, and against which the Court in *Rowe* determined whether the legislature could shorten the timeframe between calling the election and closing the electoral roll.

Focusing on how the Court determined that such a broad franchise is protected reveals the significance of legislative indications of membership in defining the constitutional meaning of 'the people'. Gleeson CJ is the most explicit in his use of legislation. He states that universal adult franchise is protected by ss 7 and

---

18   The settled doctrine relating to this freedom was established in a unanimous judgment in *Lange v Australian Broadcasting Corporation* (1997) 189 CLR 520, as refined in *Coleman v Power* (2004) 220 CLR 1 and accepted in recent cases such as *Attorney-General (SA) v Corporation of the City of Adelaide* [2013] HCA 3 and *Monis v The Queen; Droudis v the Queen* [2013] HCA 4. *Lange* followed on from earlier cases including *Australian Capital Television Pty Ltd v Commonwealth* (1992) 177 CLR 106, *Nationwide News Pty Ltd v Wills* (1992) 177 CLR 1.

19   *Roach v Electoral Commissioner* (2007) 233 CLR 162.

20   *Rowe v Electoral Commissioner* (2010) 243 CLR 1.

24.[21] This is because 'long established universal adult suffrage' is 'an historical development of constitutional significance'.[22] What this means is that, because of changed historical circumstances, ss 7 and 24 'have come to be a constitutional protection of the right to vote'.[23]

Significantly, included in those historical circumstances is 'legislative history'.[24] The relevant legislative history addressed in the case is that relating to the federal franchise. Today there is an almost universal adult franchise. Adult citizens have a right to vote unless they fall into a number of discrete and non-arbitrary categories, and only a small, closed category of adult non-citizens have a right to vote.[25] The remainder of Gleeson CJ's judgment is about what exceptions are allowed from that general right to vote, and how they can be justified. The conclusion in *Roach* was that the blanket disenfranchisement went too far, but that disenfranchisement of prisoners with a minimum sentence of three years was valid.[26]

The joint majority judgment of Gummow, Kirby and Crennan JJ displays the same method. They approach the question by looking at the central conception of representative government. The implied freedom of political communication, discussed above, is one aspect of that system. However, these judges say that voting is even more central; it is at the heart of the system of representative government. In identifying the centrality of voting to the constitutional system of government, they state that '[g]iven the particular Australian experience with the expansion of the franchise in the nineteenth century, well in advance of that in the United Kingdom, this hardly could be otherwise'.[27] This statement comes after their having outlined the details of the legislative changes from colonial times to today, with respect to the franchise.

The joint judgment then moves to what was Gleeson CJ's second step in his reasoning, stating: 'The question with respect to legislative disqualification *from what otherwise is adult suffrage* … thus becomes a not unfamiliar one. Is the disqualification for a substantial reason?'[28] Thus, Gummow, Kirby and Crennan JJ also accept the 'bedrock' of universal adult franchise, which has achieved that status due to changed legislation over time, and anything abrogating that rule must be justified.

---

21   *Roach v Electoral Commissioner* (2007) 233 CLR 162, 173–4 [6].
22   ibid 174 [7].
23   ibid.
24   ibid.
25   See current manifestation in the *Commonwealth Electoral Act 1918* (Cth).
26   This suggests something about the normative nature of 'the people', in privileging 'good' behaviour and penalising 'bad' behaviour — see the reference to 'conduct which manifests such a rejection of civic responsibility as to warrant temporary withdrawal of a civic right' in *Roach v Electoral Commissioner* (2007) 233 CLR 162, 174-5 [8] (Gleeson CJ).
27   *Roach v Electoral Commissioner* (2007) 233 CLR 162, 198 [80]–[81].
28   ibid 199 [85], (emphasis added).

In the case of *Rowe*, which followed three years after *Roach*, the majority once again deferred to legislative indications of membership of 'the people'. Chief Justice French was most explicit about this. Early in his judgment, French CJ stated: 'The content of the constitutional concept of "chosen by the people" has evolved since 1901 and is now informed by the universal adult-citizen franchise which is prescribed by Commonwealth law.' He continued, stating that the constitutional concept of choice by the people has acquired 'a more democratic content than existed at Federation. That content, being constitutional in character, although it may be subject to adjustment from time to time, cannot now be diminished.'[29]

French CJ was indicating that the meaning of choice by the people has changed. But he goes further and makes it clear that it is the changes in *legislation* over time that have determined the changed constitutional meaning. He refers to McTiernan and Jacobs JJ's judgment in *Attorney-General of the Commonwealth; ex rel McKinlay v the Commonwealth*,[30] which Gleeson CJ had referred to in *Roach*. The joint judgment in *McKinlay* had, in turn, referred to the constitutional meaning being linked to the 'common understanding of the time'.[31] French CJ states that 'common understanding' is not 'judicial understanding'.[32] This seems to be a distinction between the views of the community generally (the 'common understanding'), compared with the view of the judiciary. French CJ says that 'durable legislative development of the franchise is a more reliable touchstone. It reflects a persistent view by the elected representatives of the people of what the term "chosen by the people" requires.'[33] Then, as in *Roach*, the remainder of his judgment is about whether the law in question breaches that command, which in this instance the majority decided was the case.

The joint judgment of Gummow and Bell JJ in *Rowe* adopts the reasoning and conclusion of Gleeson CJ in *Roach* with respect to the universal adult franchise being constitutionalised.[34] In her concurring judgment, Crennan J also refers to Gleeson CJ in *Roach*.[35] Crennan J reasons that representative government must be democratic. Democratic representation is given content by the 'common understanding', which is to come from legislative development. Crennan J then reaches her conclusion that 'a fully inclusive franchise — that is a franchise free of arbitrary exclusions based on class, gender or race', is now constitutionalised.[36]

---

29 *Rowe v Electoral Commissioner* (2010) 243 CLR 1, 18 [18].
30 *Attorney-General of the Commonwealth; ex rel McKinlay v The Commonwealth* (1975) 135 CLR 1.
31 ibid 35–37.
32 *Rowe v Electoral Commissioner* (2010) 243 CLR 1, 18 [19].
33 ibid.
34 ibid 48–9 [123].
35 ibid 107 [328].
36 ibid 117 [368].

Thus, the majority judges, in both of the most recent cases concerned with the system of representative government and the phrase 'chosen by the people', have all used legislative indications of membership to determine 'the people' who should be doing the choosing. It is the pattern of membership that the judges see in legislation which provides the meaning of the phrase 'chosen by the people', particularly, who are 'the people' who should be able to exercise a choice through a federal vote.

The reasoning in the 'alien' cases

I now turn to the second group of cases, the 'alien' cases, to demonstrate that in a separate area of constitutional jurisprudence, the Court is using legislative indications to determine membership of the constitutional community. Here the Court does so by considering who can be excluded from that community through characterisation as a constitutional 'alien'.

The status of 'alien' is provided for in 51(ixx) of the Constitution, which the Federal Parliament has used to support its migration legislation since the 1980s.[37] Cases arising under that legislation are usually about whether or not someone can be deported as an alien. In these cases, as with the cases regarding representative government addressed above, a majority of the Court uses legislative indications of membership or exclusion from membership, in the course of reaching a conclusion about whether someone is a constitutional alien.

The cases are consistent in identifying allegiance as the touchstone of alien status. If a person has no allegiance to any state, then that person is an alien. This includes stateless people, as seen in *Al-Kateb v Godwin*.[38] If a person has allegiance to a foreign nation, then he or she can also be classed as an alien, as seen in the example of British subjects since 1986 in the cases of *Shaw v Minister for Immigration and Multicultural Affairs*[39] and *Nolan v Minister for Immigration and Ethnic Affairs*.[40]

Significant for my argument here is how the Court determines a person's allegiance. Members of the majority in these alien cases look to legislation, particularly citizenship legislation. There are two ways in which this has

---

37   See the *Migration Amendment Act 1983* (Cth), which came into effect on 2 April 1984. Prior to that, the immigration power in s 51(xxvii) was the foundation for that legislation. The interaction between the two powers and the doctrine of absorption is beyond the scope of this chapter, but for noting that absorption into the Australian community (which makes someone a non-immigrant) does not necessarily make an alien a non-alien and therefore immune from deportation: Genevieve Ebbeck, 'A Constitutional Concept of Australian Citizenship' (2004) 25(2) *Adelaide Law Review* 137, 145-153.

38   *Al-Kateb v Godwin* (2004) 219 CLR 562.

39   *Shaw v Minister for Immigration and Multicultural Affairs* (2003) 218 CLR 28.

40   *Nolan v Minister of State for Immigration and Ethnic Affairs* (1988) 165 CLR 178.

occurred. The first is by considering how alienage was understood at federation and concluding that it was a status which was inherently given meaning at that time through legislation. When the Court refers or defers to the meaning at federation in order to understand the current application of the constitutional term, it has adopted the meaning as affected by legislation of that era. The second approach is the Court ascribing constitutional significance to legislation in the post-federation era, by looking to Australian legislation since the enactment of the Constitution, in order to give the meaning of 'alien' current content. In this part, I address those two approaches, as well as noting a more specific use of an individual piece of legislation, to demonstrate the ability of the Parliament to determine, at least to some extent, the constitutional meaning of 'alien'.

Before proceeding, I note the relationship between constitutional 'alien' at the heart of these cases and the concept of 'the people'. 'The people' is a reference to the constitutional community. Aliens are those outside that community. By understanding what makes someone an alien, and therefore an outsider, we can understand who is *not* an alien and therefore an *insider* — one of 'the people'.

Using pre-federation legislation

The first way in which the Court uses legislative indications of the constitutional meaning of 'alien' is when it looks to the meaning of that term at the time of the federation of the Australian colonies. It is well-accepted that historical materials can be used in interpreting the Australian Constitution.[41] Despite the many disagreements and nuances regarding the use of such materials,[42] some regard for historical meaning is common to most exercises of constitutional interpretation.[43]

---

41 See for example the statement regarding use of convention debates in *Cole v Whitfield* (1988) 165 CLR 360. However, note that there are problems with using such materials, as well as other historical materials. See Helen Irving, 'Constitutional Interpretation, the High Court, and the Discipline of History' (2013) 41(1) *Federal Law Review*.

42 See for example the debate regarding originalism, both in Australia and in the US: Philip Bobbitt, *Constitutional Interpretation* (Blackwell, 1991); Greg Craven, 'Original Intent and Australian Constitution: Coming Soon to a Court Near You?' (1990) 1(2) *Public Law Review* 166; Jeffrey Goldsworthy, 'Originalism in Constitutional Interpretation' (1997) 25(1) *Federal Law* Review 1; Simon Evans, 'The Meaning of Constitutional Terms: Essential Features, Family Resemblance and Theory-Based Approaches' (2006) 29(3) *University of New South Wales Law Journal* 207.

43 I avoid using the term originalism here, as there is a distinction made in the literature between using historical materials for the purpose of establishing an originalist understanding of the Constitution, and using materials from the time of enactment to determine the meaning in a textualist sense. See the recent debate between Antonin Scalia and Richard Posner, in Antonin Scalia and Bryan A Garner, *Reading Law: The Interpretation of Legal Texts* (Thomson/West, 2012) and Richard A Posner, 'The Incoherence of Antonin Scalia' (2012) *New Republic*, http://www.newrepublic.com/article/magazine/books-and-arts/106441/scalia-garner-reading-the-law-textual-originalism. My interest in materials from the past is focused on the use of legislation, not the competing arguments regarding the different schools of interpretation.

The argument I make here is that the Court uses pre-federation legislation in order to understand the current meaning of 'alien'. The legislation in question is related to the law of nationality and citizenship. The history of that law as it now applies in Australia extends back to common law doctrines in Britain. The doctrine relating to subject and alien status in the United Kingdom developed over time into a statutory creature, with legislative incursions into the common law principles in Britain, in the Australian colonies prior to federation and then in Commonwealth law post-federation.[44]

The joint judgment of Gummow, Hayne and Heydon JJ in *Singh v Commonwealth*[45] provides an example of the use of pre-federation legislation. That judgment focused on the development of nationality laws in the UK prior to federation, in order to conclude that the meaning of 'alien' was not fixed by the common law. In that case, Tania Singh, a girl born in Australia of non-citizen parents, was resisting characterisation as an alien. The joint judgment in that case said that history shows that legislative changes had affected the meaning of 'alien' as understood at federation. That led to the majority in that case coming to the conclusion that Tanya Singh could be considered an alien, despite her birth in Australia.[46]

The relevance of pre-federation legislation is seen in the majority's view that the law of British subject status was in flux, with significant legislative incursions into the common law principles. They therefore rejected the idea that birth within the realm necessarily made someone a subject,[47] who could not be an alien, because legislation had interfered with that principle.

Using post-federation legislation

It is not only pre-federation legislation which has an impact on the Court's understanding of constitutional alienage. Australian legislation post-federation was a factor in determining the status of British subjects who were not Australian citizens, with the conclusion that they are now aliens. This is seen most clearly in the judgment in *Nolan*,[48] which concerned Therrence Nolan's challenge to the federal government's attempt to deport him. Nolan was a British subject but not an Australian citizen. The government argued he was an alien for the purpose of

---

44 For an overview, see Kim Rubenstein, *Australian Citizenship Law in Context* (Lawbook Co, 2002).

45 (2004) 222 CLR 322.

46 McHugh J, in dissent, concluded that the rule he saw in the British history and later developments was that birth in the realm meant a person could *not* be an alien. The distinction between McHugh J's reasoning and that of the majority highlights the possibility of different interpretations of the same legal materials. See McHugh J's summary in *Singh v Commonwealth* (2004) 222 CLR 322, 342-3.

47 See the discussion of this principle in David A Wishart, 'Allegiance and Citizenship as Concepts in Constitutional Law' (1986) 15 *Melbourne University Law Review* 662.

48 *Nolan v Minister of State for Immigration and Ethnic Affairs* (1988) 165 CLR 178.

the Constitution, and was therefore subject to deportation. Nolan resisted that characterisation by claiming that he owed a relevant allegiance and therefore could not be deported.

In determining whether he was a constitutional alien, the majority in *Nolan* focused on the legislative introduction of Australian citizenship from 1948.[49] From that time, Australians retained their earlier status as British subjects, which had applied as common law since the British imposed their law on this continent. However, a new status under legislation began to exist alongside that — the status of Australian citizenship. Over four decades, legislation reduced the significance of British subject status, until it disappeared as a reference to legal status in the mid-1980s.[50] The majority in the case of *Nolan*, relying on that legislative change and development, therefore concluded that the concept of 'alien' could, from 1986 at the latest, apply to British subjects who were non-citizens.[51]

Another specific example of legislation affecting constitutional status

The cases of *Singh* and *Nolan* show that legislative incursions into the law of nationality have affected the constitutional meaning of 'alien'. The majority of the Court in each case used legislation to interpret the current meaning of 'alien'. The status of 'alien' marks the boundary of the constitutional people, whereby aliens can be deported while 'the people' are the members of the constitutional community and are protected from removal.[52] In using legislative indications to understand constitutional aliens, the Court is also providing guidance as to the meaning of 'the people'.

The cases above reveal the use of legislation in the sense of indicating a pattern of development in status. There is one further example, which indicates the ability of one legislative enactment to affect constitutional membership, again by reference to the concept of 'alien'. The example is the case of *Re Minister for Immigration and Multicultural and Indigenous Affairs; Ex parte Ame*.[53] Amos

49   See *Nationality and Citizenship Act 1948* (Cth), which came into effect on 26 January 1949.
50   The only significant reference now is in provisions of Commonwealth electoral legislation allowing some British subjects who are not Australian citizens to retain their federal vote. See *Commonwealth Electoral Act 1918* (Cth) s 93(1)(b)(ii).
51   Note that in an earlier case, the Court had concluded that the United Kingdom is now a 'foreign power' for the purpose of s 44(i), even though it could not have been so considered at federation: *Sue v Hill* (1999) 199 CLR 462.
52   See Helen Irving, 'Still Call Australia Home: The Constitution and the Citizen's Right of Abode' (2008) 30 *Sydney Law Review* 133, note here I am equating 'the people' as understood in this chapter with constitutional citizenship discussed in that article.
53   *Re Minister for Immigration and Multicultural and Indigenous Affairs; Ex parte Ame* (2005) 222 CLR 439.

Ame was born in Papua while it was an Australian territory.[54] In 1975, Papua and New Guinea were unified and became an independent country, Papua New Guinea (PNG). In the process of becoming independent, PNG had to determine its citizenship laws and decided against allowing dual nationality. This became a political difficulty because Ame, and others, were Australian citizens under Australian law, although they did not have an automatic right to enter the Australian mainland. After independence, Ame entered the Australian mainland with a visa and sought to stay. The Australian government sought to deport him as an alien once his visa had expired.

In that case, the Commonwealth successfully argued that Ame was an alien, because the federal executive had passed a regulation stating that all persons who were Australian citizens but who became citizens of the independent state of PNG on Independence Day, ceased to be Australian citizens on that day.[55] The Court upheld the validity of that regulation and found that, in applying the idea of allegiance, Ame was an alien because he owed no allegiance to Australia; he was no longer a citizen, rather he owed allegiance to a foreign power because Australian legislation said he was a foreign citizen. Once again, the majority of the Court determined that legislation[56] led to his status as an alien — a constitutional status.

Despite several statements by the Court to the effect that the legislature cannot treat someone who is not truly an alien as an alien, that is, that the legislature cannot determine conclusively who is a constitutional alien, the majority of the Court has adopted what the legislature has said about citizenship as the basis for determining the meaning of constitutional 'alien'.[57]

I have outlined how the Court is going about its work in this area: it is relying, at least in part, on legislative indications of the meaning of constitutional expressions regarding membership of the constitutional people — either as electors in a system of representative government referred to in ss 7 and 24 — or as those excluded by being constitutional aliens. In the following section, I

---

54   For the history of Papua, as compared to New Guinea, see Alan Kerr, *A Federation in These Seas: An Account of the Acquisition by Australia of its External territories, With Selected Documents* (Attorney General's Department, 2009).

55   See *Papua New Guinea Independence (Australian Citizenship) Regulations 1975* (Cth) reg 4.

56   The focus of the reasoning was the validity of the Australian law at issue, but factually and politically it interacted with PNG legislation and policy. See the *Constitution of the Independent State of Papua New Guinea 1975* s 64 regarding dual citizenship.

57   On this occasion, the Court emphasised the relevance of s 122 of the Constitution, the 'territories' power, which is understood as a broad power of the federal Parliament. Just as the Parliament can accept new territories under that power, so it can also divest itself of former ones. The consequence of doing so is that the Parliament can therefore affect the status of the people of those territories. The Court sought to limit its conclusions in this case to only some territories. See *Re Minister for Immigration and Multicultural and Indigenous Affairs; Ex parte Ame* (2005) 222 CLR 439, 457 [28], [30] (Gleeson CJ, McHugh, Gummow, Hayne, Callinan, Heydon JJ).

address the implications of this form of reasoning by considering the objections to this method. I then turn to a more positive reading of the way in which the Court is interpreting membership of the constitutional community.

The implications: Objections and a positive reading

The reasoning discussed above indicates the process by which the High Court is using legislative indications of membership or exclusion in determining the constitutional meaning of 'the people'. The objections to this form of reasoning are obvious. First, by using legislative indications of constitutional membership, it appears that the Court is allowing the Parliament to define a constitutional term for itself, which appears to breach the separation of the roles of the legislature and the judiciary. The Parliament makes the laws; the judiciary should determine the validity of those laws.[58]

One response to this objection is that it is not any one legislative enactment which determines constitutional meaning. Parliament cannot identify the constitutional content of a term within one piece of legislation and then enact law upon that basis. Instead, it is a series of enactments which, over time, are interpreted by the Court as indicating a development in constitutional meaning, according to an identifiable pattern.[59]

However, this leads to questioning of how the development is identified by the Court, to what extent exceptions and anomalous aspects of the legislation affect the identification of a pattern, and at what point something becomes a well-established pattern or principle through legislation. The legislative development of the franchise at the federal level, as well as at the State and earlier colonial levels, is complex and filled with discrepancies, temporary inclusions and exclusions.[60] The development of nationality and citizenship laws is likewise

---

58   This was outlined most clearly in *Australian Communist Party v Commonwealth* (1951) 83 CLR 1.

59   The *Ame* case does not necessarily constitute an exception to this. That case can be understood as the High Court applying the meaning of alien which is equivalent to non-citizen, derived from the earlier cases which focused on the legislative incursions on the common law status of subject. In this instance, the Court is upholding the executive's power to withdraw the status of citizen, and therefore the consequent constitutional implication that the person becomes an alien and therefore subject to deportation. That power of removal of legislated status which affects constitutional status requires closer interrogation, but that was not done in the *Ame* case, nor is it addressed in this chapter.

60   See for example Anne Twomey, 'The Federal Constitutional Right to Vote in Australia' (2000) 28 *Federal Law Review* 125 and for an indication of the complexity, see Murray Goot, 'The Aboriginal Franchise and its Consequences' (2006) 52(4) *Australian Journal of Politics and History* 517.

not a simple coherent trajectory regarding membership.[61] How the legislative developments in either area are understood and characterised in terms of an identifiable pattern is open to debate.

Further, the focus on a pattern of legislative development as indicating constitutional meaning may have the problem of 'ratcheting'.[62] This allows a cumulative erosion of the sovereignty of Parliament, which operates as follows: the Court has constitutionalised the universal adult franchise and stated that reintroduction of disqualifications on the basis of religion, race, gender and property, amongst others, would likely be invalid because of their inconsistency with the mandate of 'choice by the people'.[63] What that does is limit the ability of the Parliament to determine the franchise from time to time, by not allowing a return to a more restrictive franchise. This means the franchise must forever expand, it cannot contract — this is the 'ratcheting' problem. By establishing this rule of a universal adult franchise on the basis of a consideration of a legislative pattern discerned by the Court, Parliaments in the past have, therefore, through a cumulative effect of a number of pieces of legislation, bound Parliaments into the future — this is the parliamentary sovereignty problem.

However, there is an interpretation of this method of reasoning which is more positive and indicates that the Court is allowing 'the people' to determine their own constitutional identity. First, a reminder that the primary textual indications of 'the people' in the Constitution connect to the system of representative government — ss 7 and 24. 'The people' choose the Parliament, the Parliament therefore represents 'the people' and its legislation is deemed to be the will of 'the people' through that representative system. Choice by the people has been referred to as the constitutional 'bedrock' of representative government.

Considered in this way, the legislation of Federal Parliament is the voice of the people. Thus, the Court, by adopting, deferring to, or reflecting legislative choices regarding membership of the constitutional people, is picking up on the people's own view of themselves. The Court is adopting the people's view of who they want to be included in the constitutional community and who they want excluded. The method of reasoning of the Court therefore has a measure of democratic legitimacy, by reflecting the constitutive power of the people to establish their own identity, through their representative institution, the Federal Parliament.

---

61 See further discussion of this in Kim Rubenstein, *Australian Citizenship Law in Context* (Lawbook Co, 2002).

62 'Ratcheting' applies to the reasoning in the representative government cases. Different problems arise from the reasoning in the 'aliens' cases, which are beyond the scope of this chapter.

63 See in *Roach v Electoral Commissioner* (2007) 233 CLR 162 and *Rowe v Electoral Commissioner* (2010) 243 CLR 1.

The Court is seeking the meaning of constitutional terms, and acknowledges that the meaning of those terms may change, and that their application may change over time, due to national and international social, political and legal developments. What could the Court look to in order to determine the changed meaning over time? A majority is using legislation. While not completely satisfactory, at least legislation is identifiable, and can be seen as a reflection of the Australian polity's view of themselves.

Conclusions

This chapter has discussed the High Court's method of reasoning in addressing the meaning of the constitutional 'people'. I have identified that a majority of the Court, in two areas of constitutional jurisprudence, is using legislative indications of membership in order to define 'the people' who exercise the federal vote, and constitutional 'aliens' who are excluded from membership of 'the people'. This method of reasoning is surprising in that it seems to give the legislature the power, through cumulative indications, of defining the meaning of constitutional expressions. However, this method can also be understood as the Court giving 'the people' some indirect power of self-definition.

Whether we prefer deferral to Parliamentary choices over time or the judicial application of standards seen in some other external source, depends not on an absolute rule regarding constitutional interpretation but rather on classic differences of viewpoint regarding the role of judicial review. In the context of determining the meaning of the constitutional people, it comes down to figuring out to what extent we, the people, want to be playing a part in that determination.

The outstanding questions are then: what are the limits beyond which the Court will not allow the Parliament to go, and what alternatives exist for the Court in making these kinds of judgments regarding membership of the constitutional community? These are questions that go beyond the scope of this chapter, but that indicate that deferral to 'the people', while democratically legitimate, does not resolve the difficult questions regarding the division of power between the Legislature and the Court. The ongoing dialogue between those institutions will determine the meaning of 'the people' from time to time.

3. Thick and Thin Citizenship as Measures of Australian Democracy

Kim Rubenstein[1] and Niamh Lenagh-Maguire[2]

The importance of Australian citizenship can be obscured by its relatively sparse legal foundations, and by the omission of an expressly defined concept of citizenship from the Australian Constitution. However, one of the ways in which the legal status of citizenship is elevated beyond an empty label and given substance is the linking of citizenship with the structures of Australian democracy. This connection between a statutory label and Australia's constitutionally-mandated system of representative government also lends citizenship an important constitutional dimension that otherwise might be lacking. With limited exceptions, it is citizens who vote to elect governments at local, state and federal level, and in that sense these fundamental democratic mechanisms depend on a legal distinction between citizens and non-citizens. In turn, the connection between citizenship and the franchise adds critically important substance to the otherwise fairly bare notion of Australian citizenship as a legal category.

This chapter begins by examining the place of citizenship in Australia's democratic structure before moving on to examine the important High Court decision in *Re MIMIA; ex parte Ame* ('Ame').[3] We argue that the Court's approach to citizenship in that case reflects a narrow or 'thin' conception of democratic citizenship, tied predominantly to voting rights. Drawing upon the scholarship of US academic Linda Bosniak, this chapter outlines a fuller conception of citizenship, considering notions of rights, political participation and identity to argue that there is potential for Australians to hold a 'thicker' understanding of citizenship and providing an opportunity to expand the narrower judicial conception developed through the High Court's jurisprudence and conceptions of Australian democracy.

---

1   kim.rubenstein@anu.edu.au.
2   niamh.lenagh.maguire@gmail.com.
3   (2005) 222 CLR 439.

What kind of citizenship? Big 'C' or small 'c', thick or thin?

A distinction is commonly drawn between the formal side of citizenship and its content or consequences (what Peter Schuck has described as 'what citizenship really means'[4]). Understanding and accounting for the various dimensions of citizenship besides its formal, status-based element has been a consuming project for contemporary citizenship theory, particularly in the 60 years since the publication of TH Marshall's influential essay *Citizenship and Social Class*.[5] Marshall identified three 'elements' of citizenship — the civil, political and social:

> The civil element is composed of the rights necessary for individual freedom — liberty of the person; freedom of speech, thought and faith; the right to own property and to conclude valid contracts; and the right to justice ... By the political element I mean the right to participate in the exercise of political power, as a member of a body invested with political authority or as an elector of the members of such a body ... By the social element I mean the whole range from the right to a modicum of economic welfare and security to the right to share to the full in the social heritage and to live the life of a civilized being ...[6]

In Marshall's account, these elements had at one point been held simultaneously, but were 'unbundled' from citizenship during the Middle Ages and were only re-integrated into the concept gradually, beginning with civil rights in the 17th century, followed by political rights in the 18th century, and social rights in the 20th century.

The citizenship literature is replete with taxonomies of citizenship's substantive content, many of which owe an explicit debt to Marshall's pioneering categorisation of the elements of citizenship. Prominent examples include Joseph Carens's description of three dimensions of citizenship — legal, psychological and political — which he suggests are incompatible with a conception of the nation-state as a 'culturally homogenous form of political community in which citizenship is treated primarily as a legal status that is universal, equal and democratic'.[7] Linda Bosniak's influential paper, 'Citizenship Denationalized',[8] describes four types of citizenship — citizenship as legal status, citizenship as

---

4   Peter Schuck, 'Citizenship in Federal Systems' (2000) 48 *American Journal of Comparative Law* 393.
5   TH Marshall, *Citizenship and Social Class: Class, Citizenship, and Social Development* (New York, 1965).
6   ibid 75.
7   Joseph Carens, *Culture, Citizenship, and Community: A Contextual Exploration of Justice as Evenhandedness* (2000) 161.
8   Linda Bosniak, 'Citizenship Denationalized' (2000) 7 *Indiana Journal of Global Legal Studies* 447.

rights (following Marshall), citizenship as political participation, and citizenship as identity or solidarity, that is, 'the quality of belonging, the felt aspects of community membership'.[9] Changes in the composition of national communities and the relationship between individual citizens and the nation-state have also prompted further re-examinations of what it means to be a 'citizen' in a diverse, multicultural society such as Australia. This re-examination has occurred both in terms of the liberal democratic challenges described influentially by Will Kymlicka,[10] and in the narrower sense of citizenship as a legal status that needs to adapt to the changing needs of those who hold it.[11]

As Kim Rubenstein explains, normative conceptions of citizenship are 'not only concerned with legal citizens, but with people and the way people should act and be treated as members of a community'.[12] The Australian Citizenship Council distinguished between 'large-C' and 'small-c' citizenship, to reflect this distinction between citizenship as a legal concept and its political, philosophical and social meanings.[13] The latter conceptions of 'citizenship as desirable activity'[14] tend to be based on membership and participation in a community, rather than legal status — the citizen is seen as 'a member of a political community, entitled to whatever prerogatives and encumbered with whatever responsibilities are attached to membership'.[15]

It is also important to recognise that there are connections between the legal and normative dimensions of citizenship. The status of the (large-C) Citizen is not simply a formality; citizenship carries with it a range of rights and obligations to participate in the life of the state that are denied to those who are not citizens. The legal status of Australian citizen is, in this respect, a 'gate-keeping' or exclusionary mechanism. Access to formal citizenship can determine whether a person can remain present in the Australian community and the extent to which a person can participate fully in Australian society.[16]

---

9   ibid 479.

10   Will Kymlicka, *Multicultural Citizenship: A Liberal Theory of Minority Rights* (Clarendon Press, 1995).

11   See for example Peter Spiro's work on citizenship in the context of global movement: Peter Spiro, 'Dual Citizenship as Human Right' (2010) 8 *International Journal of Constitutional Law* 111; Peter Spiro, 'Embracing Dual Nationality' in Randall Hansen and Patrick Weill (eds), *Dual Nationality, Social Rights and Federal Citizenship in the US and Europe: the Reinvention of Citizenship* (2001). For further discussion of the changing significance of Australian citizenship see Kim Rubenstein and Niamh Lenagh-Maguire, 'More or Less Secure?: Nationality Questions, Deportation and Dual Nationality' (Cambridge University Press, 2014) Kim Rubenstein and Niamh Lenagh-Maguire, 'Citizenship and the Boundaries of the Constitution' in Rosalind Dixon and Tom Ginsburg (eds), *The Research Handbook in Comparative Constitutional Law* (Edward Elgar, 2011).

12   Kim Rubenstein, *Australian Citizenship Law in Context* (Lawbook, 2002) 6.

13   Australian Citizenship Council, 'Australian Citizenship for a New Century' (Report, Australian Citizenship Council, 2000) 7.

14   Will Kymlicka and Wayne Norman, 'Return of the Citizen: A Survey of Recent Work on Citizenship Theory' (1994) 104 *Ethics* 352, 353.

15   Michael Walzer, 'Citizenship' in Terence Ball, James Farr and Russell Hanson (eds), *Political Innovation and Conceptual Change* (Cambridge University Press, 1989) 211.

16   See *Migration Act 1958* (Cth) ss 14, 198.

Looking beyond the technicalities of citizenship as a legal status can also be an attempt to develop a 'thick description' of what citizenship means as a social phenomenon, a political dynamic and, importantly, as a personal experience. The language of 'thick description' is in part an extrapolation from the approach to ethnography advocated by Clifford Geertz.[17] Geertz describes ethnography as 'an elaborate venture in ... "thick description"'.[18] Borrowing an example from Gilbert Ryle, from whom he also draws the language of 'thick' and 'thin' description, Geertz describes some of the different ways in which a seemingly simple act of constricting one eyelid, whether involuntarily or deliberately, so as to 'wink', carries social meaning:

> [B]etween ... the 'thin description' of what the rehearse (parodist, winker, twitcher ...) is doing ('rapidly contracting his right eyelids') and the 'thick description' of what he is doing ('practicing a burlesque of a friend faking a wink to deceive an innocent into thinking a conspiracy is in motion') lies the object of ethnography: a stratified hierarchy of meaningful structures ...[19]

In a very different disciplinary setting, we argue that a focus on the formal aspects of citizenship, in particular on the allocation of the statutory label of 'citizen' and on the distribution of formal political rights like voting, generates a fairly thin or superficial understanding of what it means to be a citizen. While those legal and structural aspects of citizenship are critically important, they are not the whole story of a person's experience as a citizen.

Australian citizenship as a legal status

'Australian citizenship' is, on its face, a statutory rather than constitutional status. As we argue later in this chapter, the fact that so much of the legal architecture of Australian citizenship rests on an inherently malleable statutory foundation may contribute to its relative 'thinness' as a legal concept. As Kirby J explained in *DJL v Central Authority*:

> The Australian Constitution does not refer to the status of 'citizen' in relation to native born or naturalized people of the Commonwealth. The 'people' are referred to in several places. Elsewhere the people who are

---

17   Clifford Geertz, 'Thick Description: Toward an Interpretive Theory of Culture' in Clifford Geertz, *The Interpretation of Cultures* (Basic Books, 1973) 3.

18   ibid 6.

19   ibid 7.

entitled to vote are described as 'electors'. In harmony with the notions of the time, the Constitution refers to the national status of Australians as that of 'a subject of the Queen'.[20]

The word 'citizen' appears only once in the Australian Constitution, in a provision dealing with the disqualification of a 'citizen of a foreign power' from being elected to the Federal Parliament.[21] While the Constitution does not include a definition of Australian citizenship, it does classify people according to other statuses — as 'subjects of the Queen',[22] 'residents of a state' (reflecting the federal structure of the Commonwealth of Australia)[23] and 'aliens'.[24]

Prior to the creation of a statutory form of Australian citizenship in 1948, 'the major distinction of membership in Australia ... was between British subjects and aliens'.[25] A person born or naturalised in Australia was a British subject.[26] Relying on its power to make laws with respect to 'naturalisation and aliens' (the aliens power), in 1948 the Federal Parliament enacted a statutory form of Australian citizenship.[27] The Parliament has also relied on the aliens power to make laws dealing with the terms on which 'non-citizens' may enter and remain in Australia and the removal of 'unlawful non-citizens'.[28] The *Australian Citizenship Act 2007* (Cth) (the *Citizenship Act*) currently determines who is entitled to Australian citizenship, including provisions for citizenship by descent and by naturalisation, but that Act is silent as to the rights and duties that flow from the status of 'Australian citizen'.

The substance of citizenship in Australia: Democracy and voting rights

The Australian *Citizenship Act* creates and confers the bare legal status of Australian citizenship. The Constitution, and other laws of the Commonwealth

---

20 (2000) 201 CLR 226, 277 (Kirby J).

21 *Australian Constitution* s 44.

22 ibid ss 34, 117.

23 ibid ss 25, 75, 117.

24 ibid s 51(xix).

25 Rubenstein, above n 12, 47.

26 ibid 47–9.

27 See *Naturalisation Act 1903–1920* (Cth); *Nationality Act 1920* (Cth); *Australian Citizenship Act 1948* (Cth); *Australian Citizenship Act 2007* (Cth).

28 For an overview of migration legislation in Australia post-Federation, see Mary Crock, *Immigration and Refugee Law in Australia* (Federation Press, 1998); John Vrachnas, Kim Boyd et al., *Migration and Refugee Law: Principles and Practice in Australia* (Cambridge University Press, 2005) ch 2.

and the States and Territories, give that status its legal substance.[29] In this chapter we focus on the relationship between the status of citizen and Australia's democratic system of government.

Notwithstanding its omission from the Constitution, Australian citizenship has a constitutional dimension. In *Chu Kheng Lim v Minister for Immigration, Local Government and Ethnic Affairs*,[30] Gaudron J recognised that the statutory concept of citizenship is both constitutionally unnecessary and constitutionally useful:

> Citizenship, so far as this country is concerned, is a concept which is entirely statutory, originating as recently as 1948. It is a concept which is and can be pressed into service for a number of constitutional purposes. But it is not a concept which is constitutionally necessary, which is immutable or which has some immutable core element ensuring its lasting relevance for constitutional purposes ...[31]

As we explain in this chapter, one of the ways in which the concept of citizenship is 'pressed into service' in a constitutional context is in determining who is entitled to take part in Australian democracy as an 'elector'.

Statutory framework: The relationship between citizenship and the franchise

The Constitution gives the Federal Parliament the power to make laws dealing with the qualification of electors. 'That Australia came to have universal adult suffrage was the result of legislative action.'[32] That legislative choice now has a constitutional dimension; as the High Court made clear most recently in *Rowe v Electoral Commissioner*,[33] the Parliament is not free to abandon universal suffrage. Subject to limited exceptions, Australian citizens are required to enrol as electors on the federal electoral roll and to cast votes at federal elections.[34]

This legislative choice reveals something of the connection between citizenship and the exercise of political rights in Australia, in particular the idea that a certain kind of connection with the Australian nation beyond, for example, mere presence in the community, is required before a person should be allowed to elect a national or sub-national government, and that citizenship carries with it important obligations to take an active part in the democratic process. In this

---

29 Rubenstein, above n 12, ch 5.
30 (1992) 176 CLR 1.
31 ibid 54.
32 *Roach v Electoral Commissioner* (2007) 233 CLR 162 at 173 (Gleeson CJ).
33 *Rowe v Electoral Commissioner* (2010) 243 CLR 1.
34 *Commonwealth Electoral Act 1918* (Cth) s 93.

way, the statutory status of citizen elevates a person's standing in the community above that of a long-term resident in a way that is not the case in many other areas of public life (taxation or employment rights, for example).

While the rule that an elector needs to be a citizen, and that a citizen is entitled to be an elector, tells us something about the substantive content of citizenship as a legal status, the exceptions to that rule also shed light on what it means to be a citizen. Here, we focus on two such exceptions — a category of non-citizens who are entitled to vote, and a category of citizens who are not. Turning to the first special category of exceptions, British subjects who were on the electoral roll immediately before 26 January 1984 continue to be entitled to enrolment under the *Commonwealth Electoral Act*.[35] This is a class of long-term residents of the Australian community who do not possess statutory citizenship but who had been entitled to vote on the basis of their British subject status and satisfaction of a minimum six-month residence criterion. Australia's growing constitutional independence from the United Kingdom has meant that British subjecthood is legally and constitutionally distinct from Australian citizenship, so a British subject who settled in Australia after 1984 would not be entitled to vote (and, indeed, would be subject to laws made under the aliens power).[36] The Parliament's choice to adopt citizenship as an essential criterion for the federal franchise and effectively to abandon qualification for non-citizens on the basis of a minimum period of residence, elevates the possession of formal citizenship over even very long-term membership of the Australian community. Something more than a long period of residence in Australia is required before a person should be entitled to vote; rather, this fundamental political right is reserved for those with a deeper, or at least more formal, connection with the Australian community. Maintaining a 'grandfathered' entitlement for British subjects resident in Australia before 1984 can be seen simply as a matter of fairness — having at one stage enjoyed one of the central rights of citizenship it would arguably be unfair to deprive this class of person of their right to vote. These arrangements can also be seen as a recognition of the particular historical resonance of 'British subject' status in Australia and a reminder of a time when 'British subject' status was worth as much as, if not more than, the status of 'Australian citizen'.

Of course it is also possible for an Australian citizen to lose the right to vote: if they are incapable of understanding the nature and significance of enrolment and voting, are convicted of treason or treachery or, more controversially, if

---

35   ibid.

36   *Shaw v Minister for Immigration & Multicultural Affairs* (2003) 218 CLR 28; *Re Patterson; Ex parte Taylor* (2001) 207 CLR 391; *Nolan v Minister for Immigration & Ethnic Affairs* (1988) 165 CLR 178.

they are serving a sentence of imprisonment for three years or longer. There has seemingly been little argument about the first two of these grounds of disqualification. As Gleeson CJ put it in *Roach v Electoral Commissioner*,[37]

> The rationale for excluding persons of unsound mind is obvious, although the application of the criterion of exclusion may be imprecise, and could be contentious in some cases. The rationale is related to the capacity to exercise choice. People who engage in acts of treason may be regarded as having no just claim to participate in the community's self-governance.[38]

The question whether prisoners ought to be allowed to vote has attracted more critical attention, and was considered by the High Court in 2007 in *Roach*. In that case, which Elisa Arcioni has considered in greater detail in this volume, the Court was asked to decide whether a law disenfranchising a person serving a prison sentence, irrespective of the length of their sentence, was constitutionally valid. The judgments in this case shed light on what it means to deprive a citizen of their right to vote, and on the critical importance of voting as one of the indicia of full civic membership. In considering the possible justifications of such a law, Gleeson CJ held that

> the rationale for the exclusion must be that serious offending represents such a form of civic irresponsibility that it is appropriate for Parliament to mark such behaviour as anti-social and to direct that physical separation from the community will be accompanied by symbolic separation in the form of loss of a fundamental political right ... Serious offending may warrant temporary suspension of one of the rights of membership, that is, the right to vote.

His Honour had earlier reasoned:

> It is consistent with our constitutional concept of choice by the people for Parliament to treat those who have been imprisoned for serious criminal offences as having suffered a temporary suspension of their connection with the community, reflected at the physical level in incarceration, and reflected also in temporary deprivation of the right to participate by voting in the political life of the community. It is also for Parliament, consistently with the rationale for exclusion, to decide the basis upon which to identify incarcerated offenders whose serious criminal wrongdoing warrants temporary suspension of a right of citizenship.

---

37 *Roach* (2007) 233 CLR 162, 182 (Gleeson CJ).
38 ibid, 179 (Gleeson CJ).

The seriousness of a person's wrongdoing was a central consideration in the reasoning of the majority judges in *Roach*, who held invalid the blanket ban on prisoners voting but accepted that it would be valid to exclude prisoners serving sentences of at least three years. As the joint majority judgment of Gummow, Kirby and Crennan JJ observed:

[I]n the federal system established and maintained by the Constitution, the exercise of the franchise is the means by which those living under that system of government participate in the selection of both legislative chambers, as one of the people of the relevant State and as one of the people of the Commonwealth. In this way, the existence and exercise of the franchise reflects notions of citizenship and membership of the Australian federal body politic.

Such notions are not extinguished by the mere fact of imprisonment. Prisoners who are citizens and members of the Australian community remain so. Their interest in, and duty to, their society and its governance survives incarceration. Indeed, upon one view, the Constitution envisages their ongoing obligations to the body politic to which, in due course, the overwhelming majority of them will be returned following completion of their sentence.[39]

A test case: Can 'real' citizenship exist without voting rights?

In 2005, the High Court held in *Ame*[40] that Australian citizens born in Papua, who had held the legal status of citizen under the Australian *Citizenship Act* from the Act's inception in 1948[41] until 1975, could have that status unilaterally stripped from them by regulations because that citizenship was not 'real'[42] was only a 'technical' status[43], was 'largely nominal'[44] was 'not in fact or law full

---

39   ibid 199 (Gummow, Kirby, Crennan JJ).

40   (2005) 222 CLR 439.

41   Before that time Papuans were British subjects under the authority of the Commonwealth of Australian by Letters Patent and accepted as the Territory of Papua by s 5 of the *Papua Act 1905* (Cth).

42   *Re Minister for Immigration and Multicultural and Indigenous Affairs; Ex parte Ame* (2005) 222 CLR 439, 449 (Gleeson CJ, McHugh, Gummow, Hayne, Callinan and Heydon JJ).

43   ibid.

44   ibid, 470 (Kirby J).

or real citizenship',[45] was a 'veneer of Australian citizenship',[46] was a 'flawed citizenship',[47] was of a 'fragile and strictly limited character',[48] and was more like a 'shadow… of mere appearances and title'.[49]

Background: Papuan independence and loss of citizenship

Papua was an Australian territory from 1906–1975.[50] Until the introduction of a statutory Australian citizenship, both Australians and Papuans were formally British subjects.[51] Under the *Citizenship Act*, 'Australia' was defined to include Norfolk Island and the Territory of Papua. A person born in Papua after the passage of the *Citizenship Act* was therefore born in Australia for the purposes of the Act and acquired the status of 'Australian citizen'.[52] However, the substantive rights attached to Papuans' citizenship were not equivalent to those enjoyed by other Australian citizens. Papua was not part of Australia for the purposes of the *Migration Act 1958* (Cth) ('the *Migration Act*'),[53] and its inhabitants were required to obtain a permit before entering mainland Australia, in contrast to the free right of entry enjoyed by most other Australian citizens.[54]

In 1975, Papua became part of the newly independent Papua New Guinea (PNG). The *Papua New Guinea Constitution* did not permit dual citizenship, and provided that a person who was 'a real foreign citizen' at the time that PNG became independent would not acquire citizenship of PNG.[55] A person who held Australian citizenship but had no right to enter and reside in Australia did not have 'real foreign citizenship' for this purpose.[56] In response, the *Papua New Guinea Independence (Australian Citizenship) Regulations 1975* (Cth) ('the Independence Regulations') stripped Australian citizenship from anyone who became a PNG citizen at the date of PNG's independence (16 September 1975).[57]

---

45   ibid.

46   ibid, 474 (Kirby J).

47   ibid.

48   ibid 483 (Kirby J).

49   ibid.

50   *Papua Act 1905* (Cth). Prior to Federation, the Colony of Queensland had attempted to annex Papua in order to provide a 'buffer' between it and German-controlled New Guinea: Richard Herr, 'Australia, Security and the Pacific Islands: From Empire to Commonwealth' (2006) 95 *The Round Table* 705, 707.

51   *Ame* (2005) 222 CLR 439, 467.

52   *Nationality and Citizenship Act 1948* (Cth) s 10.

53   See *Acts Interpretation Act 1901* (Cth) s 17.

54   *Migration Act 1958* (Cth) ss 6–7. Counsel for the applicant submitted that the requirement that Papuans obtain an entry permit was based on a desire to exclude non-white inhabitants of Australian territory from the mainland: Transcript of Proceedings, *Re MIMIA; Ex parte Ame* (High Court of Australia, K Rubenstein, 3 March 2005).

55   *Constitution of the Independent State of Papua New Guinea*, ss 64-5.

56   ibid.

57   *Papua New Guinea Independence (Australian Citizenship) Regulations 1975* (Cth).

Thus, Papuans who had not obtained residence rights in Australia became PNG nationals under that country's new Constitution, and upon acquiring that status lost their Australian citizenship.

Ame's case: What makes a 'real' citizen?

A Papuan man, Amos Bode Ame, argued in the High Court in 2005 that the regulations which purported to take away his Australian citizenship could not validly apply to him, nor could the *Migration Act* restrict his right to enter and remain on the Australian mainland.[58] Mr Ame challenged the distinction between 'real' citizens and the residents of external territories, and asserted that the Commonwealth could not treat him as an immigrant or an alien when he sought to enter Australia, and could not unilaterally withdraw his citizenship.

The High Court held that Papuans had held a form of citizenship that was qualitatively different from other forms of Australian citizenship:

> [I]t was no more than nominal citizenship, applicable for limited purposes … It conferred few rights and specifically no rights freely to enter the States and internal territories of Australia, as other Australian citizens might do. Nor did it permit its holders to enjoy permanent residence in the States and internal territories …[59]

Mr Ame's contention that he was a 'real' Australian citizen failed, on the basis that his was a 'hollow' form of citizenship which did not equate to the rights held by inhabitants of mainland Australia. The Court acknowledged the clear intention on the part of the Federal Parliament to restrict the rights afforded to Papuan-born Australian citizens, and held that

> [t]he Constitution does not require that all inhabitants of all external territories acquired by Australia should have an unfettered right of entry into, and residence in, mainland Australia. There is no reason why Parliament cannot treat such an inhabitant as an immigrant.[60]

The High Court upheld the Commonwealth legislation that stripped Papuan Australians of their citizenship on the basis that the laws were validly made under the territories power. Section 122 of the Constitution gives the Commonwealth power to legislate 'for the government' of a Territory 'placed by the Queen under the authority of and accepted by the Commonwealth', of which Papua

---

58   *Ame* (2005) 222 CLR 439, 441–2.
59   ibid 471.
60   ibid 458 (Gleeson CJ, McHugh, Gummow, Hayne, Callinan and Heydon JJ).

was an example. The High Court confirmed that the territories power allowed the Commonwealth to confer citizenship on the inhabitants of a territory, and conversely allowed that citizenship to be withdrawn:

> Parliament is not obliged to confer Australian citizenship upon all inhabitants of all external territories. Furthermore, the powers under which it may legislate to confer such citizenship when a Territory is acquired enable Parliament to legislate to withdraw such citizenship when rights of sovereignty or rights of administration in respect of such Territory come to an end.[61]

As a consequence, Mr Ame could be deprived of his citizenship and thereafter treated as a non-citizen under the *Migration Act*.[62]

The Court felt compelled to use these characterisations devaluing the status of citizenship held by those Papuans because Papuan Australian citizens did not have a right to enter the mainland of Australia,[63] or reside in mainland Australia,[64] and Ame, '[a]lthough a citizen, had no right (still less a duty) to vote in Australian elections and referenda. He could perform no jury or other civic service in Australia'.[65] Indeed, despite his status of a citizen, he and his fellow country-men and women were, to all intents and purposes 'treated as ... foreigner[s]'.[66]

The language of the Court's decision strikingly resembles an infamous United States Supreme Court decision of almost 150 years earlier. In *Dred Scott v Sanford*[67] the Supreme Court held that an emancipated former slave was not a 'citizen of a State' entitled to invoke the Court's diversity jurisdiction under Article III of the US Constitution. The Court held that African slaves and their descendants, whether or not they had been emancipated,

> are not included, and were not intended to be included, under the word 'citizens' in the Constitution, and can therefore claim none of the rights and privileges which that instrument provides for and secures to citizens of the United States. On the contrary, they were at that time considered as a subordinate and inferior class of beings who had been subjugated by the dominant race, and, whether emancipated or not, yet

---

61 ibid.
62 ibid 459.
63 ibid 449 (Gleeson CJ, McHugh, Gummow, Hayne, Callinan and Heydon JJ).
64 ibid 470 (Kirby J).
65 ibid 481 (Kirby J).
66 ibid.
67 60 US 393 (1857).

remained subject to their authority, and had no rights or privileges but such as those who held the power and the Government might choose to grant them.[68]

In part, the Court reached this conclusion because it was understood that citizens of a state were free to move about the country and enjoyed certain fundamental rights when in another state — a situation that simply did not apply as a matter of law to 'those persons who are the descendants of Africans who were imported into this country and sold as slaves'.[69]

In Ame's case, the practical disjuncture between rights and status effectively enabled the High Court to affirm that as a matter of law someone could hold the legal status of citizen, without any claim to rights associated with that status. The High Court was able to deny Mr Ame's claim to Australian citizenship because the kind of citizenship he had once held was flimsy and lacking in many of the aspects of citizenship that typically lend it meaning and value. It was important to all of the judges that Papuans had held a form of Australian citizenship that was deficient in many formal, legal respects. Whilst the scope of the Federal Parliament's power with respect to external territories would, on its face, have remained the same, we can speculate that had Mr Ame and his compatriots been full and active citizens of Australia with the same rights of entry and residence as other Australians, or had they enjoyed rights of democratic participation in Australia, the Court might have been less willing to uphold the Parliament's effort to strip them of those rights.

When citizenship lacks substance/depth

In this final section, we consider Ame's case through the prism of Linda Bosniak's analysis of citizenship as a legal status, as a source of rights, as a form of political activity, and as an identity. As we noted at the beginning of this chapter, there are different ways in which citizenship is 'pressed into service'[70] and these differences reflect the different ends to which the concept of citizenship is invoked. As Bosniak explains so thoughtfully in her article, 'Citizenship Denationalised',[71] there are four different ways in which scholars write about citizenship. The first is 'citizenship as legal status',[72] the second is 'citizenship

---

68   ibid 404–5.
69   ibid 403.
70   This is the term used above by Justice Gaudron in *Chu Kheng Lim v Minister for Immigration, Local Government and Ethnic Affairs* (1992) 176 CLR 1, 54.
71   Linda Bosniak, 'Citizenship Denationalized' (2000) 7 *Indiana Journal of Global Legal Studies* 447.
72   ibid 456–63.

as rights',[73] the third is 'citizenship as political activity',[74] and finally there is writing about 'citizenship as identity'.[75] Of course, some of the scholarship uses these terms in overlapping ways, but her distinctions are helpful in thinking through the way in which legal status sits with other conceptions of citizenship as rights, as political activity and as identity.

Citizenship as 'legal status' is what is important to the nation state. The legal status represents legal recognition of membership of an 'organized political community'.[76] The nation state determines who has that legal status, and debates — including those about automatic citizenship, acquisition of citizenship, rights to citizenship by descent, and indeed rights associated with change of territory and citizenship — revolve around this legal status. For the nation state, citizenship has been primarily about legal status. In Australia, the legal status of 'citizen' did not exist until 1949 and its scope has changed as Parliament so desired, through legislative amendment over time. Returning to Justice Gaudron's earlier cited statement in *Lim*, there has been no 'immutable core element[s] ensuring its lasting relevance for constitutional purposes'.[77] In contrast, for the new state of Papua New Guinea, there was a desire, from the experience of the shallow, formal status of the statutory version of their Australian citizenship to bestow upon the Papua New Guinea citizenship a status of constitutional value. There was a commitment to give citizenship 'real' meaning. Connected with this was a belief in Papua New Guinea that citizenship had to be singular. Both the joint judgment and Kirby J's separate opinion in *Ame* refer to the figurative language used in the Report of the Constitutional Planning Committee which was considering the preparation of the new PNG constitution: 'no man, it is said, can stand in more than one canoe'.[78] Accordingly, dual citizenship was constitutionally prohibited. If a person was a Papua New Guinean citizen, then they could not also be an Australian citizen.

For Mr Ame, and those like him born in Australian territory, that legal status at birth was significant. Holding that legal status meant something to them. They held a belief that there would be rights associated with that status. Indeed, this leads us to Bosniak's second characterization of 'citizenship as rights'. Echoing the work of TH Marshall referred to earlier in this chapter, Bosniak argues:

> In twentieth century social theory, the notion of citizenship has been most closely associated with the enjoyment of certain important rights and entitlements. In this conception of citizenship, the enjoyment of

---

73   ibid 463–70.
74   ibid 470–79.
75   ibid 479–88.
76   ibid 456.
77   *Chu Kheng Lim v Minister for Immigration, Local Government and Ethnic Affairs* (1992) 176 CLR 1, 54.
78   *Ame* (2005) 222 CLR 439, 448 (Gleeson CJ, McHugh, Gummow, Hayne, Callinan and Heydon JJ), 464 (Kirby J).

rights is the defining feature of societal membership: citizenship requires the possession of rights, and those who possess the rights are usually presumed thereby to enjoy citizenship.[79]

However, this approach to citizenship highlights exclusion and second-class citizenship, 'and the ways that racial subordination has painfully distorted formally egalitarian polities'.[80] This is indeed what happened in Australia, both in relation to its own Indigenous peoples[81] and in the experience of Papuan citizens upon PNG independence. Australia did not create an equal or egalitarian status of Australian citizen — different citizens had different rights and the Papuan Australian citizens felt the legacy of that profoundly. So much so that in creating a new Papua New Guinea state, there was an overt desire to distinguish itself from Australia to ensure a full and equal Papua New Guinean status of citizen.[82]

Moreover, it was the fact that different 'rights' were accorded to some Australian citizens as opposed to others that became relevant to the High Court's decision to deny the claim to Australian citizenship status by Mr Ame. Indeed, it is the next category of citizenship that Bosniak refers to that was fatal to Mr Ame's claim. Bosniak separates 'citizenship as political activity' from rights in her categorization. In doing this she is highlighting the large political theory literature that uses the term 'citizenship' to denote 'active engagement in the life of the political community',[83] and she links it to civic republican theory and participatory democratic principles about an active, engaged citizenship. This idea revolves around the ideal political society where all citizens are encouraged to be 'good citizens'. It views political involvement in a polity as a positive normative ideal. However, in order to be an active citizen, one needs to have the political rights to do so, and this is where Mr Ame and his colleagues fell down in their claim to Australian citizenship.

The fact that the Australian Parliament denied the political rights normally linked to citizenship from Papuans — such as voting, jury service, and freedom of movement in and out of the mainland — meant that the High Court could determine they did not hold a 'real citizenship'. This largely tautological framing of citizenship (those who have citizenship rights are citizens and those who don't are not) gives enormous power to the state to manipulate membership of the community.

---

79 Linda Bosniak, 'Citizenship Denationalized' (2000) 7 *Indiana Journal of Global Legal Studies* 447, 463–464.

80 ibid 465.

81 As stated earlier, there is another story that parallels the PNG–Australia story that is closer to home: that of indigenous Australians and their claims to citizenship. See John Chesterman and Brian Galligan, *Citizens Without Rights: Aborigines and Australian Citizenship* (Cambridge University Press, 1997).

82 See *Ame* (2005) 222 CLR 439, 470 (Kirby J).

83 Linda Bosniak, 'Citizenship Denationalized' (2000) 7 *Indiana Journal of Global Legal Studies* 447, 470.

For Papua New Guinea, the fact that Australia had narrowed the meaning of citizenship to enable it as a state to discriminate between Papuan Australian citizens and mainland Australian citizens was one of the drivers to be explicit about making citizenship more meaningful and 'equal' in the new state of Papua New Guinea. This resolve to use the term 'real citizenship' became a further reason for the High Court of Australia to deny Mr Ame and those like him any force to their claim of citizenship and any rights flowing from it.

For Mr Ame and those like him, any sense of connection to Australia from birth in Australian territory or sense of Australian identity from growing up in Australian territory, was not relevant to the High Court's conceptual framework. Bosniak's fourth categorization of citizenship as 'identity/solidarity' had no voice or outlet in this legal story. This understanding of citizenship is often referred to as the 'psychological dimension, that part of citizenship that describes the affective ties of identification and solidarity that we maintain with groups of other people around the world'.[84] This is where those Papuans born in Australian territory, with Australian birth certificates, had a feeling of citizenship that was not fully recognized by the state,[85] even though the state had put out legal markers such as legal status and other attributes of citizenship to assist in creating that feeling and sense of connection.

The joint judgment of the majority in *Ame* does not take account of this aspect of citizenship — the fact that at least some Papuan Australians personally identified as Australian citizens. Perhaps this is because identity is too malleable, too fluid, too non-determinant, non-concrete and non-fixed as a concept for law, in this instance, to take hold of and use for assisting in the determination of disputes. Why did the fact that these Papuans were given no choice in determining their own citizenship identity, with the change over of sovereignty, not gain currency? And how does that sit with the fact that the legal status is also malleable, in that there is little to claim with it, that it can be easily changed and modified, while at the same time it has the potential for great aspirational value? While Kirby J in his separate opinion recognized some of the normative force of the applicant's claim, His Honour was swayed by the international context of the impugned law. The fact that similar measures had been part of other countries' experience of decolonisation assisted him in making his decision. Morevoer, the force of what the people of Papua New Guinea had been seeking to achieve when they

---

84   ibid 479.

85   This point is also made out strongly in another Papuan–Australian citizenship matter involving Susan Walsh that led to a special leave application in the High Court of Australia, prior to the Ame matter. See Kim Rubenstein, 'The Lottery of Citizenship: The Changing Significance of Birthplace, Territory and Residence to the Australian Membership Prize' (2005) 22(2) *Law in Context* 45.

substituted full and effective citizenship of the newly unified and independent state for the clearly inferior citizenship that Australia had previously offered to Papuans were persuasive, in his view, against the applicant's case.[86]

This final point brings us back to the idea of 'thick' and 'thin' descriptions of citizenship. Conceiving of Australian citizenship solely as a matter of legal status results in a very 'thin', superficial account of what it means to be a citizen. Concentrating on the legal status of citizenship, and its legal incidents such as voting rights and rights of entry and residence, is clearly the method preferred by lawyers and courts called upon to determine whether a person is entitled to call themselves an Australian citizen. However, the rules governing access to citizenship and likewise to the franchise or to rights of entry into Australia do not explain all of what it means, at a personal level, to be a citizen. Neither do they provide a complete explanation of the social significance of citizenship as a label denoting full and effective membership of a community. In general, a citizen is a person who is entitled to various social and political rights, including the right to vote and to enter and remain in Australia. So much is clear from the cases and statutes. However, for many people citizenship also connotes a sense of belonging, of identifying as a citizen of a particular nation (or of several nations), or as Bosniak puts it, a sense of 'solidarity' with a national community. Incorporating these facets of citizenship 'thickens' our description of a complex social, political and personal phenomenon.

Conclusion

Ame is an instance in which the High Court recognized what citizenship theorists have long argued — that citizenship can mean different things, and that to say that a person holds the formal legal status of citizen is only the beginning of an explanation of what their citizenship means. In that case, the Court inferred from the fact that Papuan-born Australian citizens did not possess the same political rights as Australian citizens in the States and internal Territories that their statutory citizenship was not real. It was taken to be so thin as to be defeasible. While the High Court was at pains to emphasise that what happened to Mr Ame and his fellow Papuans could not so easily happen to Australian citizens who do not live in an external Territory, this reasoning is premised on an understanding that for most of them, Australian citizenship carries with it a set of political and social rights that cannot easily be stripped away.

---

86   *Ame* (2005) 222 CLR 439, 473–5 (Kirby J).

4. The Right to Participate: Revisiting *Roach* and *Rowe*

Glenn Patmore[1]

As is well known, the Constitution does not refer to the words 'democracy', 'representative democracy', 'representative government' or 'referendum democracy'. Nonetheless the High Court has been willing to imply recognition of these foundational principles. Most of the cases have considered the implied freedom of political communication. More recently, the High Court recognised a constitutional protection of a right to vote and to participate in membership of the political community.[2]

This is a significant development in the jurisprudence of the High Court, but it remains a relatively limited conception of the right to participate.[3] This chapter outlines a broader conception — the right to participate in collective decision-making. The chapter therefore examines and expands upon the High Court's more confined approach. It explains how this latter right is protected by the Constitution and legislation, how it operates in practice, and how it is recognised in political traditions.

For citizens to make collective decisions there must be a set of political institutions and rules which determine 'who is authorised to make' those decisions and 'which procedures ought to be applied'.[4] Insofar as that power 'is authorized by the basic law of the constitution, [it] becomes a right' for all qualified citizens.[5] Thus the capacity to exercise the power to make political decisions is an entitlement recognised as a basic norm of the Constitution. There can be little doubt that the legal authorisation of participation in collective decision-making is an entitlement recognised in law. The view that the Constitution confers

1   g.patmore@unimelb.edu.au. I wish to thank for their assistance, Mr Tom Appleby, Mr Benjamin Hine and Ms Candice Parr who read material to me and provided research assistance. Their work was much appreciated. A special debt is owed to Ms Sarah Shrubb who read the paper and offered comments. Special thanks must also be given to the Melbourne Law Research Service.
2   *Roach v Electoral Commissioner* (2007) 233 CLR 162; *Rowe v Electoral Commissioner* (2010) 243 CLR 1. For a similar view in the US, see Louis Fisher and Katy J Harriger, 'Political Participation' in *American Constitutional Law* (Carolina Academic Press, 8th ed, 2009) 949.
3   This is perhaps inevitable given the judicial duty only to decide matters brought before the court.
4   Norberto Bobbio, *The Future of Democracy* (Roger Griffin trans, University of Minnesota Press, 1987) 24.
5   ibid.

rights on all the people has also been recently recognised. In *Rowe*, French CJ noted that the requirement of a direct choice in ss 7 and 24 of the Constitution 'confers rights on "the people of the Commonwealth"[6] as a whole'.[7]

This chapter has two parts. The first part explains the legal rules and political practices that provide for participation by citizens in collective decision-making. Drawing upon the democratic literature, the chapter identifies the basic legal rules necessary for democracy to function.[8] It also briefly refers to the history of the democratisation of Westminster government and highlights some judicial opinion that has provided support for a broad understanding of constitutional democracy. Secondly, the chapter examines how these legal rules and political practices are and may be better recognised in the law, including in the Australian Constitution, constitutional conventions and legislation. It also considers the recent High Court decisions referring to the constitutional protection of the right to vote and to participate in the political life of the community.

Rights and freedoms to make collective decisions

Right to participate

Since the late 18th century, citizens have been regarded as having a 'right to participate in the determination of the collective will through the medium of elected representatives'.[9] By the end of the 19th century, citizens were regarded as having a right to participate in referendums and plebiscites. Today, the right to participate can be expressed as three principles, which provide the procedure for making the most important collective decisions and find expression in the Australian Constitution. The first principle is that electors directly choose representatives in periodic elections. This principle is recognised in the Australian Constitution, as the High Court explained in *Lange*:

---

6   *Langer v Commonwealth* (1996) 186 CLR 302, 343 per McHugh J.

7   *Rowe v Electoral Commissioner* (2010) 243 CLR 1, 12.

8   My analysis of the Australian Constitution and electoral legislation draws upon elite theories of democracy which are well known to political scientists. While this form of democracy has been criticised as limited, it is nonetheless useful in providing a focus on collective decision-making recognised by the law. See for example Henry Mayo, *An Introduction to Democratic Theory* (Oxford University Press, 1960) and David Held 'Competitive Elitism and the Technocratic Vision' in *Models of Democracy* (Polity, 3rd ed, 2006) 125.

9   Norberto Bobbio, *Democracy and Dictatorship* (Polity, 1989) 144; David Held, *Models of Democracy* (Polity, 3rd ed, 2006) 94.

Sections 7 and 24 of the Constitution, read in context, require the members of the Senate and the House of Representatives to be directly chosen at periodic elections by the people of the States and of the Commonwealth respectively.[10]

This principle is seen as the one indispensable requirement of modern democracies,[11] because a direct choice provides for popular control of representatives. As Gummow J explained in *McGinty*: 'What is necessary is the broadly identified requirement of ultimate control by the people, exercised by representatives who are elected periodically'.[12]

Second, once elected, representatives alone make legislative[13] and executive[14] decisions[15] on behalf of citizens.[16] In Westminster systems like Australia's, Ministers of State exercise executive power, which is the final power of political decision. In other words, they make public policy decisions. They must also be members of Parliament, and are accountable to it.[17] As Mayo pointed out many years ago:

> On the whole, no democratic system operates on the principle that voters directly decide public policies at elections. The control over policy is much more indirect — through the representatives.[18]

Of course Ministers are responsive to the views of electors, since 'popular influence over policy occurs day in day out'.[19] This influence may take different forms, such as through the popular media, community and interest groups, elites, and even state parliamentarians. Indeed the effect of popular influence and control is contemplated by the very system of responsible government. This principle, amongst other things, requires that members of the executive are responsible to Parliament and ultimately to the people, at an election. As

---

10   *Lange v Australian Broadcasting Corporation* (1997) 189 CLR 520, 557.

11   Mayo, above n 8; Bobbio, above n 4.

12   *McGinty v Western Australia* (1990) 186 CLR 140, 285.

13   Legislative power most obviously refers to the power of a Parliament to enact legislation. Members and senators for instance have the power to vote on legislation and participate in the process and procedures of the legislature. See, for example, the *Australian Constitution* ss 23 and 40.

14   Executive power refers to the power of the executive to administer the law and to manage the government, especially government departments. Ministers administer government departments and make collective decisions in cabinet. See, for example, *Australian Constitution* ss 61 and 64.

15   These powers are conferred solely on office holders, such as senators, members and ministers. The Queen and Governor-General, as members of the executive, do not make political decisions according to constitutional conventions.

16   See Suri Ratnapala and Jonathan Crowe, *Australian Constitutional Law: Foundations and Theory* (Oxford University Press, 3rd ed, 2012) 37.

17   The principle of responsible government inter alia requires that members of the executive are responsible to Parliament and ultimately to the people at an election. The executive includes Ministers, who must sit in Parliament. See the *Australian Constitution* ss 61 and 64.

18   Mayo, above n 8, 61.

19   ibid.

the court in *Lange* explained, 'the attitudes of electors to the conduct of the Executive may be a significant determinant of the contemporary practice of responsible government'.[20]

The third principle is that electors directly make policy decisions through the occasional use of referenda and plebiscites. In plebiscites, the electors are asked to vote on a question of national importance, whereas in a referendum to amend the Australian Constitution,[21] electors are asked to vote on a law that is referred to them for their final approval.[22] When voting in referendums to change the Constitution, electors make a policy choice; they exert control over the final decision whether or not to alter the Constitution. Even though the question is framed by the Federal Parliament through a referendum bill, it is not simply a choice offered to the people, but one in which they are typically engaged throughout the entire process of change. The Prime Minister and Cabinet usually initiate the constitutional change, the question to be asked is formulated and approved by the Parliament, opportunities for participation and discussion are created and, ultimately, the people are given their say. While the third principle is regarded as an exception to the second principle of participation, it is, as we have seen, more complex. There is a vital intersection between representative and referendum democracy. The Parliament proposes and the electors decide.

The right to participate, expressed as three principles, helps us understand that the Constitution provides legal entitlements to participate in collective decisions. There are also more specific rights and limitations recognised in the Constitution and legislation.

The democratic rights

The so-called democratic rights or the 'rights of representatives'[23] were developed through struggles over several centuries, but crystallised in the 19th century, in the well-known Chartist movement in the United Kingdom.[24] Their Charter had six basic points that were included in petitions to the UK Parliament

---

20 *Lange v Australian Broadcasting Corporation* (1997) 189 CLR 520, 559.

21 *Australian Constitution* s 128.

22 As Professor Orr notes: 'Terminology is often loosely used in this area.' Orr defines a referendum as 'a binding poll: one that is a necessary part of some legislative or constitutional process'. Conversely, he employs the term plebiscite 'for a poll that is essentially indicative only'. See Orr, 'The Conduct of Referenda and Plebiscites in Australia: A Legal Perspective' (2000) 11 *Public Law Review* 117.

23 Some of these rights are also explicitly recognised in other Constitutions such as the Canadian Constitution (1982): *Canada Act 1982* (UK) ('*Canadian Charter of Rights and Freedoms*').

24 'Chartism', in John Cannon (ed), *Oxford Companion to British History* (Oxford University Press, 2002) 193; Dorothy Thompson, *The Chartists* (Temple Smith, 1984).

in 1839, 1842 and 1848. Five of those points evolved into five rules: universal adult suffrage, the secret ballot,[25] no property qualification to vote or to sit in Parliament,[26] payment of members of Parliament,[27] and equal electorate sizes.[28]

The sixth point of the Charter, demanding annual elections to Parliament, was never implemented in the United Kingdom; nor has it been implemented in Australia. But the requirement for periodic elections has endured and reflects the view that representatives should be regularly accountable to the electorate.

The Chartist movement influenced the development of colonial democracy in Australia and the British Empire. As Justice Crennan explained in an extrajudicial speech, the struggle for 'full and fair representation', especially relating to manhood suffrage, became what is known as the 'imperial framework' and 'reveals the values which lie behind, and are expressed in the Constitution, in the phrase "directly chosen by the people"'.[29]

As noted, the first five points demanded by the Chartists are now included in either Australian electoral legislation or the Australian Constitution, and in UK electoral legislation. They are concerned with the authorisation of those who are to make collective decisions, providing who shall choose and be chosen as representatives (according to the universal franchise), how they shall be chosen (through a secret ballot from electorates of equal size), and with removing limits on that choice based on property and wealth qualifications. Overall, the law authorises the whole people to participate in making collective decisions and confers legal rights 'to participate directly or indirectly in the making' of those decisions.[30] But more is required for democracy to function.

Fundamental freedoms

There is a third condition necessary for collective decisions to be made: electors and representatives must be offered real alternatives, and have the freedom to choose between them.[31] This condition is guaranteed by the fundamental

---

25 *Commonwealth Electoral Act 1918* (Cth) s 323.

26 Various property qualifications lowered or repealed from 1851 onwards. No longer applicable under federal law.

27 *Commonwealth of Australia Constitution Act 1900* (UK) s 48.

28 *Commonwealth Electoral Act 1918* (Cth) s 56.

29 Justice Susan Crennan, 'Reflections on Sections 7 and 24 of the Constitution' (Speech delivered at Gilbert & Tobin Centre of Public Law, Constitutional Law Dinner, New South Wales, 8 February 2008). In the later decision of *Rowe*, her Honour, echoing some of her earlier views in this speech, acknowledged that '"choice by the people" of parliamentary representatives is a constitutional notion signifying individual citizens having a share in political power through a democratic franchise'. This view was expressly agreed with by Gummow and Bell JJ in that case, *Rowe v Electoral Commissioner* (2010) 243 CLR 1, 48.

30 Bobbio, above n 4, 25.

31 ibid.

freedoms of speech, association and assembly.[32] These freedoms draw on the philosophical tradition of the inviolable rights of the individual, as expressed in the French and American revolutions and in contemporary human rights movements. Whatever be their philosophical justifications, though, these freedoms are regarded as the necessary preconditions for the predominantly procedural rules of democracy to function effectively.[33] These freedoms form the basis not only of the liberal state, but also of the democratic state, and when 'political liberties and the legitimate opposition are gone, so, too, is democracy'.[34]

In sum, these procedural rules are regarded as the preconditions for the game, not the game itself.[35] What, then, is the game? The game is the elite competition for power which occurs in Western representative democracies. The competition takes place not only during elections, of course, but through the whole term of the Parliament. Representative democracy is by definition elite, confined to only the small number of individuals who are elected as representatives. The game itself also imposes responsibilities for representatives in a democracy.

Responsibilities of representatives

Mayo recognises three responsibilities as forming the rules of the game for representatives.[36] First, the government, formed by the majority of representatives, makes its policy decisions subject to the existence of the fundamental freedoms. These freedoms limit the capacity of the government to silence the opposition, the critics and those who dissent. It is axiomatic that in Western democracy there is a government and there is an opposition. Political liberties may not be removed by the government within or outside Parliament. This does not mean that governments may not coerce the opposition into obedience to law, nor ill-treat their opponents. Rather, the fundamental freedoms guarantee the opportunity for the opposition and the dissenters to be heard, to protest and to organise.[37] Thus this rule is an inhibition on majority rule.

Second, the opposition will obey the law, even though it might be difficult because the law is disliked.[38] While obeying the law, oppositions habitually work to change the policy and ultimately to change the government and become

---

32 ibid.

33 ibid.

34 Mayo, above n 8, 68.

35 Bobbio, above n 4, 25.

36 Mayo, above n 8, 68.

37 ibid.

38 This is subject to circumstances when there are opportunities for civil disobedience. Opportunities for civil disobedience raise controversial and complex issues of legal obligation. See Lord Lloyd of Hampstead and MDA Freeman, *Lloyd's Introduction to Jurisprudence* (Law Book Co Ltd, 5th ed, 1985); Ronald Dworkin, *Taking Rights Seriously* (Harvard University Press, 1978) ch 7–8; MR Macguigan, 'Obligation and Obedience' in Pennock and Chapman (eds), *Political and Legal Obligations* (Nomos XII, 1970).

a majority — but only by peaceful means.[39] Third, when there is a change of government the new government is subject to the same fundamental freedoms and the new opposition is bound by the same obligations.[40] As Mayo explains, '[t]he minority also agrees beforehand that they, too, will extend the same political freedoms and follow the same rules of the game should they arrive in the seats of office'.[41] The game continues again, with new actors and office holders, according to these rules.

These responsibilities are regarded as necessary for the continuity of democracy. There are of course other social conditions necessary for the peaceful transfer of power and functioning of democracy.[42] However, as Mayo says, these three rules represent the 'formal conditions' necessary to be met 'for majorities and minorities in the legislature if democracy is to work *at all*'.[43] Mayo regards these rules respectively as an inhibition, an obligation and an agreement. In constitutional discourse they would be regarded as constitutional practices or traditions. These responsibilities can also be implied from the express constitutional provisions authorising representatives to make legislative and executive decisions. As these responsibilities may be implied from the text of the Constitution, each may be regarded as a constitutional obligation.[44]

Recognition in law of the rules for collective decision-making

I have examined the right to participate in collective decision-making by explaining the key legal rules, principles and norms upon which the right rests. These provide who is authorised to make collective decisions and the procedures to be applied. But how, you might ask, are these rules recognised in law? In passing, I have already briefly indicated how these rules are acknowledged in law, but some further explanation is required. I address this topic in two ways: first, by briefly analysing how the rules for making collective decisions are recognised in traditional sources of law such as the Constitution, constitutional conventions and legislation; and second, by examining how legislative rights are recognised and may become protected by the Constitution.

---

39   Mayo, above n 8, 32.
40   ibid.
41   ibid 68.
42   ibid.
43   ibid.
44   Mayo identifies a problem here, where a minority party uses political freedom to abolish democracy itself. This problem is addressed in contemporary literature. See for example S Issacharoff, 'Fragile Democracies' (2007) 120(6) *Harvard Law Review* 1406–23

Recognition in traditional sources of law of the rules for collective decision-making

Democratic rights and freedoms are protected by the juridical state. This is the state which is governed not only *sub lege* — or under law — but also according to constitutional limits.[45] The right to participate and the 'democratic rights' of representatives may be inferred from express provisions in the Constitution. Some are imposed as institutional obligations on the legislature: 'There shall be a session of the Parliament once at least in every year', for example.[46] Others are expressed as rights of representatives: 'each member and senator ... shall receive an allowance of',[47] and each member and senator 'shall have one vote', and 'questions arising ... shall be determined by a majority of votes' in the respective houses of Parliament.[48] Some are expressed as individual rights and freedoms. The fundamental freedoms are typically recognised in constitutional bills of rights and statutory charters.

The rule that legislation must be passed subject to the fundamental freedoms receives explicit recognition where there is a statutory or constitutional bill of rights.[49] In Australia, at the federal level, where there is no constitutional bill of rights, freedom of political communication has now been recognised as an implied limit under the Constitution. The freedom confers an immunity from the operation of legislative and executive power.[50] Other fundamental freedoms may also be recognised by the High Court.[51]

The responsibilities for representatives have for a long time been regarded as rules of political practice, and might be regarded as constitutional conventions. These are traditions, not rules of law.[52] They enable the words of the Constitution to be understood in the context of rules induced from political practice. The conventions are principally concerned with the relationship between the Prime Minister, the Ministers and the Governor-General.[53] The responsibilities for

---

45 Bobbio, above n 4, 25.

46 *Australian Constitution* s 6.

47 ibid s 48.

48 ibid s 23.

49 See for example *Victorian Charter of Rights and Responsibilities Act 2006* (Vic) pt 2; those in the US Constitutional Amendment I; and Canadian Charter of Rights and Freedoms s 2.

50 *Lange v Australian Broadcasting Corporation* (1997) 189 CLR 520.

51 *McGinty v the State of WA* (1996) 186 CLR 140, 202; *ACTV v Commonwealth* (1992) 177 CLR 106, 231–32; *Kruger v Commonwealth* (1997) 190 CLR 1, 229; *Wainohu v New South Wales* (2011) 243 CLR 181, 230.

52 They are non-justiciable (that is, they are not capable of being settled by a court of law) and are often described as constitutional conventions. James Clarke, Patrick Keyzer and James Stellios, *Hank's Constitutional Law: Materials and Commentary* (LexisNexis, 2009) 1046-47. Breach of these rules may have real consequences for political actors, the Crown, the Ministers and the Parliament, who have responsibility for administering them. Clarke et al., *Hank's Constitutional Law* (LexisNexis, 2009) 1046.

53 Glenn Patmore, 'The Head of State Debate: A Response to Sir David Smith and Professor David Flint' (2012) 58(2) *Australian Journal of History and Politics* 251.

representatives have not been expressly recognised as conventions in Australia.[54] Nonetheless, they might be acknowledged as conventions in the same way that conventions were recognised by Gibbs CJ in *FAI Insurance Ltd v Winneke*.[55] In this case the question was whether or not the rules of natural justice applied to the Governor in Council. Gibbs CJ relied on the constitutional convention of responsible government to apply the rules of natural justice. His argument ran this way: the Governor in Council must act on the advice of Ministers, who are subject to the rules of natural justice. Therefore the rules of natural justice apply to the Governor in Council in exercising a statutory function. There was also no reason why the Governor in Council should not be subject to the rules of natural justice.[56]

Similarly, the principle of responsible government requires that the government be formed by the party which has the confidence of a majority of members in the lower house of Parliament. If there is to be a new majority or the majority is to be tested, the government must respect the conditions which allow a new majority to be formed. Accordingly, members of Parliament are subject to the responsibilities of representatives to obey the law and make decisions subject to the fundamental freedoms.[57]

Constitutional conventions are political practices or traditions subject only to political pressure. There is a difference in attitude towards conventions in Australia and Britain. For example, Marshall notes that 'the most obvious and undisputed convention of the British constitutional system is that Parliament does not use its unlimited powers of legislation in an oppressive and tyrannical way'.[58] In this way conventions act as an inhibition on the conduct of representatives in the United Kingdom. By contrast, in Australia such a convention has not always been followed. Conventions may be overridden by legislation, as they are not principles of law. Laws which have sought to restrict freedom of association have been passed at both the Commonwealth and State levels. Examples include the Menzies legislation banning the Communist Party[59] and recent NSW legislation to control union payment of membership dues to political parties.[60]

---

54 See for example the *Resolutions Adopted at the Australian Constitutional Convention*, Parliament House, Brisbane, 29 July to 1 August 1985, 312.

55 (1982) 151 CLR 342.

56 *FAI Insurance Ltd v Winneke* (1982) 151 CLR 342, 349. There was also precedent supporting the application of the rules of natural justice to the Governor in Council, see *Roebuck v Borough of Geelong West* (1876) 2 VLR (L) 189; *Shire of Kowree v Shire of Lowan* (1897) 19 ALT 143.

57 The responsibilities for representatives may also meet the test of conventions as propounded by authors such as Marshall. See Geoffrey Marshall, *Constitutional Conventions* (Clarendon Press, 1984).

58 ibid 9.

59 *Australian Communist Party v Commonwealth* (1951) 83 CLR 1.

60 See the *Election Funding, Expenditure and Disclosures Act 1981* div 2A, 4A, ss 87, 95E, 96D–E; *Unions NSW v NSW* [2013] HCA 58.

Whether or not Mayo's responsibilities of representatives are now recognised as conventions, some judges have recognised elements of the responsibilities of representation, though not the responsibilities themselves. Their Honours have focused on the words in ss 7 and 24 that require a direct choice by the people of senators and members (respectively) as imposing limits on the legislature and the government. Accordingly, the legislature and government may not limit a free choice among the available candidates in an election, nor the freedom of political communication.

Several High Court decisions illustrate the scope of these limits. In describing the constitutional system of representative government, the High Court in *Lange* observed that 'the elections to [the Parliament] must be free, with all that this implies in the way of freedom of speech and political organisation'.[61] In *Mulholland*, Gleeson CJ maintained

> that the choice required by the Constitution is a true choice with 'an opportunity to gain an appreciation of the available alternatives' and that a ballot paper that discriminated in favour of a government candidate 'might so distort the process of choice as to fail to satisfy the test' laid down in the Constitution.[62]

In *Langer*, the High Court upheld the system of full preferential voting,[63] where voters number their ballot paper sequentially in accordance with their preference for candidates. Brennan CJ affirmed the validity of preferential voting on the grounds that it provided 'a method of freely choosing members of the House of Representatives' from amongst the available alternatives and 'permits a voter to make a discriminating choice among the candidates for election to the House of Representatives'.[64] In sum, the rules for making collective decisions are to be found in a variety of legal sources, including the Constitution and legislation. Some political practices have not yet been recognised as constitutional conventions, whilst other legal rules have not been fully developed.

Legislative rights recognised and protected as constitutional rights

I now turn to my second issue: how legislative rights may be recognised and entrenched by the Constitution. The so-called democratic rights which draw upon the Chartist movement in the United Kingdom, and that movement's legacy in countries such as Australia, have been expressly recognised in either

---

61   *Lange v Australian Broadcasting Corporation* (1997) 189 CLR 520, 559 (quoting Birch).
62   *Mulholland v Australian Electoral Commission* (2004) 220 CLR 181, 191–2.
63   *Commonwealth Electoral Act 1918* (Cth) s 240.
64   *Langer v Commonwealth* (1996) 186 CLR 302, 317.

the Australian Constitution or in electoral legislation. There is contention over whether the rights are merely recognised in legislation, or may also now be protected by the Constitution.

This issue arose in relation to the *Commonwealth Electoral Act*'s regulation of electorate sizes. The argument that ss 7 and 24 requiring a direct choice by the people requires equal electoral sizes in Commonwealth legislation was rejected by a majority of the High Court in *McKinlay*.[65] At best, some judges in *McKinlay* and *McGinty*[66] made *obiter dicta* statements that these provisions prohibit gross disparities in electorate size or other forms of electoral inequality. At some point such disparities could not be regarded as a direct choice by the people. Nonetheless, the *Commonwealth Electoral Act* now requires equality of electorate sizes, plus or minus ten per cent.[67]

More recently, members of the High Court have referred to a constitutional protection of the right to vote and participate in the political life of the community. The constitutional protection of the right to vote has been controversial. Professor Twomey, relying on Kiefel J in *Rowe*, has argued that ss 7 and 24 do not give rise to a personal right to vote.[68] Professors Blackshield and Williams maintain that the requirement for a direct choice of representatives by the people in ss 7 and 24 arguably supports an *implied* right to vote.[69] In this part, I briefly address two questions in relation to this controversy. First, what form of constitutional protection has been accorded to the right to vote by a majority of the High Court? Second, what is the relationship between the constitutional protection and legislation?

The Federal Parliament has enacted the franchise, which refers to a statutory right to vote. The Parliament has a plenary constitutional power to enact laws for elections and for the qualifications of electors.[70] The first federal electoral act provided a franchise for all adult male and female persons qualified to vote.[71] However, it excluded, on the basis of race, Aboriginal people, Torres Straight Islanders and persons of African and Asian descent.[72] These disqualifications

---

65   *Attorney-General (Cth); Ex rel McKinlay v Commonwealth* (1975) 135 CLR 1.

66   *McGinty v Western Australia* (1996) 186 CLR 140.

67   *Commonwealth Electoral Act 1918* (Cth) s 59(10).

68   Anne Twomey, '*Rowe v Electoral Commissioner* — Evolution or Creationism?' (2012) 31(2) *University of Queensland Law Review* 181, 196.

69   Tony Blackshield and George Williams, *Australian Constitutional Law and Theory* (Federation Press, 5th ed, 2010) 375.

70   *Australian Constitution* ss 8, 10, 29, 30, 31, and 51(xxxvi).

71   *Commonwealth Franchise Act 1902* (Cth) s 3.

72   ibid s 4 provided: 'No aboriginal native of Australia Asia Africa or the Islands of the Pacific except New Zealand shall be entitled to have his name placed on an Electoral Roll unless so entitled under section forty-one of the Constitution.' This was replaced by the *Commonwealth Electoral Act 1918* (Cth) s 39(5).

were not removed until the early 1960s.[73] The universal franchise now means that the legislative right to vote is conferred without restrictions based on race, gender and property. It was not until the 21st century that the High Court decided whether or not the Constitution protected the universal franchise.

The recognition of constitutional protection of the right to vote was accepted by Gleeson CJ in *Roach*[74] and French CJ, Gummow, Crennan and Bell JJ in *Rowe*. In *Roach* the High Court considered a challenge to legislation that banned all prisoners voting.

In *Roach*, the Chief Justice concluded 'that ... the words of ss 7 and 24, because of changed historical circumstances including legislative history, have come to be a constitutional protection of the right to vote'.[75]

His Honour drew on the philosophy of the universal franchise to define the meaning of the right to participate in the political life of the community:[76]

> Because the franchise is critical to representative government, and lies at the centre of our concept of participation in the life of the community, and of citizenship, disenfranchisement of any group of adult citizens on a basis that does not constitute a substantial reason for exclusion from such participation would not be consistent with choice by the people.

He accepted that a substantial reason required 'a rational connection with the identification of community membership or with the capacity to exercise free choice'.[77] In this case, his Honour concluded that the legislative ban on all prisoners voting was arbitrary because it did not distinguish non-serious from serious offences; only serious offences would warrant disenfranchisement.[78]

He noted that the rationale for 'the exclusion from the franchise' must be 'related to the right to participate in political membership of the community'.[79] Chief Justice Gleeson expressly referred to this right, defined broadly, regarding it as protecting the right to vote, which is one of the political rights of citizenship, which in turn provides for full membership of the community. His focus in the

---

73 *Commonwealth Electoral Act 1961* (Cth) s 4 repealed s 39(5) of the 1918 Act; *Commonwealth Electoral Act 1962* (Cth) s 2 removed s 39(6) a provision which restricted enrolment by Aboriginal people.

74 *Roach v Electoral Commissioner* (2007) 233 CLR 162.

75 ibid 174.

76 ibid. Interestingly, in addressing the legislative ban on all prisoners voting in this case his honour said: 'Since what is involved is not an additional form of punishment, and since deprivation of the franchise takes away a right associated with citizenship, that is, with full membership of the community, the rationale for the exclusion must be that serious offending represents such a form of civic irresponsibility that it is appropriate for Parliament (177) to mark such behaviour as anti-social and to direct that physical separation from the community will be accompanied by symbolic separation in the form of loss of a fundamental political right.' *Roach v Electoral Commissioner* (2007) 233 CLR 162, 176–7.

77 ibid 174.

78 ibid.

79 ibid.

judgment, though, was on the right to participate as protecting the right to vote, which he regarded as a fundamental right. However, the Chief Justice's acceptance of the constitutional protection of the right to vote was not adopted by the other judges in *Roach*.

In *Rowe*, the existence of the right to vote was again considered by the High Court. In dissent, Kiefel J argued that ss 7 and 24 did not give rise to a personal right to vote. Her Honour construed the view of Gleeson CJ as a reference to 'an incident of universal adult suffrage, rather than an individualised view of "the franchise"'.[80] However, none of the majority judgments in *Rowe* adopted her approach. In fact, Chief Justice Gleeson's reference to the 'Constitutional protection of the right to vote' was quoted with approval by four judges — French CJ, Crennan, Gummow and Bell JJ.[81] Moreover, each advanced their own distinct understanding of the constitutional protection of the right.

French CJ recognised that ss 7 and 24 conferred rights on the whole people of the Commonwealth. This is because the right to vote was of concern to all the people[82] and individual voting rights and duties to enrol are made in aid of a direct choice, required by ss 7 and 24.[83] Chief Justice French quoted Gleeson CJ's views to justify the irreversible evolution of 'chosen by the people' as protecting the universal adult-citizen franchise. Justices Gummow and Bell noted that

> legislative development always was to be overseen by the imperative of popular choice found in ss 7 and 24 of the Constitution ... One result is explained in the following passage from the reasons of Gleeson CJ in *Roach v Electoral Commissioner*: ... [That] the words of ss 7 and 24 ... have come to be a constitutional protection of the right to vote.

Justice Crennan expressly recognised that 'the relevant words of ss 7 and 24 have always constrained Parliament'[84] and, in Gleeson CJ's words, 'have come to be a constitutional protection of the right to vote'.[85] This, she said,

> mandates a franchise which will result in a democratic representative government ... that is, a franchise free of arbitrary exclusions based on class, gender or race. To recognise that ss 7 and 24 mandate a democratic

80   *Rowe v Electoral Commissioner* (2010) 243 CLR 1, 127.
81   Gleeson CJ, Crennan, Gummow and Bell JJ.
82   *Rowe v Electoral Commissioner* (2010) 243 CLR 1.
83   ibid.
84   ibid, 107.
85   ibid.

franchise, for the purposes of the popular elections which they prescribe, is to recognise the embedding of the right to vote in the constitutional imperative of choice by the people of parliamentary representatives.[86]

In sum, each judge in the majority referred to the constitutional protection of the right to vote, rather than a requirement or incident of representative government. In a recent review of *Roach* and *Rowe*, the Federal Court in *Holmdahl v Australian Electoral Commission (No. 2)*[87] held that the Constitution conferred a public right to vote, not a personal right to vote.[88] Justice Gray quoted with approval Justice McHugh's view in *Langer*:[89]

> The 'rights' conferred by the section are given to 'the people of the Commonwealth' — not individuals, although by necessary implication a member of the public may bring an action to declare void legislation that is contrary to the terms of s 24 or what is necessarily implied by it. Whether or not a member has been 'chosen by the people' depends on a judgment, based on the common understanding of the time, as to whether the people as a class have elected the member. It does not depend on the concrete wishes or desires of individual electors.

Thus a person has a legal entitlement to enforce the public right. Presumably they are acting as representatives of the people of the Commonwealth. However, the right to vote is only conferred on individual persons as members of 'the people'. It is only a right exercised by the people as a class. Due to this complexity the distinction between personal and public right may prove difficult to discern in theory and application. While Justice Gray provided a persuasive opinion, he omitted to quote directly from Chief Justice Gleeson in *Roach*. His honour preferred Justice Kiefel's characterisation in *Rowe* of the Chief Justice's approach. Thus Gleeson CJ's justifications relied on by the majority in *Rowe* were not fully explored in *Holmdahl*.[90] The precise nature of the constitutional protection of the right to vote remains contentious. But there is now, at least, clear judicial support for a constitutional protection of the right to vote.

The judgments of the majority in *Rowe* are of significance to the emergence of an interpretive relationship between the Constitution and longstanding legislation. The High Court's discussion of the relationship is of particular importance to an understanding of the regulatory limits of the Constitution. The aspects of that relationship that will be considered are the effect of the Constitution on legislation and the effect of legislation upon the Constitution. Special

---

86   ibid 117 (emphasis added).
87   *Holmdahl v Australian Electoral Commission (No 2)* [2012] SASCFC 110.
88   ibid, 125 Kourakis CJ and Sulan J concurred with Grey J.
89   *Langer v The Commonwealth* (1995) 186 CLR 302, 342-43; see also, *Langer v The Commonwealth* (1995) 186 CLR 302, 349 (Gummow J).
90   Leave to appeal to the High Court from the Federal Court in *Holmdahl* was denied on 12 April 2013.

attention will be given to the idea of 'permeability' between the Constitution and legislation: the use of constitutional principles as interpretive tools for the direct or indirect protection of rights under legislation and the applicability of legislative provisions as normative principles to enhance the constitutionally prescribed system of representative and responsible government.[91]

My inquiry will focus upon the openness and potential flow of normative principles between the Constitution and legislation. It is important to note that while there is a permeability between these two instruments, the Constitution is supreme law and is not in any way dependent for its authority upon legislation. The possibility for an interpretation that strengthens the right to vote will be emphasised.

A legislative limit on the implied right to participate was at issue in *Rowe*, where the Court considered an amendment to the enrolment procedures.[92] Since 1983, Commonwealth legislation provided that after the election was called, there would be a grace period of seven days to enrol for the first time, or to transfer enrolment if a person had changed their address. In 2006, legislation removed the grace period for new enrolments entirely, and reduced the period to three days for transfer of enrolments.[93] The Electoral Commission estimated that reinstatement of the seven day grace period might affect approximately 100,000 people who lodged claims in the seven day period after the writs were issued. A majority in *Rowe* held that the amendment was invalid.

Effect of the Constitution on legislation

Four justices[94] accepted that the right to vote was protected by the Constitution and regarded it as a limit on the legislative power of the Commonwealth. Chief Justice French held that the *Australian Electoral Act* provisions for grace periods of seven days for enrolment and 3 days for transfer of enrolment could not be restricted due to the 'collateral damage to the extent of participation by qualified persons'.[95] Even though some people failed to fulfil their duties under the Act, limiting their own opportunities, the damage was still a detriment 'of concern to

---

91 This definition is derived from the definition advanced by Craig Scott in an article in which he puts forward his definition of permeability as 'one means of giving practical legal effect to the abstract doctrine of interdependence which has, thus far in its lifespan, existed as little more than a rhetorical slogan'. Craig Scott, 'The Interdependence and Permeability of Human Rights Norms: With Special Reference to the International Covenants on Human Rights' (1989) 27 *Osgoode Hall Law Journal* 769, 771.

92 *Rowe v Electoral Commissioner* (2010) 243 CLR 1.

93 See *Commonwealth Electoral Act 1918* (Cth) see especially s 102 (4AA) which were amendments made by the *Electoral and Referendum Amendment (Electoral Integrity and Other Measures) Act 2006* (Cth). See also ss 101, 102(4) and 115 of the *Commonwealth Electoral Act 1918* (Cth).

94 French CJ, Gummow and Bell JJ, and Crennan J.

95 *Rowe v Electoral Commissioner* (2010) 243 CLR 1, 22.

the whole Commonwealth'.[96] In sum, he saw the legal effect of the amendment as diminishing the opportunities for enrolment and transfer of enrolment that existed prior to their enactment.

Justices Gummow and Bell believed the method of choice adopted by the legislative amendment failed as a means to what should be the end; that is, making elections as expressive of popular choice as practical considerations properly permit — popular choice being guaranteed by ss 7 and 24.[97] They maintained that '[t]he position then is reached that the 2006 Act has the practical operation of effecting a legislative disqualification from what otherwise is the popular choice mandated by the Constitution.'[98] Their Honours also adopted a substantive view of the right, rejecting the argument of the Commonwealth that enrolment was merely a procedure, because it affected the rights of electors.

Justice Crennan accepted that 'the centrality of the franchise, to a citizen's participation in the life of the community and membership of the Australian body politic, was recognised in *Roach*'.[99] Her Honour also maintained that 'persons' had a 'right to participate in choosing parliamentary representatives', against which her Honour assessed the challenged legislation.[100] She said:

> It can be accepted that the impugned provisions ... operate to disentitle or exclude persons (otherwise legally eligible) from the right to vote and the right to participate in choosing parliamentary representatives for the State and Subdivision in which they reside. It can also be accepted that achieving and maintaining Electoral Rolls of integrity is a purpose which is compatible with ss 7 and 24.

Her Honour held that the Amendment Act was not appropriate or necessary to protect the integrity of the Electoral Rolls. Moreover, 'to seek to discourage a surge of late claims for enrolment by disentitling or excluding those making them [under the Amendment Act] constitutes a failure to recognise the centrality of the franchise to a citizen's participation in the political life of the community'.[101]

Thus their Honours recognise three different norms protecting participation and voting. The franchise may not be limited in a way that is detrimental or damaging to participation by 'qualified persons',[102] or by 'disqualifying', 'disentitling' or 'excluding' of citizens, and should enhance the popular choice to participate in elections to the maximum extent that is practical.

---

96   ibid.
97   ibid 57.
98   ibid 58.
99   ibid 112.
100   Twomey, above n 68, 192.
101   *Rowe v Electoral Commissioner* (2010) 243 CLR 1, 120.
102   ibid 22.

Effect of legislation on the Constitution

Significantly, it appears that the meaning of the constitutional text is in part defined by reference to legislation. In *Rowe*, French CJ explained that the universal franchise had become part of the content of the constitutional concept of 'chosen by the people' in ss 7 and 24. He maintained that this constitutional content was developed according to the common understandings of the time, which his Honour said was best expressed in 'durable legislative development[s]'. Justices Gummow and Bell maintained that legislative objectives may give effect to constitutional requirements: 'Section 245(1) states that it "shall be the duty of every elector to vote at each election". This legislatively stated duty furthers the constitutional system of representative government by popular choice.'[103] Thus legislative rights to participate may augment or permeate into the meaning of a direct choice by the people in ss 7 and 24. In *Rowe*, this occurred in two ways: first, the recognition of the right to a seven day grace period for enrolment and a 3 day transfer of enrolment after the election was called; and second, a right to a grace period for failure to enrol or transfer enrolment at a later time. The first grace period became constitutionally entrenched, and the second justified that entrenchment. Chief Justice French, Gummow and Bell JJ referred to s 101 of the *Commonwealth Electoral Act 1918* (Cth), which imposes an obligation to enrol and transfer enrolment.[104] If a person fails to comply, a criminal sanction is imposed, except where a person sends or delivers a late claim for enrolment or transfer to the Electoral Commissioner. Chief Justice French noted that the penalty provisions 'are designed not to punish, but to encourage maximum participation by persons qualified to vote'.[105] Justices Gummow and Bell believed that the provision was designed to encourage maximum enrolment.[106] The legislation encouraging maximum participation or enrolment was in the context of grace periods. It followed, in French CJ's words, that these durable legislative developments were a declaration of the common understanding of the right to vote and to participate in the political decisions of the community.[107]

The permeability of norms between the Constitution and legislation has significance for other legislative rights and freedoms mentioned in this chapter but not currently recognised as protected by the Constitution. Significantly, the so-called democratic rights or the 'rights of representatives' which give effect to a choice by the people have endured in legislation. The majority judgments

---

103   ibid 50.

104   *Commonwealth Electoral Act 1918* (Cth) s 101.

105   *Rowe v Electoral Commissioner* (2010) 243 CLR 1, 29.

106   ibid 58.

107   Justice Crennan's consideration of the effect of legislation on the Constitution was different to the other majority judges. Her Honour refers to the history of the franchise more generally, rather than focusing on legislative developments. The colonial franchises by federation, she noted, were designed to produce democratic lower houses, providing the genesis for the understanding of the constitutional protection given to the right to vote.

in *Rowe* offer approaches that may see further democratic legislative rights protected. However, it is notable that the protection given by the majority to the right to vote pertained to the denial of individuals' opportunities to participate in an election. Not all voting methods may attract such protection: compulsory or preferential voting, which are concerned with Parliament's choice of electoral system, are one example.[108]

Conclusion

The High Court has now recognised a constitutional protection of the right to vote and participate in the political life of the community. The permeability of norms between the Constitution and legislation helps us better understand the nature and scope of that right. However, it has been argued that there is a broader conception of the right to participate in collective decisions which is recognised in constitutional principles, augmented by legislation and possibly constitutional conventions. This includes participation in legislative and executive decisions, not just voting in elections. Whether or not this broader right is recognised by the courts, it will remain of the utmost significance to the practice and proper functioning of Australian constitutional democracy.

---

108   The view that compulsory voting was required by the Constitution was expressly rejected in *Rowe* by Hayne and Kiefel JJ: *Rowe v Electoral Commissioner* (2010) 243 CLR 1, 75, 131; see also Heydon at [313]. Moreover, it may be inferred from Brennan's judgment in *Langer* that preferential voting is constitutional, though not necessarily required. See also *Holmdahl v Australian Electoral Commission* (2012) 277 FLR 101.

II. Accountability and Responsible Government

5. Ministerial Advisers: Democracy and Accountability

Yee-Fui Ng[1]

Ministerial advisers, personally appointed by Ministers, and working out of their private offices, have become an integral part of the political landscape over the last 40 years.

At federation, the very idea of ministerial advisers would have been denigrated, as the framers of the Constitution did not believe in 'making room for political friends'.[2] They believed that it would lead to the 'spoils system' in the United States, where high and low official positions were used to reward friends and offer incentives to work for the political party, resulting in a system that was corrupt and inefficient.

Despite this, the role of ministerial advisers is now deeply entrenched in the political system. It all started with the informal 'kitchen cabinets', where a small group of trusted friends and advisers of the Minister gathered around the kitchen table to discuss political strategies. This has since become formalised and institutionalised into the role of the partisan ministerial adviser, as distinct from the impartial public service. The number of ministerial staff increased from 155 in April 1972 to 407 in June 2011; an increase of 163 per cent.[3]

There has been a distinct shift from federation, where the idea of ministerial advisers would have been derided, to a situation where ministerial advisers are now an integral and institutionalised aspect of governing the nation. Their position has been legislatively recognised and their salaries have been appropriated from public funds since 1980.[4]

There are questions about the democratic accountability of ministerial advisers. Ministerial advisers are not elected and are often derived from political party ranks and arguably do not enhance a participatory form of democracy. As such, a closer analysis of the democratic accountability of ministerial advisers is central to the theme of how law and democracy can interrelate to face new challenges.

---

1   Law Lecturer, RMIT. yeefui@gmail.com.
2   *Official Report of the National Australasian Convention Debates*, Adelaide, 19 April 1897, 916–7.
3   Anne Tiernan, *Power Without Responsibility: Ministerial Staffers in Australian Governments from Whitlam to Howard* (UNSW Press, 2007) 244; Australian Government Department of Finance and Deregulation, *Members of Parliament (Staff) Act 1984 Annual Report 2010–11*, http://www.finance.gov.au/publications/mops_annual_reports/2010-2011/docs/MOPS_Annual_Report.pdf.
4   *Members of Parliament (Staff) Act 1984* (Cth). See *Appropriation Act (No 1) 2012-13* (Cth) Schedule 1; *Appropriation Act (No 1) 1980-81* (Cth).

In this chapter, I will first examine the issues that ministerial advisers pose to democracy. I then consider how relevant legal accountability mechanisms can be extended to ministerial advisers.

I argue that ministerial advisers are increasingly exercising executive power beyond what is allowed in the Statement of Standards for Ministerial Staff[5] and should therefore be subject to legal accountability mechanisms such as appearing before parliamentary committees and judicial review under section 75(v) of the Constitution.

Ministerial advisers and democracy

As ministerial advisers are relatively new actors within the operation of the executive, it is necessary to examine the democratic issues relating to their role.

It can be argued that ministerial advisers enhance participatory democracy in two ways. First, it could be said that the mere existence of the position of ministerial adviser increases public participation in political processes. This is because members of the public can become ministerial advisers and seek to directly influence the political process.

However, ministerial advisers tend to come from a party political background.[6] This means that although a greater number of people are able to influence the political process through becoming ministerial advisers, it tends to be party participation that predominates, rather than a broader form of public participation. In fact, this may exacerbate decision-making on purely political grounds, such as ministerial handouts to win marginal seats.

It may even be argued that there may be questionable actions by ministerial advisers that could be seen to indirectly undermine responsible government. An example of this is the actions of a United Kingdom special adviser, Damian McBride, who collaborated in setting up a blog disseminating fabricated rumours about the sex lives of Conservative politicians in order to undermine their reputations.[7] This kind of purely self-interested, party political activity may be seen to indirectly undermine responsible government by distracting political debate and parliamentary scrutiny of executive action from substantive policy issues towards fabricated issues about politicians' private lives.

---

5   Statement of Standards for Ministerial Staff, http://www.smos.gov.au/resources/statement-of-standards.html.
6   Maria Maley, *Partisans at the Centre of Government: the Role of Ministerial Advisers in the Keating Government 1991–96* (PhD Thesis, The Australian National University, 2002) 211–12; Benito Folino, *A Government of Advisers: The Role, Influence and Accountability of Ministerial Advisers in the New South Wales Political System* (PhD Thesis, University of New South Wales, 2010) 120–3.
7   'Damian McBride's Departure Marks the End of a Bumpy Whitehall Career', *Guardian*, (United Kingdom) 13 April 2009, http://www.guardian.co.uk/politics/2009/apr/13/labour-damian-mcbride-resignation.

Secondly, ministerial advisers can be seen to benefit democracy because they interact with interest groups on behalf of their Minister. This means that there are a wider range of interest groups that can lobby the Minister through the conduit of ministerial advisers, which may increase participatory democracy. However, ministerial advisers also filter information that reaches the Minister. Thus, it is unclear whether the presence of ministerial advisers does increase the number of interest groups reaching the attention of the Minister.

It is necessary to consider the democratic accountability of ministerial advisers. The Australian constitutional system operates within a framework of democratic accountability. Democratic accountability can be explained through a vertical principal–agent relationship, where the 'principal' is 'the people' who agree to be governed by its 'agents' (the elected politicians, executive, judiciary, legislature) in exchange for the protection of individual rights (the protection of life, liberty and property).[8] The principal holds the agents accountable through various means, such as elections or legal mechanisms.[9] Therefore, the sovereign position in a democracy is the public, and accountability focuses on the obligation of officials to justify their public decisions and their exercises of public power to the people.[10]

In addition, there are also horizontal accountability structures, which are a system of checks and balances between government agents and institutions,[11] such as ministerial advisers. As ministerial advisers are not elected by the people, there is no direct link between the 'agent' (ministerial advisers) that should respond to the needs of the 'principal' (the public). Despite this, ministerial advisers operate as significant actors within the executive. Therefore, there have to be systems in place ensuring that ministerial advisers are accountable, much like the elected representatives.

This chapter will examine the current regulation of ministerial advisers. The chapter will also identify accountability gaps and suggest how these can be addressed.

---

8   Christine B Harrington and Z Umut Turem, 'Accounting for Accountability in Neoliberal Regulatory Regimes' in Michael W Dowdle (ed), *Public Accountability: Designs, Dilemmas and Experiences* (Cambridge University Press, 2006) 198–9.
9   ibid 199.
10   ibid.
11   ibid.

Accountability of ministerial advisers

There have been concerns about the accountability of ministerial advisers as seen by prominent events such as the 'Children Overboard' incident.[12]

In the 'Children Overboard' incident in 2001, Ministers made public statements that asylum seekers had thrown their own children overboard. For instance, the Prime Minister said, 'I don't want people like that in Australia. Genuine refugees don't do that ... They hang on to their children.'[13]

Within a few days, several public servants found out that the children overboard story was false.[14] They notified a ministerial adviser of the Defence Minister about this.[15] Nonetheless, Ministers continued to make public statements about asylum seekers throwing children overboard as part of an election campaign. When pressed for evidence, the press secretary of the Defence Minister asked a public servant to email two photographs to him.[16] The photos were actually of two brave navy sailors who rescued terrified asylum seekers and their children in the open sea when their boat sank. The press secretary was informed soon after that the photos were not of the children overboard incident, but of the rescue operation.[17]

Despite this, the press secretary asked a public servant for another copy of the photo. He was insistent that the photo be emailed immediately. 'I am your boss', he said to the public servant. He refused to hang up until the photos were emailed to him. The Ministers released these photographs to the media as evidence of children being thrown overboard.[18] A Senate Select Committee was formed to investigate the 'Children Overboard' incident. The government refused to allow ministerial advisers to appear before the Senate Committee. The Senate Committee was highly critical of this, stating that '[s]uch bans and refusals are anathema to accountability'.[19] Despite this, the Senate Committee

---

12 There are other incidents at State level such as the Hotel Windsor incident and the 'leaked tapes' crisis in Victoria. See Ombudsman Victoria, 'Ombudsman Investigation into the Probity of the Hotel Windsor Redevelopment' (2011), http://www.ombudsman.vic.gov.au/resources/documents/Ombudsman_investigation_into_the_probity_of_The_Hotel_Windsor_redevelopment.pdf; James Campbell, 'Tony Nutt told Police Minister Peter Ryan "to put a sock in it"', *The Herald Sun (Melbourne)*, 4 March 2013, http://www.heraldsun.com.au/news/victoria/tony-nutt-told-police-minister-peter-ryan-to-put-a-sock-in-it/story-e6frf7kx-1226589560123.

13 Christine B Harrington and Z Umut Turem, 'Accounting for Accountability in Neoliberal Regulatory Regimes' in Michael W Dowdle (ed), *Public Accountability: Designs, Dilemmas and Experiences* (Cambridge University Press, 2006) 251.

14 Commonwealth Senate Select Committee, *A Certain Maritime Incident* (2002) xxxvi.

15 Patrick Weller, *Don't Tell the Prime Minister* (Scribe Publications, 2002) 26.

16 David Marr and Marian Wilkinson, *Dark Victory* (Allen & Unwin, 2nd ed, 2004) 266–7.

17 ibid.

18 ibid 35.

19 Commonwealth Senate Select Committee, *A Certain Maritime Incident* (2002) xxxiv.

did not seek to compel the attendance of ministerial advisers, stating that it would be unjust to impose a penalty on a ministerial adviser who did not appear on the direction of their Minister.[20]

In 2004, one of these ministerial advisers, Mike Scrafton, wrote an article in a newspaper stating that he told the Prime Minister that claims of children being thrown overboard were unsubstantiated before the federal election, contrary to the Prime Minister's denials.[21] A special Senate inquiry was established to hear his evidence. Scrafton passed a polygraph test for his statutory declaration.[22] The report indicated that the ministerial adviser had briefed the Ministers on the falsity of the children overboard allegations prior to the elections and the Ministers had chosen not to correct the public record.[23]

This example highlights an accountability gap, making it necessary to examine the current regulation of ministerial advisers and how further accountability mechanisms can be applied to them.

Current regulation of ministerial advisers

Ministerial advisers are employed under the *Members of Parliament (Staff) Act 1984* (Cth).[24] The terms and conditions of employment of ministerial advisers are subject to the determination of the employing Minister,[25] with the Prime Minister being able to vary the employment terms and conditions.[26]

Section 31 of the Act requires the Prime Minister to table a yearly report to Parliament setting out the name of each consultant engaged by all Ministers, the period of engagement of the consultant, and the tasks specified.[27] Ministerial advisers are not engaged as consultants and therefore do not fall within the scope of this provision. Nevertheless, since 2007–08, the government has tabled annual reports providing information about the numbers of ministerial advisers employed, their classification levels, and their salaries and benefits.[28]

Ministerial advisers are also subject to a Statement of Standards, setting out the standards that they are expected to meet in performing their duties.[29] The

---

20 Commonwealth Senate Select Committee, *A Certain Maritime Incident* (2002) xxxiv–xxxv.
21 Commonwealth Senate Select Committee on the Scrafton Evidence, Report (2004) 1–2.
22 ibid 68; Text of Mike Scrafton's Letter to the Australia of 4 September 2004, Appendix 4 of Commonwealth Senate Select Committee on the Scrafton Evidence, Report (2004).
23 Commonwealth Senate Select Committee on the Scrafton Evidence, Report (2004) 1–2, 48.
24 *Members of Parliament (Staff) Act 1984* (Cth) s 13 ('MOPS Act').
25 ibid s 14(1).
26 ibid s 14(3).
27 ibid s 31.
28 See Members of Parliament (Staff) Act 1984 Annual Reports, http://www.finance.gov.au/publications/mops_annual_reports/index.html.
29 Statement of Standards for Ministerial Staff, http://www.smos.gov.au/resources/statement-of-standards.html.

Statement of Standards include acknowledgement that ministerial staff do not have the power to direct public servants in their own right.[30] In addition, it recognises that executive decisions are the preserve of Ministers and public servants, and not ministerial staff acting in their own right.[31] Further, ministerial advisers have the duty to facilitate direct and effective communication between their Minister's department and their Minister.[32] Implementation and sanctions under the Standards are handled internally by the executive through the Prime Minister's Office.[33] This means that any breaches of the Standards by ministerial advisers such as those in the 'Children Overboard' incident would be handled behind closed doors, without the scrutiny of Parliament or any external bodies.

The Statement of Standards seems to suggest that ministerial advisers have a very limited role and are merely conduits between the Ministers and the public service. Nevertheless, ministerial advisers have increasingly extensive roles, including advising on public policy, media, political, parliamentary management and party management matters.[34]

Tony Nutt, the former Chief of Staff of the Victorian Premier, in the leaked conversations to the *Herald Sun*, sums it up very colourfully:

> [A] ministerial adviser deals with the press. A ministerial adviser handles the politics. A ministerial adviser talks to the union. All of that happens every day of the week, everywhere in Australia all the time. Including frankly, the odd bit of, you know, ancient Spanish practices and a bit of bastardry on the way through. That's all the nature of politics.[35]

Significantly, there are instances where certain ministerial advisers act on behalf of their Minister and potentially exercise executive power. Dr Maria Maley referred to this as advisers becoming 'surrogates' and making minor decisions in the Minister's name,[36] while Jack Waterford noted that some Ministers 'effectively delegate parts of their work to individual staffers, expecting them to make

---

30   ibid cl 11.

31   ibid cl 12.

32   ibid cl 13.

33   ibid. Implementation of the Standards is the responsibility of the Prime Minister's Office and the Government Staffing Committee. Sanctions imposed under the Standards are determined after consultation with the relevant Minister by the Prime Minister's Chief of Staff, acting on advice from the Government Staffing Committee.

34   *The Herald and Weekly Times Pty Limited v The Office of the Premier (General)* [2012] VCAT 967 [22].

35   James Campbell, 'Tony Nutt told Police Minister Peter Ryan "to put a sock in it"', *The Herald Sun* (Melbourne), 4 March 2013, http://www.heraldsun.com.au/news/victoria/tony-nutt-told-police-minister-peter-ryan-to-put-a-sock-in-it/story-e6frf7kx-1226589560123.

36   Maria Maley, *Partisans at the Centre of Government: the Role of Ministerial Advisers in the Keating Government 1991–96* (PhD Thesis, The Australian National University, 2002) 123. Cited in Commonwealth Senate, Finance and Public Administration References Committee, Staff Employed under the *Members of Parliament (Staff) Act 1984* (2003) 16.

routine decisions and to process approvals without any need for consultation'.[37] Harry Evans, a former Clerk of the Senate, has stated that ministerial advisers 'act as de facto assistant ministers and participate in government activities as such'.[38] Further, the Senate Committee for the 'Children Overboard' incident found that 'it can no longer be assumed that [ministerial] advisers act at the express direction of ministers and/or with their knowledge and consent. Increasingly, advisers are wielding executive power in their own right.'[39]

In this chapter, I focus on ministerial advisers with the role of acting on behalf of the Minister, as this is their most controversial role. I will consider whether in some situations ministerial advisers exercise executive power.

Do ministerial advisers exercise executive power?

The constitutional framework for the executive is characterised by large gaps and eloquent silences. The content of Commonwealth executive power was deliberately not expressly defined by the drafters of the Constitution. Sir Alfred Deakin stated in relation to section 61:

> No exhaustive definition is attempted in the Constitution — obviously because any such attempt would have involved a risk of undue, and perhaps unintentional, limitation of the executive power. Had it been intended to limit the scope of the executive power to matters on which the Commonwealth Parliament had legislated, nothing would have been easier than to say so.[40]

Therefore, executive power is an elusive and slippery concept defying the strictures of precise definition.[41] Even the scope of executive power is uncertain, with only incremental clarification through case law over the years.

Technically, according to section 61 of the Constitution, the Commonwealth's executive power is vested in the Queen and is exercisable by the Governor-General. However, there is a constitutional convention that the Governor-

---

37   Jack Waterford, 'Reining in Political Staff and Outsiders', *Public Sector Informer* (*Canberra Times*) December 2001, 6. Cited in Commonwealth Senate, Finance and Public Administration References Committee, Staff Employed under the *Members of Parliament (Staff) Act 1984* (2003) 16.
38   Clerk of the Senate, Correspondence to Senator Cook, 22 March 2002, 4.
39   Commonwealth Senate Select Committee, *A Certain Maritime Incident* (2002) xxxvii.
40   Alfred Deakin, 'Channel of Communication with Imperial Government: Position of Consuls: Executive Power of Commonwealth', in P Brazil and M Mitchell (eds), *Opinions of Attorneys-General of the Commonwealth of Australia: Volume 1: 1901–14* (Canberra, AGPS, 1981) 129, 130.
41   In *Davis v Commonwealth* (1988) 166 CLR 79, 92, Mason CJ, Deane and Gaudron JJ acknowledged that the scope of the executive power of the Commonwealth had 'often been discussed but never defined'. In *Pape v Commissioner of Taxation* (2009) 238 CLR 1, the judges do not attempt a full discussion on the scope of executive power.

General only exercises executive power on the advice of Ministers.[42] Thus, in practice, executive power is exercised by Ministers, as the government acts through Ministers who administer government departments under section 64 of the Constitution.[43] In addition, Ministers may exercise executive power conferred by statute.[44] However, it is recognised that efficient government administration may require in many circumstances that a Minister act through another person.[45] As stated by Staughton LJ in *R v Secretary of State for the Home Department; Ex parte Doody*:

> Parliament frequently confers powers on a minister who is the political head of a department. Much less frequently, it confers powers on an official of a particular description or grade ... But it is absurd to suppose that every power which is conferred on the political head of a department must be exercised by him and him alone. It is in general sufficient that the power is exercised by a junior minister or an official on his behalf.[46]

Ministers do not have to personally make all decisions themselves. Legislation may confer the ability for Ministers to delegate their powers.[47] Alternatively, legislation may specify that a public servant is to exercise powers under the statute.[48] Therefore, public servants may exercise executive power by virtue of authority granted by statute or power delegated by the Minister.

The Statement of Standards for ministerial advisers seems to envisage that executive power is solely the province of Ministers and public servants, not ministerial advisers.[49] However, I argue that, in certain circumstances, ministerial advisers can and do exercise executive power. In particular, according to the *Carltona* or 'alter ego' principle,[50] Ministers may have agents who are authorised to carry out certain tasks without having a formal delegation to do so. According to this principle, constitutionally the agent's decision is deemed

---

42   Ian Killey, *Constitutional Conventions in Australia: An Introduction to the Unwritten Rules of Australia's Constitution* (Australian Scholarly Publishing, 2nd ed, 2012) 130.

43   *Ryder v Foley* (1906) 4 CLR 422, 432–3. See P H Lane, *Lane's Commentary on the Australian Constitution* (LBC Information Services, 2nd ed, 1997) 433.

44   P H Lane, *Lane's Commentary on the Australian Constitution* (LBC Information Services, 2nd ed, 1997) 433.

45   *R v Secretary of State for the Home Department; Ex parte Doody* [1993] QB 157, 194, *R v Secretary of State for the Home Department; Ex parte Doody* [1994] 1 AC 531, 566. Applied in Australia by *Attorney General v Foster* (1999) 84 FCR 582.

46   [1993] QB 157, 194. *R v Secretary of State for the Home Department; Ex parte Doody* [1993] QB 157, 194, adopted on appeal in the House of Lords in *R v Secretary of State for the Home Department; Ex parte Doody* [1994] 1 AC 531, 566. Cited with approval in *Attorney General v Foster* (1999) 84 FCR 582.

47   *R v Secretary of State for the Home Department; Ex parte Doody* [1993] QB 157, 194.

48   ibid.

49   Statement of Standards for Ministerial Staff, http://www.smos.gov.au/resources/statement-of-standards.html.

50   *Carltona Ltd v Commissioners of Works* [1943] 2 All ER 560, 563. Applied in Australia by *O'Reilly v State Bank of Victoria Commissioner* (1983) 153 CLR 1, 11.

to be the Minister's decision.[51] The Minister remains responsible and answerable to Parliament for anything his/her officials have done under the Minister's authority.[52]

This is illustrated by the case of *Ozmanian v Minister for Immigration, Local Government and Ethnic Affairs*.[53] In this case, the Minister authorised procedures for dealing with the large number of requests for ministerial interventions to grant protection visas 'in the public interest'. A Senior Adviser of the Minister would sign a letter on behalf of the Minister about whether the Minister would consider the application for a protection visa. This meant that a ministerial adviser was in effect signing letters determining substantive issues affecting the rights of asylum-seekers. In *Ozmanian*, although the letter was said to be sent at the request of the Minister, the Minister had in fact never seen the letter.[54] This would be an exercise of executive power if it was held to be valid.

At first instance, Merkel J held that the Senior Adviser made the decision on behalf of the Minister.[55] Although the decision was not made by the Minister, it was a decision made under the authority of the *Migration Act 1958* (Cth) ('*Migration Act*') as it was in accordance with the general procedures established with the Minister's authority.[56]

Despite this, Merkel J stated that the *Migration Act* detailed powers of delegation making it less likely that the *Carltona* principle would apply.[57] Further, courts are reluctant to utilise the *Carltona* principle where the exercise of that power may have drastic consequences upon an individual, such as visa decisions.[58] Hence, the power under the *Migration Act* had to be exercised by the Minister personally or an authorised delegate.[59] This means that the decision made by the Senior Adviser was invalid.[60]

Merkel J's decision was overturned by the Full Federal Court on other grounds. The Full Court did not find it necessary to determine the ministerial adviser issue.[61] Therefore the law in this area is not settled.

Ozmanian is an instance of a ministerial adviser exercising executive power, contrary to the Statement of Standards. However, there are no external

---

51 *Carltona Ltd v Commissioners of Works* [1943] 2 All ER 560, 563.
52 ibid.
53 (1996) 41 ALD 293.
54 *Ozmanian v Minister for Immigration, Local Government and Ethnic Affairs* (1996) 41 ALD 293, 300.
55 ibid 305.
56 ibid.
57 ibid 309.
58 ibid.
59 ibid. This part of the decision was overturned by the Full Court of the Federal Court in *Bedlington v Chong* (1998) 87 FCR 75; *Raikua v Minister for Immigration and Multicultural and Indigenous Affairs* (2007) 158 FCR 510, 523.
60 *Ozmanian v Minister for Immigration, Local Government and Ethnic Affairs* (1996) 41 ALD 293, 310.
61 *Minister for Immigration and Multicultural Affairs v Ozmanian* (1996) 71 FCR 1.

enforcement mechanisms under the Standards, and the Standards are not legislatively enshrined. Therefore, courts do not take the Standards into account. Nevertheless, the courts have the jurisdiction to police the boundaries of executive power. The courts have a few options. First, the courts could decide that a particular aspect of executive power is non-delegable to ministerial advisers, akin to Merkel J's judgment. This is more likely in decisions with drastic consequences for individuals and where there are existing powers of delegation within the legislation. Decisions involving fundamental rights of life and liberty should arguably only be exercised by the Minister or an authorised delegate due to the potentially significant negative impact on individuals. The power of delegation within legislation suggests that delegation should be conducted within the legislative framework. Where the court decides that decisions are non-delegable, the decisions of ministerial advisers are invalid.

Alternately, the courts may decide that the *Carltona* principle may apply to ministerial advisers based on statutory interpretation. In this situation, ministerial advisers are acting as the informal agent of the Minister and are able to make executive decisions on the Minister's behalf. According to case law, the person exercising the power must be an 'appropriate' official.[62] Mark Campbell has found that, in general, courts have accepted that it is for the Minister to decide who is an appropriate official to exercise power,[63] and the court tends to defer to the Minister's choice. As *Carltona* indicates, even if the Minister gave responsibility to an official who is too junior, it is the Minister who would answer for this in Parliament.[64] This suggests that courts would not supervise the selection of the official, even if the official is junior.

However, as Professor Mark Freedland argues, *Carltona* was decided in a legal and constitutional environment where 'extreme importance' was attached to ministerial responsibility.[65] *Carltona* is predicated upon the Minister actually taking responsibility in Parliament for the wrong choice of an official. However, the application of ministerial responsibility in Australia has been watered down significantly.[66] Thus it is reasonable to more cautiously apply *Carltona* in modern times and not simply assume that all public officials would be covered by this principle.

---

62 *Carltona Ltd v Commissioners of Works* [1943] 2 All ER 560; *Re Golden Chemical Products Ltd* [1976] 2 All ER 543; *R v Secretary of State for the Home Department; Ex parte Oladehinde* [1991] AC 254; *R (on the application of Chief Constable of West Midlands) v Birmingham Justices* [2002] EWHC 1087 [10].

63 Mark Campbell, 'The Carltona Doctrine' (2007) 18 *Public Law Review* 251, 261. *R v NDT Ventures Ltd* (2001) 4 Admin LR 110 (4th); *Re Golden Chemical Products Ltd* [1976] 2 All ER 543.

64 *Carltona Ltd v Commissioners of Works* [1943] 2 All ER 560, 563.

65 Mark Freedland, 'The Rule against Delegation and the Carltona Doctrine in an Agency Context' (1996) *Public Law* 19, 24–5.

66 See Ian Killey, *Constitutional Conventions in Australia: An Introduction to the Unwritten Rules of Australia's Constitution* (Australian Scholarly Publishing, 2nd ed, 2012) 87.

There are limits to the Minister's choice of agent. The courts are likely to inquire into the identity of the Minister's agent if the Minister's choice was irrational or beyond the Minister's powers.[67] If an Immigration Minister authorised a low level administrative assistant from the Department of Tourism to make visa decisions, for example, the courts would be likely to intercede, as this decision would be illogical and unreasonable: the Minister has qualified staff in his/her department to handle visa matters and it does not make sense for an assistant in the Department of Tourism without the requisite skills to make migration decisions.[68]

In addition, where the decision affects individual rights and liberties and involves coercive powers, the courts may also look more closely at the Minister's choice of agent. This is because executive and statutory decisions depriving an individual of rights and liberties are grave and should not be entrusted to unqualified individuals. For instance, if an Immigration Minister authorised a low-ranking administrative assistant to make deportation decisions, which have grave consequences for individuals, this activity would not be upheld by the courts. However, if the Immigration Minister granted the same power to a senior ministerial adviser, the courts would tend not to question the choice of the adviser.

In short, *Ozmanian* demonstrates that there are instances where ministerial advisers in effect exercise executive power. Where ministerial advisers exercise executive power, they are operating as part of the executive. Therefore, they should be subject to appropriate accountability mechanisms. I will now briefly outline two possible options for accountability: to Parliament and to the courts.

Accountability to Parliament

The recent High Court decision of *Williams v Commonwealth* ('*Williams*') emphasises the concept of responsible government, with six judges utilising responsible government as the basis of their decisions.[69] The majority of French CJ, Gummow, Bell and Crennan JJ utilised responsible government to hold that the Commonwealth needs statutory authority to enter into contracts and spend public money, subject to limited exceptions.[70] French CJ held that a broad conception of the Commonwealth executive's power to contract would undermine parliamentary control of the executive branch and weaken the

---

67   Mark Campbell, 'The Carltona Doctrine' (2007) 18 *Public Law Review* 261. *R (on the application of Chief Constable of West Midlands) v Birmingham Justices* [2002] EWHC 1087 (Admin) [16].

68   See Mark Campbell, 'The Carltona Doctrine' (2007) 18 *Public Law Review* 262.

69   *Williams v Commonwealth* (2012) 248 CLR 156, 179-80 [4] French CJ, 239 [161] Gummow and Bell JJ, 357-8 [542]-[544] (Crennan J).

70   ibid. The exceptions include prerogative powers, ordinary and well-recognised functions of government, nationhood power and incidental power. *Williams* (2012) 248 CLR 156,191 [34] French CJ, 342 [484] Crennan J.

role of the Senate.[71] Crennan J also emphasised the institution of responsible government, where the executive's primary responsibility in its prosecution of government is owed to Parliament.[72] Crennan J noted that this accountability came to be expressed in terms of the need for the executive to enjoy the confidence of Parliament in dealing with finance, as the arm of government most immediately representing and therefore responsible to the people (the electors).[73] Gummow and Bell JJ held that an unqualified executive power to contract and to spend would undermine the basic assumption of legislative predominance inherited from the United Kingdom and would distort the relationship between Chapter I and Chapter II of the Constitution.[74]

In *Williams*, responsible government is more central to the reasoning process of the judges than in *Lange v Australian Broadcasting Corporation* ('*Lange*').[75] According to the High Court in *Lange*, responsible government could create limits on executive power, not just legislative power.[76] This concept of responsible government being a fetter on executive power was taken further in *Williams*, as the High Court utilised responsible government as a restraint on the Commonwealth Executive's ability to circumvent parliamentary processes. This resulted in a substantive limitation, that is, a significant reduction of Commonwealth executive power in contracting without statutory authority.

Therefore, *Williams* may represent a resurgence of responsible government and the utilisation of parliamentary accountability as a mechanism for constraining the actions of the Commonwealth executive.

Under the doctrine of responsible government, the executive is responsible to the legislature. As the High Court stated in *Egan v Willis*, the contemporary position in Australia is that while 'the primary role of Parliament is to pass laws, it also has important functions to question and criticise the government on behalf of the people', and 'to secure accountability of government activity is the very essence of responsible government'.[77] According to John Stuart Mill, the task of the Legislature is to 'watch and control the government: to throw the light of publicity on its acts'.[78]

Sir Samuel Griffith provided an explanation about the main principles of responsible government, that is, the Crown does not act on its own volition, but

---

71   ibid [60].
72   ibid [509].
73   ibid [509].
74   ibid [136].
75   (1997) 189 CLR 520.
76   *Lange v Australian Broadcasting Corporation* (1997) 189 CLR 520, 561.
77   *Egan v Willis* (1998) 195 CLR 424, [42–3] (Gaudron, Gummow and Hayne JJ).
78   John Stuart Mill, *Considerations on Representative Government* (Parker, Son and Bourn, 1861) 104.

rather follows advice of Ministers.[79] Therefore Ministers bear the responsibility for the decisions that they make. Ministers are responsible to Parliament and can only hold their position with the confidence of the people, reflected by the House of Representatives in Parliament.[80] The requirement of confidence from the House of Representatives is based on the principle that the House of Representatives is the people's house, and represents the interests of the people, while the Senate is the State's house. As Sir John Quick and Sir Robert Garran said: 'The Senate represents the States as political units. The House represents the people as individual units.'[81] Therefore, the principle of responsible government has a democratic element and is linked with the concept of representative democracy as it provides that the executive government is accountable, through the mechanisms of Parliament, to the people who elected the executive.

In terms of ministerial advisers, I argue that because their salary is appropriated from public funds[82] and as they may increasingly be exercising executive power, the principles of responsible government apply to them. Hence, ministerial advisers should be accountable to Parliament by being required to appear before parliamentary committees, such as those established for the 'Children Overboard' incident.

At the Commonwealth level, parliamentary privileges and immunities are governed by the *Parliamentary Privileges Act 1987* (Cth). This Act preserves the operation of section 49 of the Constitution, that Commonwealth Members of Parliament have the powers, privileges and immunities of the United Kingdom House of Commons existing on 1 January 1901.[83] According to *Lange*, section 49 of the Constitution provides the source of coercive authority for each House of Parliament to 'summon witnesses, or to require the production of documents, under pain of punishment for contempt'.[84] Therefore, at the Commonwealth level, the Senate has the power to compel the production of persons and documents. This includes the power to compel ministerial advisers to attend, to give evidence and produce documents to a Senate Committee.

---

79   Samuel Griffith, 'Notes on Australian Federation: Its Nature and Probable Effects' (paper presented to the Government of Queensland, 1896) 17–8, http://adc.library.usyd.edu.au/data-2/fed0017.pdf.

80   ibid.

81   John Quick and Robert Randolph Garran, *The Annotated Constitution of the Australian Commonwealth* (Angus & Robertson, 1901) 447.

82   There has been a yearly appropriation of ministerial adviser salaries in Parliament since 1980 as part of the 'ordinary services of government'. See for example *Appropriation Act (No 1) 1980–81* (Cth), *Appropriation Act (No 1) 2012–13* (Cth) Schedule 1, Department of Finance and Administration, Outcome 3.

83   *Parliamentary Privileges Act 1987* (Cth) s 5.

84   *Lange* (1997) 189 CLR 520, 557–9. See also Parliament of Australia, Orders for Production of Documents (2005), http://www.aph.gov.au/About_Parliament/Senate/Powers_practice_n_procedures/guides/briefno11.

Traditionally ministerial advisers are seen to be accountable to their Minister personally, while Ministers are accountable to Parliament.[85] It has been argued that ministerial advisers are thus not required to appear before parliamentary committees. As a result, ministerial advisers have generally tended not to appear before parliamentary committees based on the instructions of their Minister.

However, this argument is weak, as public servants are similarly accountable to their Minister, who is then linked by the chain of accountability to Parliament. Unlike ministerial advisers, public servants routinely appear before parliamentary committees. Their presence is to give an *account* of their actions to Parliament, while *responsibility* for their actions fall on their Minister, who may be censured in Parliament.[86] The appearance of ministerial advisers before parliamentary committees would be to perform a similar function.

In situations such as the 'Children Overboard' incident, the fact that ministerial advisers did not appear before the parliamentary committees allowed the Ministers to escape accountability by claiming they were not advised of the fact that no children had been thrown overboard, while ministerial advisers did not present their account as they did not appear before Parliament. This creates an accountability gap, where Ministers are able to plead ignorance to controversial policies and decisions and escape accountability in Parliament. Therefore, in accordance with recommendations of a Senate Committee, ministerial advisers should appear before parliamentary committees, particularly where a Minister has renounced a ministerial adviser's action, refused to answer questions regarding the conduct of a ministerial adviser, critical information has been received from a Minister's office but is not communicated to a Minister, or critical instructions have emanated from a Minister's office and not the Minister.[87]

There is no strong rationale why ministerial advisers do not appear before parliamentary committees. The best way for this to happen is with the agreement between Parliament and the government for ministerial advisers to appear based on negotiated guidelines. This has previously been done for public servants.[88] Otherwise, there will be a perpetual battle of wills between Parliament, with their strong powers, and government, with their fondness for political escapism.

---

85   H Collins, 'What Shall We Do With the Westminster Model?' in R Smith and P Weller (eds), *Public Service Inquiries in Australia* (University of Queensland Press, 1978) 366.

86   Senate Finance and Public Administration References Committee, 'Staff Employed Under the *Members of Parliament (Staff) Act 1984*' (2003) xii.

87   ibid.

88   See Government Guidelines for Official Witnesses before Parliamentary Committees and Related Matters, http://www.dpmc.gov.au/guidelines/.

Accountability to the courts

Another potential accountability mechanism is if courts are able to judicially review the executive actions of ministerial advisers. To this end, it can be argued that ministerial advisers are 'officers of the Commonwealth' under section 75(v) of the Constitution. Section 75(v) is said to entrench a minimum provision of judicial review.[89] This means that Parliament is unable to remove the jurisdiction of the High Court 'by any form of words or any device'.[90]

It is clear that Ministers,[91] public servants[92] and Minister's delegates[93] are 'officers of the Commonwealth'. However, this issue has not been determined for ministerial advisers.

According to case law, an 'officer of the Commonwealth' has to have an office of some conceivable tenure, be directly appointed by the Commonwealth, accept office and salary from the Commonwealth, and be removable by the Commonwealth.[94] In *R v Murray and Cormie; Ex parte Commonwealth*, Isaacs J stated:

> The expression 'officer of the Commonwealth' has not a fictional meaning. It has a real meaning that the person referred to is individually appointed by the Commonwealth; and therefore the Constitution takes his Commonwealth official position as in itself a sufficient element to attract the original jurisdiction of the High Court.[95]

In *Williams*, the fact that Commonwealth funding was used to employ school chaplains was not considered enough for the school chaplains to hold an office under the Commonwealth under section 116 of the Constitution.[96]

Gummow and Bell JJ, with French CJ, Crennan and Kiefel JJ agreeing, held that the school chaplains were not 'offices ... under the Commonwealth' under section 116 of the Constitution.[97] For these judges, the presence of a contractual

---

89   *Plaintiff S157/2002 v Commonwealth* (2003) 211 CLR 476, [103] (Gaudron, McHugh, Gummow, Kirby and Hayne JJ).
90   *R v Commonwealth Court of Conciliation & Arbitration; Ex parte Brisbane Tramways Co Ltd* (1914) 18 CLR 54, 59.
91   *Church of Scientology Inc v Woodward* (1982) 154 CLR 25, 65.
92   *R v Commonwealth Court of Conciliation & Arbitration; Ex parte Brisbane Tramways Co Ltd* (1914) 18 CLR 54, 66, 86, *Church of Scientology Inc v Woodward* (1982) 154 CLR 25, 66. *Queensland Medical Laboratory v Blewett* (1988) 84 ALR 615, *Minister for Immigration and Multicultural Affairs v Jia* (2001) 205 CLR 507, 545, *Re Minister for Immigration and Multicultural Affairs; ex parte Epeabaka* (2001) 106 CLR 128, 135, *Re Patterson; ex parte Taylor* (2001) 207 CLR 291, 498.
93   *Carter v Minister for Aboriginal Affairs* (2005) 143 FCR 383, 393.
94   *R v Murray and Cormie; Ex parte Commonwealth* (1916) 22 CLR 437, 452–3, *R v Commonwealth Court of Conciliation & Arbitration; Ex parte Brisbane Tramways Co Ltd* (1914) 18 CLR 54.
95   *R v Murray and Cormie; Ex parte Commonwealth* (1916) 22 CLR 437, 452–3.
96   *Williams v Commonwealth* [2012] HCA 23 [109]. See also *Mazukov v University of Tasmania* [2002] FCAFC 166.
97   ibid (French CJ) [107]–[110] (Gummow and Bell JJ), [476] (Crennan J), [597] Kiefel J.

relationship with the Commonwealth was material.[98] For them, the term 'under' indicates a requirement for a closer connection to the Commonwealth than merely being engaged by a private body that receives funding from the Commonwealth.[99] This can also be said of the term 'officer of the Commonwealth'.

Heydon J also preferred a narrow reading of 'an office under the Commonwealth' to prevent radical expansion of the opportunities for litigation under section 75(v). He suggested that an 'officer' has to have a direct relationship with the Commonwealth, and the Commonwealth may specify qualifications before particular appointments may be made or continued.[100] Heydon J held that chaplains did not have an office under the Commonwealth due to the lack of legal relationship between the chaplains and the Commonwealth, which resulted in the inability of the Commonwealth to appoint, control and dismiss the chaplains.[101]

This suggests that a level of control by the Commonwealth is required to satisfy the criteria of 'officer of the Commonwealth'. Thus, *Williams* may indicate that there is a spectrum. On one end are Ministers and public servants with a close relationship to the Commonwealth and who are fully controlled by the Commonwealth—entities that are clearly covered by section 75(v). On the other end of the spectrum are persons or entities without a direct relationship with the Commonwealth, that are unable to be controlled by the Commonwealth, and who are not covered by section 75(v). The question is where the line is drawn for entities that fall somewhere in the middle of the spectrum, such as ministerial advisers.

Ministerial advisers are appointed by Ministers and are engaged under section 13 of the *Members of Parliament (Staff) Act 1984* (Cth) ('MOPS Act').[102] Ministerial advisers are removable by Ministers. Under section 16(3) of the MOPS Act, a Minister may at any time terminate the employment of ministerial advisers.[103] Ministers have full control of the terms and conditions of employment of ministerial advisers. Under the MOPS Act, the terms of conditions of employment of ministerial advisers are subject to the determination of the employing Minister,[104] with the Prime Minister being able to vary employment terms and conditions.[105] The Prime Minister has authorised the Special Minister of State

---

98   [443]–[447].
99   ibid.
100   ibid [443]–[447].
101   ibid.
102   MOPS Act s 13.
103   ibid s 16 (3). The Prime Minister may override the determination of Ministers to terminate ministerial advisers. MOPS Act s 16(5).
104   ibid s 14(1).
105   ibid s 14(3).

to exercise some powers under the Act.[106] Further, the salaries of ministerial advisers are appropriated from public funds. Although the Prime Minister is able to override the decision of the Minister for their ministerial advisers, the Prime Minister is part of the Commonwealth and this employment structure still demonstrates complete control by the Commonwealth over ministerial advisers.

Ministerial advisers thus fulfil the criteria in case law as they are appointed and removable by Ministers and their salaries are appropriated from public money. They are appointed as individuals and not corporations. Ministers and the Prime Minister have full control of the terms and conditions of employment of ministerial advisers. Hence the relationship between Ministers and ministerial advisers demonstrates complete control of the Ministers over their advisers such that ministerial advisers would constitute 'officers of the Commonwealth'.

In addition, the main purpose of section 75(v) is to ensure judicial supervision over the exercise of executive and statutory power.[107] This is done by ensuring that actions of officers of the Commonwealth are lawful. Griffith CJ has indicated that where the meaning of the words of section 75 is ambiguous, 'the ambiguity should be resolved in favour of the power'.[108] Barton J also suggested that the context gives section 75(v) 'a very extensive meaning'.[109] Barwick CJ said that the High Court should itself be 'jealous to preserve and maintain the scope of the power'.[110]

Therefore, there is a strong argument that ministerial advisers are 'officers of the Commonwealth'. As such, they are subject to judicial review through the original jurisdiction of the High Court when they exercise executive power. Thus, the remedies of injunction, prohibition and mandamus are available against ministerial advisers.

Conclusion

Ministerial advisers occupy an uncertain position in the operation of the executive arm of government as they are employed by Ministers personally and report directly to Ministers. It is unclear if their accountabilities extend beyond accountability to Ministers as part of a normal employment contract.

---

106   Enterprise Agreement 2012-2015, http://maps.finance.gov.au/enterprise_agreement/index.html.
107   Mark Aronson, Bruce Dyer and Matthew Groves, *Judicial Review of Administrative Action* (Thomson Reuters, 4th ed, 2009) 40.
108   *R v Commonwealth Court of Conciliation & Arbitration; ex parte Whybrow & Co* (1910) 11 CLR 1, 22.
109   *R v Commonwealth Court of Conciliation & Arbitration; Ex parte Brisbane Tramways Co Ltd* (1914) 18 CLR 54, 66.
110   *R v Judges of the Federal Court of Australia; ex parte the Western Australian National Football League (Incorporated)* (1979) 143 CLR 190, 201.

The traditional actors within the executive of the Queen, Governor-General, Ministers and public servants are no longer the only actors who engage in public functions. The scope of governmental activity has increased over the years. Some traditional functions of government have been outsourced to private entities. Governing has become more complex and demanding following the 24/7 news cycle such that Ministers are unable to cope with the workload themselves and employ ministerial advisers to assist them. Ministerial advisers clearly perform public functions affecting the governing of the nation. Nevertheless, they are external to the public service, with a separate employment framework.[111]

The idea of partisan advisers for Ministers was denigrated by the framers of the Constitution as being corrupt and undesirable.[112] The ideal of the impartial public service continues to this day in spirit, as seen in the statement of Australian Public Service Values.[113] However, the reality may not completely reflect this, given that the senior public servants of departments are now on fixed-term contracts and can be removed easily by the Ministers if they fall out of favour.[114] This means that public servants are less likely to be 'frank and fearless' and impartial in their advice than if their positions were permanent. Further, ministerial advisers have slowly and steadily grown as an institutionalised source of advice — a phenomenon that would have been considered very undesirable at federation. There has been a distinct shift in attitude towards partisan ministerial advisers being a formalised part of government, with their position officially recognised through statute.[115]

The issue of accountability is challenging for ministerial advisers. Although their salary is appropriated from public funds and they are close to the political and policy workings of the government and Parliament, they do not officially sit in the Houses of Parliament. This means that they are not directly subject to political accountability through Parliament. Further, ministerial advisers are not located within departments and statutory authorities, suggesting they are outside the traditional administrative law framework.

Although ministerial advisers are personally employed by Ministers in their private offices, they perform many public functions, including advising on public policy, media, political, parliamentary management and party management matters.[116] Increasingly, ministerial advisers also exercise executive power.

---

111 Public servants are appointed under the *Public Service Act 1999* (Cth), while ministerial advisers are appointed under the *Members of Parliament (Staff) Act 1984* (Cth).

112 *Official Report of the National Australasian Convention Debates*, Adelaide, 19 April 1897, 916–7.

113 Australian Public Service Values, http://www.apsc.gov.au/aps-employment-policy-and-advice/aps-values-and-code-of-conduct/code-of-conduct/aps-values.

114 *Barratt v Howard* (2000) 96 FCR 428, 451–452; Patrick Weller, *Australia's Mandarins: The Frank and the Fearless?* (Allen & Unwin, 2001) 33.

115 MOPS Act.

116 *The Herald and Weekly Times Pty Limited v The Office of the Premier (General)* [2012] VCAT 967 [22].

Given that ministerial advisers have become an integral part of the executive and may exercise executive power in some instances, I argue that ministerial advisers should be subject to appropriate public law accountability mechanisms. For instance, ministerial advisers should be accountable to Parliament through being made to appear before parliamentary committees. There can also be accountability through courts, utilising the mechanism of judicial review for the executive decisions of ministerial advisers. Other actors within the executive, such as Ministers and public servants, are subject to a plethora of accountability mechanisms, such as through Parliament, the courts and administrative law mechanisms, such as tribunals, ombudsmen, the Auditor-General and freedom of information legislation. However, current public law mechanisms have not yet been applied to ministerial advisers due to their relatively new status as independent and significant actors within the contemporary executive.

In conclusion, ministerial advisers are significant new institutional actors in the executive. Due to their increasing roles within the executive, I argue that ministerial advisers should be subject to public law accountability mechanisms. As ministerial advisers are now part of the operation of the executive, so too should their accountabilities increase.

6. Applied Law Schemes and Responsible Government: Some Issues

Joe Edwards

Introduction

An 'applied law scheme' is a type of cooperative legislative scheme in which one jurisdiction enacts a model law which is then 'picked up' or 'applied' by another jurisdiction or group of jurisdictions. In the 1990s, applied law schemes were the 'next big thing' in Australian federalism; a way of achieving that hallowed goal, uniformity of regulation across the nation, in circumstances where there was no political will, or constitutional power, for the enactment of a Commonwealth law. But then, in *R v Hughes*,[1] the High Court raised serious questions about the constitutional validity of the most significant applied law scheme, the Corporations Law scheme, and it seemed as though applied law schemes were, if not consigned to the dustbin of history, then at least of considerably less utility than we had thought. If regulatory uniformity was to be achieved, we were going to have to opt for a cooperative legislative scheme that was either significantly 'tighter' or significantly 'looser' than an applied law scheme.

At the 'tighter' end of the spectrum are what we call 'reference schemes', where the States refer a 'matter' to the Commonwealth Parliament under s 51(xxxvii) of the Constitution, and the Parliament then enacts a law with respect to that matter. This, of course, is how we ended up with the *Corporations Act 2001* (Cth), which superseded the Corporations Law scheme; and there have been other references of matters in the past decade, in areas such as personal property securities, consumer credit, business names, de facto financial matters and terrorism. However, it hardly need be said that reference schemes are treated with caution by the States, for the simple reason that they achieve regulatory uniformity by the transferral of legislative power to the centre. They are thus not a means of achieving regulatory uniformity except in those relatively rare cases where the need for uniformity, or the speed with which it must be attained, is (perceived to be) especially great.[2]

---

1   (2000) 202 CLR 535 ('*Hughes*').
2   See, on this point, G Williams, 'Cooperative Federalism and the Revival of the Corporations Law: *Wakim* and Beyond' (2002) 20 *Company and Securities Law Journal* 160, 168.

At the 'looser' end of the spectrum are what we call 'mirror law schemes', which involve the Commonwealth and the States and Territories (or simply the States and Territories) enacting legislation in relation to an area in the same, or substantially the same, terms. Examples of the mirror law schemes include the uniform defamation Acts, the uniform evidence Acts, the succession or wills Acts and the new work health and safety Acts. However, while mirror law schemes (generally) do not raise the same constitutional issues which, after *Hughes*, were thought to beset applied law schemes, nor present the same challenge to State 'independence' or 'autonomy' as presented by reference schemes, they also (generally) fail to achieve the kind of regulatory uniformity to which our policy makers aspire. As Chief Justice Robert French has put it, mirror law schemes create not 'one law covering the whole country', but 'a mosaic of similar laws'.[3]

However, despite the dismay that greeted the collapse of the Corporations Law scheme — despite the sense in many quarters that reference schemes or mirror law schemes were the way things were going to have to be — applied law schemes never really went away. While the Commonwealth and the States scrambled to organise the State references upon which the *Corporations Act* is based, the applied law schemes regulating less high profile areas — like agricultural and veterinary chemicals, electricity and therapeutic goods and poisons — hummed along quietly in the background.

Moreover, in the past five years or so, applied law schemes have proliferated faster than any other type of cooperative legislative scheme. Indeed, it would not be too much of an exaggeration to say that they have become the default way that the Commonwealth and the States and Territories seek to achieve regulatory uniformity.

Some of the new applied law schemes involve legislation enacted by the Commonwealth and the States and Territories. These include, for example, the applied law schemes regulating:

- consumer protection;
- gas;
- energy retail; and
- commercial shipping.

Others, however, involve legislation enacted only by the States and Territories (although the Commonwealth has often been a party to the intergovernmental agreement underpinning the scheme, and has played an important role in funding). Examples of these schemes include those for the regulation of:

---

3   See Justice R S French, 'Horizontal Arrangements: Competition Law and Cooperative Federalism' (2008) 15 *Competition and Consumer Law Journal* 255, 261, referring to the Uniform Companies Scheme, which operated in Australia between 1961 and 1981.

- health practitioners;
- early childhood education and care;
- occupational licensing;
- railways;
- co-operatives; and
- heavy vehicles.

The schemes just mentioned are only those that are already operational, or at a relatively advanced stage of development. But there are others in the works, not least of which is the proposed applied law scheme for the regulation of the legal profession.

The purpose of this chapter is two-fold. First, it will offer a primer on just what an applied law scheme is and the way in which one works. Secondly, it will explore some of the challenges posed by applied law schemes to the system of responsible government established by, and underpinning, the Constitution. In other words, it asks the question: does the use of an applied law scheme to achieve regulatory uniformity result in us all paying too high an accountability price?

What is an applied law scheme?

The starting point: An intergovernmental agreement

The starting point for most applied law schemes, particularly in recent times, has been an intergovernmental agreement in which the various interested jurisdictions — either the Commonwealth and the States and Territories, or just the States and Territories — agree that a particular area requires regulatory uniformity. The Council of Australian Governments (COAG) has often been the forum at which these agreements are made, but this is not necessarily the case. The Standing Council on Law and Justice (SCLJ) (formerly the Standing Committee of Attorneys-General (SCAG)) has also been responsible for the implementation of several high profile cooperative legislative schemes (although it has tended to favour mirror law schemes — such as the uniform defamation Acts and the uniform evidence Acts — rather than applied law schemes).

An intergovernmental agreement may, of course, deal with any matter to which the parties turn their minds. However, in the ordinary course of things, it will deal with the following issues:

- the general content of the scheme (that is, the matters that it will regulate and the manner in which it will do so);

- governance of the scheme (including, in many cases, the establishment of a Ministerial Council constituting the responsible Ministers of the relevant jurisdictions);

- division of costs between the jurisdictions (both during the transition phase and subsequently);

- timelines for the establishment of the scheme;

- reporting and accountability;

- dispute resolution; and

- withdrawal from the scheme.

Once an intergovernmental agreement has been made, it will then be up to the bureaucracies of the Commonwealth and States and Territories — policy officers, government lawyers and drafters — to make the necessary arrangements for the implementation of the applied law scheme.

Basic operation of an applied law scheme

Put simply, an applied law scheme works as follows:

- one jurisdiction (usually called the 'host jurisdiction') enacts a model law in its jurisdiction (usually as a Schedule to an Act of Parliament and, in recent times, usually called a 'National Law'); and then

- each other jurisdiction (usually called a 'participating jurisdiction') enacts an Act (an 'application Act') which applies the National Law in its jurisdiction (and, more particularly, in the 'gap' in the 'reach' or 'coverage' achieved by the exercise of legislative power of the host jurisdiction).

When the Commonwealth is the host jurisdiction (which is not always the case), it will obviously be limited to making a law which is supported by a head of legislative power.[4] So, for example, the Commonwealth could rely on the Territories power in s 122 of the Constitution to make a law applying only in the Australian Capital Territory (ACT). The States and the Northern Territory (NT) could then apply the law in the 'gap' left by the Commonwealth's exercise of legislative power — that is, outside the ACT — thus ensuring a nationwide regulatory scheme. This was how the old Corporations Law scheme worked. And it remains the way in which agricultural and veterinary chemicals are regulated.[5]

---

4 The Commonwealth Parliament may, of course, make laws only with respect to certain, discrete subject matters, such as interstate and overseas trade and commerce (s 51(i) of the Constitution), taxation (s 51(ii)), foreign, trading and financial corporations (constitutional corporations) (s 51(xx)) and external affairs (s 51(xxix)). These subject matters of legislative power are often called 'heads of power'.

5 See, in particular, the *Agricultural and Veterinary Chemicals Code Act 1994* (Cth), to which the Agricultural and Veterinary Chemicals (Agvet) Code is a Schedule.

When the Commonwealth is the host jurisdiction, it does not necessarily rely on the Territories power. In fact, it is Commonwealth policy to treat the self-governing Territories essentially as if they were States. So, the Commonwealth might rely on its power to legislate with respect to constitutional corporations and interstate and overseas trade and commerce, and then seek the agreement of the States and Territories to apply the Commonwealth law in the 'gap' left by the law; that is, to non-constitutional corporations (such as natural persons and unincorporated associations) engaged in intrastate (or intraterritory) trade and commerce. This is essentially the approach used in relation to the regulation of therapeutic goods and poisons.[6] It is also the approach used in the context of one of the most significant applied law schemes — the Australian Consumer Law — which substantially superseded the *Trade Practices Act 1975* (Cth) and the State and Territory fair trading Acts in 2010.[7]

Another, more recent, example involves the *Marine Safety (Domestic Commercial Vessel) National Law Act 2012* (Cth), which is part of a package of Acts enacted by the Commonwealth in 2012 to ensure the registration and safe operation of all commercial vessels. The Commonwealth Act applies essentially to vessels engaged in interstate trade and commerce, vessels owned by constitutional corporations, vessels covered by the implementation of international agreements, vessels that are external to Australia and vessels owned by the Commonwealth. It is proposed that the States and the NT will apply the National Law in the relatively small 'gap' left by the Commonwealth Act (essentially, in the waters within the limits of the States or the NT).

As already mentioned, the Commonwealth is not always the host jurisdiction. Sometimes it is simply a participating jurisdiction, as in the case of the three applied law schemes regulating the energy sector. Each of these applied law schemes features South Australia (SA) as the host jurisdiction.[8]

In other cases, the Commonwealth enacts no legislation at all. A number of recent applied law schemes involve one State as host jurisdiction and each other State and the Territories applying the law of the host jurisdiction in their jurisdictions. In this case, the 'gap' which is being 'filled' by the laws of the participating jurisdictions is not a result of the fact that the host jurisdiction is empowered to legislate only with respect to particular subject matters. After all, unlike the Commonwealth, the States (and the Territories) are able to legislate

---

6   See, in particular, the *Therapeutic Goods Act 1989* (Cth).

7   See, in particular, the *Competition and Consumer Act 2010* (Cth), to which the Australian Consumer Law is a Schedule.

8   See, in particular, the *National Electricity (South Australia) Act 1996* (SA), to which the National Electricity Law is a Schedule; the *National Gas (South Australia) Act 2008* (SA), to which the National Gas Law is a Schedule; and the *National Energy Retail Law (South Australia) Act 2011* (SA), to which the National Energy Retail Law is a Schedule.

with respect to essentially any subject matter.[9] Rather, the 'gap' is a result of the fact that the host jurisdiction's power to legislate extraterritorially (that is, with respect to persons, acts, omissions, events, matters, things, etc outside the host jurisdiction) is limited.[10] The applied law schemes for the regulation of early childhood education and care,[11] health practitioners,[12] occupational licensing,[13] railway safety,[14] co-operatives[15] and heavy vehicles[16] are purely State- and Territory-based applied law schemes. The still-stalled applied law scheme for the regulation of the legal profession is also in this category.

Applied law schemes and responsible government: Some issues

Introduction: The concept of responsible government

With the above overview of applied law schemes in mind, it is necessary now to return to the core question: do applied law schemes undermine responsible government? This is obviously a rather large question. So, the ensuing discussion seeks to address it by focusing on only four issues:

- First, 'application methods'; that is, the various ways in which a participating jurisdiction might apply a National Law in its jurisdiction.

---

9   A caveat to this is that s 52 of the Constitution gives the Commonwealth Parliament exclusive power with respect to a limited range of subjects. See also s 90 in relation to duties of custom and excise. Further, while the States may legislate with respect to a very wide variety of subject matters, State legislation which is inconsistent with Commonwealth legislation will, to the extent of the inconsistency, be invalid: see s 109. Territory legislation is also apt to be invalidated by Commonwealth legislation (in circumstances of 'repugnancy').

10   The States and Territories are able to enact laws with extraterritorial effect. However, there must be a 'sufficient connection' between the enacting State or Territory and the extraterritorial persons, acts, omissions, events, matters, things, etc in relation to which the State or Territory law operates. This requirement flows from the State Constitutions and the self-government Acts of the Territories, which relevantly mandate that State or Territory laws must be for the 'peace, order and good government' of the State or Territory concerned. See generally *Pearce v Florenca* (1976) 135 CLR 507, 517–8; *Union Steamship Co of Australia Pty Ltd v King* (1988) 166 CLR 1, 14; and *Port MacDonnell Professional Fishermen's Association Inc v South Australia* (1989) CLR 340, 372.

11   Victoria is the host jurisdiction for this scheme. See, in particular, the *Education and Care Services National Law Act 2010* (Vic), to which the Education and Care Services National Law is a Schedule.

12   Queensland is the host jurisdiction for this scheme. See, in particular, the *Health Practitioner Regulation National Law Act 2009* (Qld), to which the Health Practitioner Regulation National Law is a Schedule.

13   Victoria is again the host jurisdiction for this scheme. See, in particular, the *Occupational Licensing National Law Act 2010* (Vic), to which the Occupational Licensing National Law is a Schedule.

14   SA is the host jurisdiction for this scheme. See, in particular, the *Rail Safety National Law (South Australia) Act 2012* (SA), to which the Rail Safety National Law is a Schedule.

15   New South Wales (NSW) is the host jurisdiction for this scheme. See, in particular, the *Co-operatives (Adoption of National Law) Act 2012* (NSW), to which the Co-operatives National Law is a Schedule.

16   Queensland is again the host jurisdiction for this scheme. See, in particular, the *Heavy Vehicle National Law Act 2012* (Qld), to which the Heavy Vehicle National Law is a Schedule.

- Secondly, the interpretation of a National Law.
- Thirdly, the establishment of a so-called 'single national regulator' to administer and enforce a National Law.
- Finally, the treatment of a participating jurisdiction's suite of administrative laws upon the enactment of a National Law

Before turning to those issues, however, it is necessary to offer a working definition of 'responsible government'. The concept is, of course, a famously slippery one. However, in the recent case of *Williams v Commonwealth*, Kiefel J distilled its essence neatly:

> The relationship [responsible government] establishes between the Parliament and the Executive may be described as one where the former is superior to the latter.[17]

In other words, according to Kiefel J, responsible government is fundamentally about parliamentary supremacy.

Professor Cheryl Saunders has seconded Kiefel J's emphasis on parliamentary supremacy. However, she has also identified additional features. According to Saunders, responsible government assumes

> that governments are responsible to parliaments and, through parliaments, to voters; [that] the parliament makes or authorises the making of rules that create or change law; that most of the information necessary for the voters to make their electoral judgment is in the public domain; and that courts review the legality of the exercise of public power within a system of somewhat delicate checks, balances and conventional practices.[18]

In Saunders' view, then, responsible government involves more than just parliamentary supremacy. It also involves members of the public knowing what they need to know and, when aggrieved by a decision, having reasonable access to avenues of review.[19]

---

17 (2012) 248 CLR 156, [579].

18 See C Saunders, 'Collaborative Federalism' (2002) 61 *Australian Journal of Public Administration* 69, 73. See also C Saunders, 'A New Direction for Intergovernmental Arrangements' (2001) 12 *Public Law Review* 274, 276, where Saunders writes: 'Stripped to its bare essentials, parliamentary responsible government is a system in which Parliaments are directly elected by voters and governments hold office with the support of a majority in the most popular House. Between elections, the Parliament holds the government and administration accountable. Its ability to do so is reinforced by the requirements of parliamentary approval for taxing and spending. New and altered laws require the approval of Parliament. Regularly, every three or four years, voters have the opportunity to change the government by changing the parliamentary majority. To this end, voters need the capacity to evaluate the government's record.'

19 Saunders speaks of judicial review, but arguably, in the context of the modern regulatory state, administrative (merits) review is also an aspect of responsible government. Other avenues of review — such as the making of freedom of information (FOI) requests, the making of applications for review by the Ombudsman, and so forth — may also be thought to be included.

With these definitions in mind, it is necessary now to turn to the first issue mentioned above: application methods.

Application methods

As discussed above, under an applied law scheme:

- the host jurisdiction enacts a National Law; and
- each participating jurisdiction enacts an application Act which applies the National Law.

It is important to understand, however, that this description disguises considerable complexity, because participating jurisdictions may 'apply' a National Law in one of a number of ways.

In what may be described as a 'true' applied law scheme, a participating jurisdiction applies the National Law as in force in the host jurisdiction *from time to time*. An example of this approach may be seen in the *Health Practitioner Regulation National Law (Victoria) Act 2009* (Vic), which applies, as a law of Victoria, the Health Practitioner Regulation National Law enacted by Queensland. Section 4, which is the critical provision, provides as follows:

> *4 Application of Health Practitioner Regulation National Law*
>
> The Health Practitioner Regulation National Law, as in force from time to time, set out in the Schedule to the *Health Practitioner Regulation National Law Act 2009* of Queensland
>
> (a) applies as a law of Victoria; and
>
> (b) as so applying may be referred to as the Health Practitioner Regulation National Law (Victoria); and
>
> (c) so applies as if it were part of this Act.

When a participating jurisdiction applies a National Law as in force in the host jurisdiction from time to time, this means that, each time the host jurisdiction amends the National Law, the amendments apply automatically in the participating jurisdiction. There is no need for the Parliament of the participating jurisdiction itself to enact an amending Act. Nor is there any need for the amendments to be tabled or laid before the Parliament of the participating jurisdiction. In fact, parliamentarians in the participating jurisdiction may not even be aware that the National Law, as it applies in that jurisdiction, has changed.

This feature of applied law schemes — which ensures the easy maintenance of regulatory uniformity — is probably their foremost advantage. It is also what really distinguishes them from mirror law schemes. In a mirror law scheme, participating jurisdictions might agree to amend their legislation simultaneously. But often they do not. Governments change. The priority accorded to the particular amendments varies from jurisdiction to jurisdiction. And, before you know it, the legislation in, say, Queensland may be quite different to the legislation in SA.[20] However, this feature is also a controversial one, largely because it is seen as having the potential both to erode each participating jurisdiction's 'independence' or 'autonomy' (its 'sovereignty', if you will), and to undermine the role, and more importantly the supremacy, of its Parliament. As a result of these concerns, some jurisdictions have adopted alternative methods of applying a National Law.

The first alternative method is as follows:

- the participating jurisdiction enacts an application Act which applies a National Law as in force in the host jurisdiction from time to time; but

- the participating jurisdiction also includes in its application Act a provision requiring any amendments made to the National Law by the host jurisdiction to be tabled in the Parliament of the participating jurisdiction.

An example of this method may be seen in the *Education and Care Services National Law (Application) Act 2011* (Tas), which applies, as a law of Tasmania, the Education and Care Services National Law as in force in Victoria from time to time, but which also provides:

16 Tabling of amendments to Education and Care Services National Law (Tasmania)

(1) The Minister is to cause any amendment to the Education and Care Services National Law (Tasmania) to be tabled in each House of Parliament within 10 sitting-days from the date on which the amendment receives the Royal Assent in Victoria.

(2) Nothing in this section affects the operation of that amendment.

It is important to note, however, that while amendments to the National Law must be tabled in the Parliament, the Parliament is given no express power to amend the amendments, or to 'disapply' them altogether. (The process may thus be contrasted to the process, familiar in most jurisdictions, by which subordinate legislation is laid before the Parliament and may be disallowed by

---

20   See generally Justice R S French, 'Cooperative Federalism: A Constitutional Reality or a Political Slogan' (paper presented at the 'Western Australia 2029: A Shared Journey' conference, Perth, 2004) 15.

either House.[21]) As a result, the amendments still come into effect automatically. However, this strategy does ensure that parliamentarians in the participating jurisdiction are aware of the ongoing evolution of the National Law as applied in that jurisdiction.

The second alternative method is similar to the first, in that the participating jurisdiction enacts an application Act which applies the National Law as in force in the host jurisdiction from time to time. However, the application Act then provides that any amendments made to the National Law by the host jurisdiction may be disapplied or proclaimed to have no effect. An example of this method may be seen in the *Fair Trading Act 1987* (NSW), which applies, as a law of NSW, the Australian Consumer Law as in force in the Commonwealth from time to time, but which also provides:

29 Future modifications of Australian Consumer Law text

(1) A modification made by a Commonwealth law to the Australian Consumer Law text after the commencement of this section does not apply under section 28 [which is the section that applies the Australian Consumer Law in NSW] if the modification is declared by a proclamation to be excluded from the operation of that section.

It is worth noting, however, that this method invariably involves disapplication by the executive — usually by the Governor acting on the advice of the Minister or the Executive Council — rather than by the Parliament. So, while this method might go some way to ensuring the maintenance of a participating jurisdiction's sovereignty, it does not necessarily answer the concern of those worried about the relative power of the executive vis-à-vis the Parliament.

The third alternative method is quite different from the first two. It involves a participating jurisdiction enacting an application Act that applies the National Law as in force in the host jurisdiction *at a particular time* — usually the time that the participating jurisdiction's application Act commences — rather than from time to time.[22] This means, of course, that when the host jurisdiction amends the National Law, the amendments do not apply automatically in the participating jurisdiction. However, to ensure that regulatory uniformity is easily maintained, the application Act of the participating jurisdiction goes

---

21   See, for example, the *Legislative Instruments Act 2003* (Cth) pt 5.

22   In circumstances where a participating jurisdiction applies the National Law as in force in the host jurisdiction at a particular time, one may question whether the participating jurisdiction has 'applied' the National Law in any real sense. Arguably, what it has done is enact an Act which mirrors the National Law. As between the host jurisdiction and the participating jurisdiction, the resulting scheme is then best thought of as a mirror law scheme, rather than an applied law scheme. On this issue, the views of Roger Jacobs, a drafter at the Parliamentary Counsel's Office of Western Australia, would seem to be correct. See R Jacobs, 'National Applied Laws Schemes: A WA Perspective' (paper presented at the Australasian Drafting Conference, Adelaide, 2011) 26.

on to provide that, when the host jurisdiction amends the National Law, the executive of the participating jurisdiction may make regulations which amend the National Law as it applies in the participating jurisdiction. In other words, the application Act provides for 'executive amendment' or 'updating' of the National Law. Provisions of this sort are rather evocatively called 'Henry VIII clauses'. An example of such a clause may be seen in the *Occupational Licensing National Law (South Australia) Act 2011* (SA), which applies, as a law of SA, the Occupational Licensing National Law as in force in Victoria at a particular time, but which also provides:

5 Amendments to Schedule to maintain national consistency

(1) If –

(a) the Parliament of Victoria enacts an amendment to the *Occupational Licensing National Law* set out in the Schedule to the *Occupational Licensing National Law Act 2010* of Victoria; and

(b) the Governor is satisfied that an amendment that corresponds, or substantially corresponds, to the amendment made by the Parliament of Victoria should be made to the *Occupational Licensing National Law (South Australia)*, the Governor may, by regulation, amend the South Australian Occupational Licensing National Law text.

This method, like the second method, preserves jurisdictional sovereignty better than it does parliamentary supremacy.

The fourth alternative method is like the third, in that it involves a participating jurisdiction enacting an application Act that applies the National Law as in force in the host jurisdiction at a particular time, rather than from time to time. However, it differs in that the application Act does not provide for 'executive amendment' or 'updating' of the National Law. Consequently, when the host jurisdiction amends the National Law, the only way that the participating jurisdiction can 'keep up' is if its Parliament amends the National Law as it applies in the participating jurisdiction.

The fifth and final alternative method is the least like a 'true' application of a National Law. It involves a participating jurisdiction enacting an application Act that applies the National Law — either from time to time or at a particular time, although more typically the latter — and then modifies that National Law in some way in and for the participating jurisdiction. When a participating jurisdiction adopts this method, the resulting applied law scheme is necessarily non-uniform as between the host jurisdiction and the participating jurisdiction. An example of this strategy may be seen in the *Health Practitioner Regulation (Adoption of National Law) Act 2009* (NSW), which applies, as a law of NSW, the Health Practitioner Regulation National Law as in force in Queensland from time to time, but which also modifies that National Law. Section 4 of the NSW Act, which is the critical provision, provides as follows:

4 Adoption of Health Practitioner Regulation National Law

The Health Practitioner Regulation National Law, as in force from time to time, set out in the Schedule to the *Health Practitioner Regulation National Law Act 2009* of Queensland:

(a) applies as a law of this jurisdiction, with the modifications set out in Schedule 1, and

(b) as so applying may be referred to as the *Health Practitioner Regulation National Law (NSW)*, and

(c) so applies as if it were a part of this Act.

Schedule 1 then disapplies the provisions of the National Law which relate to the health, performance and conduct of health practitioners, and creates a NSW-specific regime to deal with those matters.

The fact that there are a range of ways in which participating jurisdictions may 'apply' a National Law — with different strategies favoured by different jurisdictions — means that applied law schemes will often be extremely complicated. This complexity, by itself, might be thought to raise responsible government concerns. After all, as discussed above, the concept of responsible government connotes both the ready availability of information (for the purpose of assisting members of the public to make their electoral judgment, among other purposes) and the ready accessibility of avenues of review. Arguably, the greater the complexity of the law, the less likely it is that members of the public will be able either to understand the information relevant to their judgment or (without significant time and cost) to access their review rights.[23]

Ultimately, however, what is clear from the above discussion of application methods is that there is a tension at the heart of any applied law scheme. The legal mechanisms necessary to ensure the attainment, and maintenance, of regulatory uniformity may be seen as undermining jurisdictional sovereignty and Parliamentary supremacy; while the mechanisms necessary to maintain jurisdictional sovereignty and Parliamentary supremacy will invariably undermine the goal of regulatory uniformity.

---

23 It is worth noting here that the complexity of the Corporations Law scheme attracted considerable negative comment in *Hughes*. See, for example, 551, 573.

Interpretation of an applied law scheme

Imagine a situation — one which, it must be said, rarely occurs in practice — where all participating jurisdictions apply the National Law as in force in the host jurisdiction from time to time, and without making any jurisdiction-specific modifications. Imagine also that a single national regulator is created to oversee the National Law, thus ensuring uniform administration and enforcement. (The creation of a regulator is addressed in further detail below.) Even in such a situation, ongoing regulatory uniformity could not be guaranteed. This is because the National Law as applied in each participating jurisdiction would be interpreted — by lawyers, the regulator and the courts — by reference to different interpretation Acts. The *Interpretation Act 1987* (NSW) in NSW, the *Interpretation of Legislation Act 1984* (Vic) in Victoria, the *Legislation Act 2001* (ACT) in the ACT, and so forth. Over time, subtle — but potentially significant — differences could emerge, even if the text of the National Law remained identical nationwide.

Government lawyers and drafters have been alive to this potential problem since the days of the first applied law schemes, and have sought to combat it in two main ways:

Approach 1: each participating jurisdiction disapplies its interpretation Act (insofar as the National Law is concerned) and the National Law itself includes rules for the Law's interpretation. This approach has been adopted in the context of the applied law schemes regulating electricity, gas, energy retail, early childhood education and care, health practitioners, occupational licensing, railway safety and co-operatives, among others.

Approach 2: each participating jurisdiction disapplies its interpretation Act (insofar as the National Law is concerned) and instead applies the interpretation Act of another jurisdiction. This approach has been adopted in the context of the Australian Consumer Law and the Agvet scheme.

Do either of these approaches raise any responsible government concerns? Arguably not. After all, each approach involves only the disapplication of a 'mere' interpretation Act, and that interpretation Act is being disapplied only insofar as one piece of legislation (the National Law) is concerned. However, if one considers the purpose interpretation Acts are intended to serve, the answer might be different. An interpretation Act is supposed to be the place — the one place, the common law aside — where the people living in a particular jurisdiction may look to make sense of the rest of the laws that govern them. That is, an interpretation Act plays a critical role in the 'knowability' and 'accessibility' of the law. Seen in this light, the problem with its disapplication reveals itself. The more applied law schemes a particular jurisdiction participates in, the more times its interpretation Act is disapplied. Over time, a jurisdiction's interpretation Act might go from being an important means of promoting community understanding of the law to a key that fits only every third or fourth lock.

Besides, even for those disinclined to think that the disapplication of an interpretation Act raises any real responsible government concerns, it is worth noting that two jurisdictions — Victoria and the ACT — have not just a 'standard' interpretation Act, but also an Act which requires the jurisdiction's legislation to be interpreted compatibly with human rights.[24] These Acts obviously reflect a very significant policy choice made by the jurisdictions which have adopted them. They are not Acts to be disapplied lightly.

It is true that, at least to date, neither Victoria nor the ACT has expressly disapplied its human rights Act. But there is a serious question whether each jurisdiction's human rights Act has any scope to operate in the context of an applied law scheme.[25] After all, each jurisdiction's human rights Act requires legislation to be interpreted in a way that is compatible with human rights 'so far as it is possible to do so consistently with its purpose'.[26] What is the purpose of a National Law as it applies in either Victoria or the ACT? Well, clearly a purpose — if not the primary purpose — of a National Law is to achieve a uniform nationwide scheme. So will the Victorian and ACT courts consider it 'possible' to interpret a National Law as it applies in either jurisdiction compatibly with human rights, even if such an interpretation might undermine the goal of nationwide regulatory uniformity? Or will they think it impossible? And, if the latter, could it not be said that the very significant decisions made by the legislatures of Victoria and the ACT — in enacting Acts designed to accord substantial priority to human rights issues — have been quietly undermined?

The courts do not appear to have wrestled with the issue so far. But this may simply reflect the fact that many of the existing applied law schemes entail regulation which is basically 'economic' in nature; human rights issues are thus less apt to arise. As the applied law schemes penetrate into other areas — early childhood education and care, for example, or the regulation of health practitioners — this situation may well change. It is, if nothing else, an issue to watch.

---

24   See the *Charter of Human Rights and Responsibilities Act 2006* (Vic) ('*Victorian Human Rights Charter*') and the *Human Rights Act 2004* (ACT) ('*ACT Human Rights Act*').

25   See, on this question, Parliamentary Counsel's Committee, *Protocol on Drafting National Uniform Legislation* (2008) 10. See more broadly cases such as *Australian Securities Commission v Marlborough Gold Mines Ltd* (1993) 177 CLR 485, 492, where the High Court stressed the importance of 'uniformity of decision in the interpretation of uniform national legislation'.

26   See the *Victorian Human Rights Charter* s 32 and the *ACT Human Rights Act* s 30.

Creating a single national regulator to administer and enforce an applied law scheme

Attaining and maintaining uniformity in the text of a National Law, as applied in participating jurisdictions, is obviously critical to ensuring the existence of a truly nationwide regulatory scheme. However, it is only one part of the equation. Uniformity in administration and enforcement is also vital.[27] After all, a person's 'experience' of the law is likely to be shaped as much, if not more, by how that law is translated into practice by regulators as it is by the words on the face of the statute book.[28] It is for this reason that it is generally seen as desirable for there to be a single national regulator for all participating jurisdictions, rather than a separate jurisdiction-specific regulator for each participating jurisdiction.

The creation of a single national regulator is legally complicated. However, generally speaking, there are two main approaches.

- Approach 1: the provisions establishing the regulator are not set out in the National Law, but in a separate Act of one of the participating jurisdictions (usually, but not invariably, the host jurisdiction). They are thus not applied by all participating jurisdictions. By contrast, the provisions conferring the regulator's functions and powers are set out in the National Law, and are thus applied by all participating jurisdictions.

- Approach 2: both the provisions establishing the regulator and the provisions conferring its functions and powers are set out in the National Law itself, and are thus applied by all participating jurisdictions.

The first approach is the 'traditional' approach — in the sense that it was used in many of the earlier applied law schemes, including the Corporations Law scheme — and remains the approach used in all of the applied law schemes in which the Commonwealth is a participating jurisdiction. The second approach has become the more common approach in recent years, and is the approach used in essentially all of the purely State and Territory-based applied law schemes. As will be discussed below, it is also the approach which arguably raises the more serious responsible government concerns.

The first approach was subject to detailed consideration in *Hughes*. As noted above, *Hughes* concerned the Corporations Law scheme, which involved a regulator established under a Commonwealth law purporting to perform

---

27   C Saunders, 'A New Direction for Intergovernmental Arrangements' (2001) 12 *Public Law Review* 276.

28   The issue of the interpretation, administration and enforcement of the law by regulators has received comparatively greater attention in the United States than in Australia. See, for example, R D Moss, 'Executive Branch Legal Interpretation' (2000) 52 *Administrative Law Review* 1303, 1304, where Moss observes that 'the executive branch is perpetually involved in giving the law meaning … In the vast majority of cases, moreover, executive branch interpretation is not subjected to judicial review.'

functions under State laws (namely, the State laws which applied the National Law that the Commonwealth had enacted for the ACT). Put simply, the question for the High Court was whether the Commonwealth regulator was able to perform the functions conferred under the State laws. The resulting decision is complex, or, to borrow the words of Saunders again, 'somewhat unclear'.[29] However, the case appears to stand for a number of propositions:[30]

- First, while a State may confer a function on a Commonwealth regulator, a Commonwealth law must 'authorise' or 'permit' that conferral; that is, it must authorise or permit the Commonwealth regulator to perform the State function. This is necessary to ensure that there is no inconsistency for the purposes of s 109 of the Constitution between the State conferral and any Commonwealth legislation (in particular, the Commonwealth legislation establishing the relevant regulator). It may also be necessary to 'waive' any constitutional immunity that Commonwealth bodies or officers have from State laws that purport to apply to them.

- Secondly, and more significantly, it is necessary to consider whether the Commonwealth regulator is under a duty to perform the State function:[31]

  - If there is not a duty: it seems that the Commonwealth regulator may perform the State function, whether or not there is a connection between this function and a head of Commonwealth legislative power.

  - If there is a duty: the Commonwealth law authorising or permitting the Commonwealth regulator to perform the State function will only be valid if there is a connection between the State function and a head of Commonwealth legislative power. (This is likely to be especially so in circumstances where the performance of the function is 'coercive' in some way; that is, capable of affecting the rights of individuals.)

Both of these propositions are capable of presenting problems in practice. The first proposition, for instance, makes it necessary to consider when, as a matter of statutory construction, the Commonwealth has authorised or permitted the conferral of State functions on a Commonwealth regulator. An interesting

---

29   C Saunders, 'A New Direction for Intergovernmental Arrangements' (2001) 12 *Public Law Review* 274.

30   See, in particular, the helpful analysis in G Hill, '*R v Hughes* and the Future of Cooperative Legislative Schemes' (2000) 24 *Melbourne University Law Review* 478, 490–1, upon which this chapter relies. See also D Rose and G Lindell, 'A Constitutional Perspective on *Hughes* and the Referral of Powers' (paper presented at the Corporate Law Teachers Association Conference, 3 November 2000); D Rose, 'The *Hughes* Case: The Reasoning, Uncertainties and Solutions' (2000) 29 *University of Western Australia Law Review* 180; I Govey and H Manson, 'Measures to Address *Wakim* and *Hughes*: How the Reference of Powers Will Work' (2001) 12 *Public Law Review* 1; M J Whincop, 'The National Scheme for Corporations and the Referral of Powers: A Sceptical View' (2001) 12 *Public Law Review* 263; B M Selway, '*Hughes* Case and the Referral of Powers' (2001) 12 *Public Law Review* 288; G Hill, 'Revisiting *Wakim* and *Hughes*: The Distinct Demands of Federalism' (2002) 13 *Public Law Review* 205; D Rose, 'Commonwealth-State Cooperative Schemes After *Hughes*: What Should be Done Now?' (2002) 76 *Australian Law Journal* 631; G Williams, 'Cooperative Federalism and the Revival of the Corporations Law: *Wakim* and Beyond' (2002) 20 *Company and Securities Law Journal*.

31   There is some suggestion that this might be a 'constitutional imperative'. See *Hughes* 553–4.

example of this involves s 44AI of the *Competition and Consumer Act 2010* (Cth), which authorises or permits the Australian Energy Regulator (AER), which has important responsibilities under the three applied law schemes regulating the energy sector, to perform certain State functions. Section 44AI relevantly provides:

44AI Commonwealth consent to conferral of functions etc on AER

(1) A State/Territory energy law may confer functions or powers, or impose duties, on the AER for the purposes of that law.

...

(3) The AER cannot perform a duty or function, or exercise a power, under a State/Territory energy law unless the conferral of the function or power, or the imposition of the duty, is in accordance with the Australian Energy Market Agreement, or any other relevant agreement between the Commonwealth and the State or Territory concerned.

As a result of s 44AI(3), the question whether the AER is relevantly authorised or permitted to perform a State function shifts from being a question of interpreting the relevant Commonwealth Act to a question of construing the relevant State Act: does it 'confer functions or powers, or impose duties, on the AER'? It then shifts again to become a question of interpreting the Australian Energy Market Agreement (AEMA)[32] or any other relevant intergovernmental agreement. The latter task is not always easy. In large part, this is because the AEMA, and the other relevant intergovernmental agreements, are not drafted with the precision of legislation or of ordinary contracts. Indeed, they could even be said to exhibit a certain 'wooliness' of language.[33] The upshot is that, in individual cases, it can be a complex and time-consuming process to determine whether a State conferral is 'in accordance with' the AEMA or any other relevant intergovernmental agreement, and thus, whether the Commonwealth has authorised or permitted the AER to perform the relevant State function.

The second proposition enunciated by the High Court in *Hughes* — namely, that where a Commonwealth regulator is under a duty to perform a State function, the Commonwealth law authorising or permitting this will be valid only if

---

32 The AEMA is the intergovernmental agreement which underpins the three applied law schemes regulating the energy sector.

33 The lack of precision evident in many intergovernmental agreements reflects the fact that, generally speaking, they are not intended to create, and do not create, binding legal relations. See N Seddon, *Government Contracts: Federal, State and Local* (Federation Press, 5th ed, 2013) 118–20. See further *South Australia v Commonwealth* (1961) 108 CLR 130, 154.

there is a connection between the State function and a head of Commonwealth legislative power — is also problematic. As Associate Professor Andrew Lynch and Professor George Williams explain:

> In requiring a legislative source of power to support the Commonwealth's imposition upon its [regulators] of 'powers coupled with duties ...', *Hughes* substantially curtailed the usefulness of cooperation in many instances. If the Commonwealth must have the legislative authority to support those powers conferred by the States operating as [duties] upon its [regulators], and a suitable power can be found, then, ironically, the Commonwealth may already have the means to legislate to this end without any need for State cooperation. If, conversely, no Commonwealth power can be sourced, then no agreement with the States can make good the deficiency.[34]

The Commonwealth has responded to *Hughes* by inserting into relevant Commonwealth legislation[35] clauses (*Hughes* clauses) which do a number of things:

- First, they explain when a State law will purport to impose a duty on a Commonwealth regulator.

- Secondly, they provide that, if a State purports to impose a duty on the Commonwealth regulator, the duty is taken to be imposed under State law to the extent to which this is within the legislative power of the State and consistent with relevant constitutional doctrines.

- Thirdly, they provide that, if the duty is not taken to be imposed on the Commonwealth regulator under State law (because of an absence of State legislative power or the operation of relevant constitutional doctrines), the duty is instead taken to be imposed by Commonwealth law (to the extent to which this is within the legislative power of the Commonwealth and consistent with relevant constitutional doctrines).[36]

- Fourthly, they provide that, if the imposition of the duty on the Commonwealth regulator exceeds both State and Commonwealth legislative

---

34   See A Lynch and G Williams, 'Beyond a Federal Structure: Is a Constitutional Commitment to a Federal Relationship Possible?' (2008) 31 *University of New South Wales Law Journal* 395, 419.

35   See, for one example, the *Therapeutic Goods Act 1989* (Cth) ss 6AAA–6AAC.

36   *Hughes* clauses ordinarily provide that if the relevant duty is taken to be imposed by Commonwealth law, then it is the intention of the Parliament 'to rely on all powers available to it under the Constitution to support the imposition of the duty'. One question that arises in this context is: will a court go looking for possible heads of power, or do they need to be spelled out in the legislation? See, on this point, M Farnan, 'Commonwealth-State Cooperative Schemes: Issues for Drafters' (paper presented at the Australasian Drafting Conference, Sydney, 2005) 15. The conventional view is that, notwithstanding s 15A of the *Acts Interpretation Act 1901* (Cth) ('*AI Act*'), the courts will not go looking for possible heads of power. See generally *The King v Poole; Ex parte Henry (No 2)* (1939) 61 CLR 634, 652; *Pidoto v Victoria* (1943) 68 CLR 87, 108–10; *Bank of NSW v Commonwealth* (1948) 76 CLR 1, 371; *Strickland v Rocla Concrete Pipes Ltd* (1971) 124 CLR 468, 493; *Re Dingjan; Ex parte Wagner* (1995) 183 CLR 323, 339; *Victoria v Commonwealth* (1996) 187 CLR 416, 501–3.

power or contravenes relevant constitutional doctrines, the regulator is taken to have a discretionary power (to perform the relevant function), rather than a duty.

Hughes clauses are designed to preserve the constitutional validity of applied law schemes, and to ensure that Commonwealth regulators are at least empowered (if not obliged) to administer and enforce them. However, they have not yet been tested in the High Court. The question whether the Court would regard them as fully coming to terms with the requirements identified in *Hughes* thus remains open.

Hughes issues arise only where the single national regulator is a Commonwealth officer or body. However, even where administration occurs at the State and Territory level, it is possible that constitutional issues may still arise. There is a doctrine of constitutional law — known as the *Melbourne Corporation* doctrine — which prohibits the Commonwealth from enacting laws which, in their 'substance and operation', constitute 'in a significant manner a curtailment or interference with the exercise of State constitutional power'.[37] Relevantly, the effect of the doctrine would appear to be as follows:

- The Commonwealth may confer discretionary functions and powers on a State regulator — that is, it may authorise a State regulator to do something — irrespective of whether or not the relevant State consents (assuming, of course, that the Commonwealth possesses the power to legislate in the first place).

- However, the Commonwealth may not impose obligations or duties on a State regulator — that is, it may not require a State regulator to do something — in the absence of the relevant State's consent.

The issue of what would constitute State 'consent' for the purposes of the *Melbourne Corporation* doctrine is the subject of some uncertainty. Clearly, a State could consent by enacting appropriate legislation. One would ordinarily expect this to occur in the context of an applied law scheme (although careful attention would need to be paid to drafting issues). Alternatively, it is possible that a Commonwealth–State executive agreement (that is, an intergovernmental agreement) would suffice. Chief Justice Gleeson explored this issue in *O'Donoghue v Ireland*.[38] His Honour considered that, provided there is no State legislative impediment to the conferral of the obligation on the relevant State regulator (that is, no State legislation which operates, expressly or impliedly, so that the State regulator cannot perform the relevant function), there is no apparent reason why an executive agreement between the Commonwealth and the State should

---

37   See *Austin v Commonwealth* (2003) 215 CLR 185, 245–6. More generally, see *Melbourne v Commonwealth* (1947) 74 CLR 31 (the '*Melbourne Corporation case*').
38   (2008) 234 CLR 599 ('*O'Donoghue*').

not be a sufficient manifestation of the State's consent. The High Court has not considered the issue again since *O'Donoghue*. It is unclear, therefore, whether a majority of the Court would be prepared to adopt Gleeson CJ's approach.

It is perhaps because of the complexities discussed above that attention has turned to alternative approaches to establishing, and conferring functions and powers on, the regulators of applied law schemes. However the second approach mentioned above — under which both the provisions establishing the regulator and the provisions conferring its functions and powers are set out in the National Law itself, and are thus applied by all participating jurisdictions — raises issues of its own (and arguably does nothing to address the issues raised in *Hughes*).

When the second approach is used, the National Law will include a provision along the following lines:[39]

National Regulator

(1) The National Regulator is established.

(2) The National Regulator—

(a) is a body corporate with perpetual succession; and

(b) has a common seal; and

(c) may sue and be sued in its corporate name.

(3) The National Regulator represents the [jurisdiction/State/Territory].

Based on a plain reading of this provision, it would appear that, each time it is applied by a participating jurisdiction — that is, each time a participating jurisdiction enacts an application Act which applies the National Law — a separate body corporate (having the features described in sub-ss (2) and (3)) is created in and for that participating jurisdiction.

However, the National Law will also contain a separate provision as follows:[40]

Single national entity

(1) It is the intention of the Parliament of this jurisdiction that the National Law as applied by an Act of this jurisdiction, together with the National Law as applied by Acts of other participating jurisdictions,

---

39   See, for example, the Health Practitioner Regulation National Law s 23; the Education and Care Services National Law s 224; the Occupational Licensing National Law s 97; the Rail Safety National Law s 12; and the Heavy Vehicle National Law, ss 597–8.
40   See, for example, the Health Practitioner Regulation National Law s 7; the Education and Care Services National Law s 7; the Occupational Licensing National Law s 6; the Rail Safety National Law s 9; and the Heavy Vehicle National Law s 597.

has the effect that *an entity established by the National Law is one single national entity*, with functions conferred by this Law as so applied [emphasis added].

It is not easy to read the first provision together with the second. One possibility (seemingly the more legally defensible one) is that, whatever the intention of the Parliaments of the participating jurisdictions, the provisions of the National Law are simply not effective to create a 'single national entity'. So, while the National Regulator might, as a practical matter, operate as a 'single national entity', there is, as a legal matter, a separate body corporate, bearing the name of the National Regulator, in each participating jurisdiction. The other possibility, of course, is that the provisions of the National Law succeed in creating a 'single national entity', which is clearly their intention.[41]

However, leaving this issue aside, the real question for present purposes is this: to which executive, and thus which Parliament, is a regulator established under the second approach accountable? To the executive, and thus the Parliament, of the host jurisdiction? To the executive, and thus the Parliament, of the participating jurisdiction in which the regulator is based (if that is not the host jurisdiction)? To the executives, and the Parliaments, of all of the participating jurisdictions (perhaps via the Ministerial Council which, in the context of many applied law schemes, has overall responsibility for the scheme)? And if the latter, is there a risk that the regulator, by being accountable to everyone, might be accountable to no one? What if the regulator makes a controversial decision? What if it makes a mistake? Which Minister is going to answer for it, and in which Parliament?

---

41 There is High Court authority for the proposition that one jurisdiction may, jointly with another jurisdiction, establish a single body which derives its existence, functions and powers from the legislation of both jurisdictions. See, in particular, *R v Duncan; Ex parte Australian Iron and Steel Proprietary Ltd* (1983) 158 CLR 535 ('*Duncan*') and *Re Cram; Ex parte NSW Colliery Proprietors' Association Ltd* (1987) 163 CLR 117 ('*Cram*'). In these cases — which concerned an attempt by the Commonwealth to create a body jointly with NSW — the Court placed great emphasis on how it thought the Commonwealth and NSW *intended* the relevant cooperative legislative scheme to operate. (It is, needless to say, a basic principle of statutory construction that, in interpreting the provisions of an Act, the interpretation that would best achieve the purpose or object of the Act is to be preferred over each other interpretation. See, for example, the *AI Act* s 15A.) However, even if the current Court were to regard the provisions of the National Laws in question as equivalent to the provisions at issue in *Duncan* and *Cram* (which is doubtful), it is by no means clear that it would be anywhere near as sympathetic as the *Duncan* and *Cram* courts were to appeals to the 'intention of Parliament' (or, more broadly, to appeals to the value of 'cooperation'). And even if it were prepared to be so, interesting questions would remain. For instance: would the 'single national entity' itself be a body corporate? That is, would the individual corporations established in the participating jurisdictions somehow become, by the force of parliamentary intention, a single corporation? Or would the 'single national entity' be some other kind of legal entity, its roots the individual corporations created by the participating jurisdictions? After all, as Deane J put it in *Duncan*: 'It is competent for the legislature to constitute ... an entity of a type unknown to the common law': at 587. But if this were found to have occurred, what would be the nature of this new legal entity? And would it have the powers of the individual corporations which begat it, like the power to contract or to acquire real or personal property?

These and other questions might tend to suggest that the first approach mentioned above is the better one. Because this approach is careful to avoid any ambiguity about which participating jurisdiction is responsible for establishing, and has in fact established, the regulator, political accountability is easier to locate. After all, on this approach, it is clear that the regulator will be accountable — ultimately — to the executive, and thus the Parliament, of the jurisdiction which established it. To quote Chief Justice Robert French again:

> It is reasonably arguable that accountability is optimised under a cooperative scheme when one government and one Minister has to be responsible for its administration.[42]

Hughes (and other) issues notwithstanding, it would therefore seem desirable to pursue the first, traditional approach, rather than the second, presently ascendant approach.[43]

Administrative law issues

The interpretation Acts of participating jurisdictions are not the only laws which are capable of operating 'in relation to' a National Law as applied in each participating jurisdiction in such a way as to produce different outcomes in different participating jurisdictions. A range of other laws may also have this effect.[44] Notable in this respect are what might be described broadly as 'administrative laws'.

It is necessary here to distinguish between:

- laws relating to merits and (in particular) judicial review; and
- laws relating to:

---

42   Chief Justice R S French, 'The Incredible Shrinking Federation: Voyage to a Singular State' in G Appleby, N Aroney and T John (eds), *The Future of Australian Federalism: Comparative and Interdisciplinary Perspectives* (Cambridge University Press, 2012) 63.

43   This is not to say, of course, that the first approach raises no responsible government concerns. For instance, in the context of an applied law scheme involving, say, a regulator established under SA law which performs functions and exercises powers under the laws of all other States and Territories, will the executive and the Parliament of SA — the institutions to which the regulator is ostensibly accountable — be as 'interested' in a controversial decision made by the regulator in NSW or Victoria as they would be if the same decision were made in SA? Will a person affected by a decision in NSW or Victoria have the same capacity to complain, or seek redress, as a person affected by a decision in SA? Graeme Hill has suggested that the High Court's decision in *Bond v The Queen* (2000) 201 CLR 213 — which was a precursor to *Hughes* and also concerned the Corporations Law scheme — 'exhibits some concern that lines of political accountability are still unclear' even on the first approach. See G Hill, 'Reviewing Decisions by Commonwealth Bodies Made Under State or Territory Legislation' (2006) 17 *Public Law Review* 112, 130.

44   Some commentators have described these laws as 'adjectival' or 'ancillary' laws. See, for instance, C Saunders, 'A New Direction for Intergovernmental Arrangements' (2001) 276; C Saunders, 'Cooperative Arrangements in Comparative Perspective' in G Appleby, N Aroney and T John (eds), *The Future of Australian Federalism: Comparative and Interdisciplinary Perspectives* (Cambridge University Press, 2012) 419.

- review by the Ombudsman;
- privacy;
- FOI;
- financial management and accountability (including the auditing of regulators);
- public records or archives; and
- public service, administration and management.

Turning first to merits and judicial review,[45] most of the recent applied law schemes have followed a fairly standard approach[46] under which:

- the National Law includes basic provisions about review (concerning, for example, which decisions are reviewable, the review process, etc); and
- each participating jurisdiction's application Act includes provisions prescribing which State tribunal or court is responsible for carrying out the review.[47]

This approach ensures the continuing ready accessibility of avenues of review (and thus raises no particular responsible government concerns). However, its disadvantages in terms of ongoing regulatory uniformity are manifest. Depending on the approach of each participating jurisdiction's tribunals and courts, it is possible that a person aggrieved by an administrative decision in, say, Queensland might achieve a distinctly different result to a person aggrieved by the same (or a similar) decision in Victoria. Moreover, distinctly different interpretations of the National Law might spring up in different participating jurisdictions (notwithstanding common interpretative rules). Needless to say, this approach is also not ideal from the perspective of a single national regulator, which must contend with an array of different tribunals and courts, with varying rules and procedures (most of which will remain untouched by the National Law), in respect of the same decisions.[48] Nor does this approach help to build expertise within a particular tribunal or court.

---

45 For a useful analysis of this issue, see G Hill, 'Reviewing Decisions by Commonwealth Bodies Made Under State or Territory Legislation' (2006) 17 *Public Law Review*. See also C Saunders, 'Administrative Law and Relations Between Governments: Australia and Europe Compared' (2000) 28 *Federal Law Review* 263, 269–70.

46 The adoption of this standard approach may reflect a concern not to transgress relevant constitutional limitations, in particular, the entrenched supervisory jurisdictions of the High Court and State Supreme Courts. See generally *Plaintiff S157/2002 v Commonwealth* (2003) 211 CLR 476; and *Kirk v Industrial Court of NSW* (2010) 239 CLR 531.

47 Further review or appeal will then generally occur within the hierarchy of tribunals and courts existing in the participating jurisdiction concerned.

48 This is something that applied law schemes are supposed to avoid. See K Graham, 'The Commonwealth's Response to *Re Wakim*: The *Jurisdiction of Courts Legislation Amendment Act 2000*' (2000) 26 *AIAL Forum* 33, 34. See also D O'Brien, 'Administrative Review Under the Corporations Law and the Australian Securities Commission Law' (1991) 9 *Company and Securities Law Journal* 235.

Some applied law schemes have sought to address these problems by providing for the establishment of a specialist merits review body to review all decisions made under the scheme, with judicial review by the courts of only one jurisdiction. For example, in the context of the three applied law schemes regulating the energy sector, the Australian Competition Tribunal, established by a Commonwealth Act, conducts merits review,[49] while judicial review is carried out by the federal courts under the *Administrative Decisions (Judicial Review) Act 1977* (Cth) ('*ADJR Act*').[50]

In relation to the broader package of administrative laws, the position is more complicated and (arguably) more problematic from a responsible government perspective. The standard approach in this context is one of 'disapplication and replacement'. That is, each participating jurisdiction disapplies its administrative laws (insofar as the National Law is concerned) and replaces those laws by:

- applying mutually agreed replacement rules insofar as some matters are concerned (usually financial management and accountability, auditing and the like); and

- applying the administrative laws of another jurisdiction (with necessary modifications) insofar as other matters are concerned (usually review by the Ombudsman, privacy and FOI).

This disapplication and replacement approach raises a number of responsible government concerns. For one thing, there is a question whether the functions served by the disapplied laws (functions which include ensuring the ready availability of information and the ready accessibility of avenues of review) will be properly served by whatever replaces them (assuming something does). In other words, will the mutually-agreed replacement rules, or the administrative laws of the other jurisdiction, be the equal of what they have supplanted? Even if they are, it is undeniable that the disapplication and replacement of a participating jurisdiction's administrative laws adds significant complexity to the law.[51] Even for a trained lawyer, it can be difficult to discern precisely

49 This procedure — merits review by the Australian Competition Tribunal with judicial review by the federal courts — is applicable only in relation to certain bodies with functions and powers under the relevant National Laws (in particular, the AER). Other bodies with functions and powers under the National Laws (such as the Australian Energy Market Commission and the Australian Energy Market Operator) are subject to the standard approach under which their decisions are reviewed by the (prescribed) tribunals and courts of each participating jurisdiction. As of August 2013, the Standing Council on Energy and Resources — which is the Ministerial Council overseeing the applied law schemes regulating the energy sector — was conducting a review of the so-called 'limited merits review' process established under the schemes. The current proposal envisions the continuation of (altered) merits review by the Australian Competition Tribunal and judicial review by the federal courts.
50 The *ADJR Act* sch 3 prescribes the State and Territory Acts that apply the National Electricity Law, the National Gas Law and the National Energy Retail Law as 'enactments' for the purposes of the *ADJR Act*.
51 This complexity is most evident in circumstances where one participating jurisdiction disapplies its administrative laws and applies those of another jurisdiction. For example, when the States and Territories disapply their administrative laws and apply those of the Commonwealth — which occurs frequently, even

what options are available for, say, making an application for review by the Ombudsman or making an FOI request. The barriers to entry (both in terms of time and cost) are considerable.

Other issues

The issues discussed above are not an exhaustive list of the challenges that applied law schemes pose (or potentially pose) to responsible government. Some further issues (although by no means all of them) are discussed below.

First, there is the issue of regulations. We have long since become used to the fact that the Parliament delegates significant legislative power to the executive. As a result of this practice, much of the real detail of any particular scheme is determined by the executive, via regulations or other subordinate legislation, rather than by the Parliament, via primary legislation. However, the understanding behind this practice is that the Parliament will scrutinise any regulations promulgated by the executive, and may easily disallow them. This is not necessarily the case in the context of applied law schemes. Most National Laws, like most ordinary Acts, contain broad regulation-making powers, with authority to make the regulations generally bestowed on either the relevant Ministerial Council[52] or one executive (with the unanimous consent or 'recommendation' of the others).[53] The National Laws also usually provide for the tabling of any regulations in the Parliament of each participating jurisdiction. However, the relevant disallowance provision often reflects an approach that is best described as 'majority rules'. The following provision, taken from the Health Practitioner Regulation National Law, offers an illustration:[54]

---

in the context of purely State and Territory-based applied law schemes, because the Commonwealth's laws are seen as 'neutral ground' — the Commonwealth's laws, as applied, must be modified so that, whenever they refer to a Commonwealth officer or body (such as the Australian Information Commissioner or the Commonwealth Ombudsman), the references are taken to be references to a State or Territory officer (or officers) or body (or bodies). This is necessary because, as discussed above, the States and Territories cannot unilaterally (that is, without Commonwealth consent) confer a function or power on a Commonwealth officer or body. A purported conferral of this sort would be invalid by virtue of s 109 of the Constitution and/or the Commonwealth's implied intergovernmental immunity. This is generally not the only modification that is necessary. Accordingly, it is common for National Laws to have broad regulation-making provisions which permit the regulations to modify the applied Commonwealth laws or to provide that the applied Commonwealth laws apply as if specific provisions were omitted or specific amendments to the Commonwealth laws (by the Commonwealth Parliament) had not taken effect.

52   See, for example, the Health Practitioner Regulation National Law s 245; the Education and Care Services National Law s 301; and the Occupational Licensing National Law s 160.

53   See, for example, the Rail Safety National Law s 264; the Co-operatives National Law s 612; and the Heavy Vehicle National Law s 669.

54   It is worth noting that, under the Health Practitioner Regulation National Law, Victoria is responsible for the preparation and printing of regulations made by the Ministerial Council, notwithstanding that Queensland is the host jurisdiction: see s 245 of the National Law. This is but one of the many oddities that one may expect to find when looking at an applied law scheme in any detail.

246 Parliamentary scrutiny of national regulations

(1) A regulation made under this Law may be disallowed in a participating jurisdiction by a House of the Parliament of that jurisdiction —

(a) in the same way that a regulation made under an Act of that jurisdiction may be disallowed; and

(b) as if the regulation had been tabled in the House on the first sitting day after the regulation was published by the Victorian Government Printer.

(2) A regulation disallowed under subsection (1) does not cease to have effect in the participating jurisdiction, or any other participating jurisdiction, unless the regulation is disallowed in a majority of the participating jurisdictions.

The effect of a provision like this is clear: the Parliaments of, say, SA and Tasmania, could find themselves 'out-voted' by those of the bigger States. And while the 'minority' Parliaments could presumably take extraordinary measures to disallow the regulations — up to and including 'withdrawing' from the applied law scheme altogether — it is likely that they would find themselves under considerable political pressure not to buck the horse.

Another issue concerns those jurisdictions which enact an application Act that applies the National Law but also modifies that National Law in some way in and for the participating jurisdiction. It is relatively common for these jurisdictions not to provide a 'consolidated' version of the National Law as modified by the application Act (NSW is an honourable exception to this trend). This leaves readers of the National Law with the unenviable task of trying to piece together their own 'consolidation', the National Law in one hand, the application Act in the other. This is hardly acceptable if, as discussed above, one regards responsible government as being at least in part about the 'knowability' and 'accessibility' of the law.[55]

A final issue concerns those jurisdictions, currently Victoria and the ACT, which have a human rights Act. The impact of applied law schemes on the 'interpretative duty' imposed by human rights Acts has already been mentioned. But it is also worth recalling that another key feature of human rights Acts is that they require the preparation of statements which accompany a Bill when it is introduced

---

55   The failure to provide suitable consolidations may also be seen in circumstances where participating jurisdictions apply the administrative laws of another jurisdiction (with modifications). In these circumstances, readers of the administrative laws, as applied, must have a copy of the original administrative laws, the National Law (which will usually modify the applied administrative laws to some extent) and the National Regulations (which will usually modify the applied administrative laws to a greater extent).

into the Parliament which attest to the Bill's compatibility with human rights.[56] While Victoria and the ACT have prepared statements of compatibility when they have applied a National Law for the first time, the statements have not necessarily been prepared for subsequent amendments to the Law. This is because, in circumstances where Victoria and the ACT apply a National Law as in force in the host jurisdiction from time to time (as they generally do), any amendment to the Law made by the host jurisdiction will apply automatically in Victoria and the ACT. The obligation to prepare a statement of compatibility, which arises only when a Bill is introduced to the Parliament, simply does not apply in these circumstances.[57] It is possible, then, that applied law schemes have the capacity to undermine quite seriously the intended effect of human rights Acts, detracting not only from the interpretative duty they impose, but also from their potential, via the statement of compatibility process, to get parliamentarians thinking about human rights.[58]

Conclusion

There are those who hope that policy makers will begin to interrogate more closely 'the value of national uniformity', and ultimately come to 'reflect on the advantages of diversity and innovation that federalism potentially offers Australia'.[59] Such people are likely to be waiting a long time. The consensus — be it unthinking or otherwise — that there is a strong economic and 'equality' case for regulatory uniformity seems strong and, if anything, growing stronger.

---

56   See the *Victorian Human Rights Charter* s 28 and the *ACT Human Rights Act* s 37. These statements are generally called 'statements of compatibility'.

57   This issue has attracted criticism in Victoria: see the Scrutiny of Acts and Regulations Committee, Parliament of Victoria, *Review of the Charter of Human Rights and Responsibilities Act 2006* (2011) 95–6. In its response to this review, the Victorian Government stated that it 'does not intend to require statements of compatibility … for amendments to national uniform schemes that entail the application of laws of another jurisdiction in Victoria. The initial legislation that implements a national applied law uniform scheme in Victoria is accompanied by a statement of compatibility and is subject to scrutiny by the Victorian Parliament and [the Scrutiny of Acts and Regulations Committee]. At that time, Parliament agrees to the content of the initial legislation, including the process for making amendments and regulations.' See Government of Victoria, *Review of the Charter of Human Rights and Responsibilities Act 2006: Victorian Government Response* (2012) 13–4.

58   The other main way that human rights Acts aim to promote human rights is to impose on 'public authorities' a duty to act compatibly with, and give proper consideration to, human rights. See the *Victorian Human Rights Charter* s 38 and the *ACT Human Rights Act* s 40B. Applied law schemes arguably have the potential to disrupt this obligation as well. Whether or not this is so may depend not only on the definition of 'public authority' adopted in each human rights Act, but also on the issues discussed above in relation to the establishment of a single national regulator. For example, when the second approach discussed above is utilised — that is, the approach under which both the provisions establishing the regulator and the provisions conferring its functions and powers are set out in the National Law itself, and are thus applied by all participating jurisdictions — is a separate body corporate, bearing the name of the regulator, established in each participating jurisdiction?

59   C Saunders, 'Cooperative Arrangements in Comparative Perspective' in G Appleby, N Aroney and T John (eds), *The Future of Australian Federalism: Comparative and Interdisciplinary Perspectives* (Cambridge University Press, 2012) 414, 430.

A more realistic hope is that attempts to achieve regulatory uniformity might occur in a way that is more in keeping with our underlying constitutional system. This does not necessarily mean that applied law schemes should be jettisoned in favour of 'tighter' (reference schemes) or 'looser' (mirror law schemes) cooperative legislative schemes.[60] But it does mean that, if applied law schemes are to be implemented, greater attention should be paid to what the concept of responsible government requires and implies. When a jurisdiction decides to participate in an applied law scheme, the most careful attention should be given to the method which is to be utilised to apply the law of the host jurisdiction: what role does that method give to the Parliament vis-à-vis the executive? And if that method inverts the usual power relationship between the Parliament and the executive, has the necessity of that inversion been both properly considered and properly explained to the voting public? Secondly, the relationship between the legislation necessary to enter into an applied law scheme and the balance of a jurisdiction's law — everything from its interpretation Act to its FOI Act to its public records or archives Act — must be considered. In particular, it must be recognised that the disapplication or modification of laws that are well-understood and, moreover, understood to be generally applicable, will not be consequence-free. Thirdly, and perhaps most critically, the regulators established to administer and enforce an applied law scheme must be accountable — preferably to a particular executive, and thus, a particular Parliament, and also via the courts and other scrutiny actors. Finally, at every stage, the overall complexity of the applied law scheme must not be forgotten, bearing in mind that the 'knowability' and 'accessibility' of the law are, ultimately, aspects of the rule of the law.[61] Addressing these issues may come at a price in terms of the uniformity of the resulting applied law scheme. But is the price we pay for ignoring them any lower?

---

60   Note that Saunders, in particular, has argued that reference schemes, as opposed to other kinds of cooperative legislative schemes, represent a 'mechanism for collaboration that is compatible with the rest of the constitutional system'. C Saunders, 'Collaborative Federalism' (2002) 61 *Australian Journal of Public Administration* 75.

61   See generally *Black-Clawson International Ltd v Papierwerke Waldhof-Aschaffenburg AG* [1975] AC 591, 638 (Diplock LJ): 'The acceptance of the rule of law as a constitutional principle requires that a citizen, before committing himself to any course of action, should *be able to know* in advance what are the legal consequences that will flow from it' (emphasis added).

III. Democracy, Law and Culture

7. Ritual in the Law of Electoral Democracy

Graeme Orr[1]

Theorising the law of democracy

For all its concern with power, prestige and politics, public law can be an earnest and colourless topic. The corner of public law I inhabit is the law of politics, especially electoral democracy. It is particularly dominated by a concern with process. On top of that, it is not well theorised. In part, this is because it is an emerging sub-discipline. It has been jointly sired by constitutional and administrative law, and by that branch of political science concerned with electoral systems and behaviour. But the law of politics is also under-theorised because it is seen as an essentially pragmatic venture in which even symbolism and rhetoric are sublimated. The High Court's occasional venture (or adventure) aside,[2] whether it is made ad hoc by judges or, as is more typical, explicitly by Acts of Parliament or even inferentially by electoral administrators, electoral law is proudly pragmatic.

This essay is an attempt to rectify that under-theorising of the law of electoral politics. By theorising, I mean asking the 'why' or 'what for' questions. By the law of electoral politics, I mean the rules lain down, and institutions and systems set up, to govern democracy through the process of renewing elective offices and other forms of popular voting, such as referendums. Here, I want to stake a claim for the importance of the concept of ritual in how we understand this field, particularly in considering what elections are 'for'.

Ritual is a concept familiar to anthropologists and political historians,[3] but much less so to contemporary legal or political theorists. Yet ritual naturally emerges from and illuminates the experience of democratic culture. That illumination can reflect light upon — and hence aid our understanding of — the law's role in

---

1   g.orr@law.uq.edu.au.
2   *ACTV v Commonwealth* (1992) 177 CLR 106, uncovering an implied freedom of political communication, is the best known example. The twin franchise cases of *Roach v Electoral Commissioner* (2007) 233 CLR 162 and *Rowe v Electoral Commissioner* (2010) 243 CLR 1 are more recent instances. Mild in their effect, the cases have still been savaged by champions of the originalist intention to leave the field to Parliament alone. For example, James Allan, 'The Three Rs of Recent Australian Judicial Activism: *Roach, Rowe* and (No) 'Riginalism' (2012) 36 *Melbourne University Law Review* 743.

3   For example, James Frazer, *The Golden Bough: A Study in Magic and Religion* (Macmillan, 1963); Mark W Brewin, *Celebrating Democracy: The Mass-Mediated Ritual of Election Day* (Peter Lang, 2008).

democracy. Whilst the ritual dimension may often be overlooked in rationalist accounts of law-making, it is inescapable. The laws and institutions we adopt will necessarily shape and constrain the ritual experience. Without appreciating this, we cannot fully understand the social power and place of elections and the laws and institutions that underlie them.

I will shortly offer definitions of the concept, then attempt some positive demonstration of my claims about the importance of a ritual understanding. But first, it is useful to take a quick stock of the dominant theoretical approaches and presumptions that have been applied to the law of electoral politics. Broadly put, those approaches are the realist, and the liberal. They are fairly hard-headed, in the sense that they are usually invoked to drive law reform or judicial review in the area. My desire is not to supplant the realist and liberal approaches with an approach drawing on ritual, but to augment them.

Take first the self-styled realist approach. Popular here and abroad, this strand of thought is economistic, and essentially pragmatic to the point of cynicism. In this view, electoral politics is seen as a Schumpeterian competition amongst political elites.[4] The law of electoral politics must be calibrated to minimise negative effects of gaming by self-interested incumbent MPs and parties, and to maximise positive effects such as accountability.[5] Electoral democracy in this approach is depicted as having no ends in itself; it is seen as just an institutional method to soften or compromise the elite rule of representative government. In Schumpeter's declaration: 'Democracy is a political method [i.e.] a certain type of institutional arrangement for arriving at [governmental] decisions and hence incapable of being an end in itself'.[6]

The law's role within all this is as a boundary-rider, trying to limit undemocratic harms that may arise if democracy becomes the discretionary plaything of self-interested and passing legislators and administrations. Richard Posner epitomises this approach, in his explicitly anti-trust model for regulating electoral democracy.[7] From this understanding we derive things such as the independence of electoral authorities that run elections, and the tendency for courts, worldwide, to place limits around Parliament's power to make electoral legislation.[8]

---

4   Joseph Schumpeter, in three seminal chapters in *Socialism, Capitalism and Democracy* (Routledge, new ed, 1994) chs 21–23, laid out his critique of classical liberal democracy.

5   Electoral accountability is crude, but without it other forms of accountability (for example, parliamentary and media oversight of government, or the reflexive attention of leaders to public opinion) would be much weaker.

6   Joseph Schumpeter, *Socialism, Capitalism and Democracy* (Routledge, new ed, 1994) 242. Posner explicitly embraces Schumpeter, though he paints his approach as pragmatic rather than elite democracy. See Richard A Posner, *Law, Pragmatism and Democracy* (Harvard University Press, 2003) chs 4–6.

7   Richard A Posner, *Law, Pragmatism and Democracy* (Harvard University Press, 2003) chs 4–6. See Richard Pildes, 'Competitive, Deliberative and Rights-Oriented Democracy' (2004) 3 *Election Law Journal* 685.

8   Even absent an explicit bill of rights. See *ACTV v Commonwealth* (1992) 177 CLR 106, *Roach v Electoral Commissioner* (2007) 233 CLR 162 and *Rowe v Electoral Commissioner* (2010) 243 CLR 1. Such cases manifest

In the other, liberal approach, the law plays a more normatively constructive, rather than a merely boundary-riding role. The law is depicted as part of a quest for deeper values or loftier purposes, derived from liberal political philosophy. These purposes are political liberty, equality and deliberation. That is, the law can aim to encourage participation and political freedoms, it can seek to advance political equality in an otherwise unequal society and it can seek to foster informed and reflective public deliberation (although this last role is often overlooked or sublimated).[9] Now there is obviously room for tension amongst these goals, especially between liberty and equality. (For example, how far can we restrain money in politics in the interests of egalitarianism, and is it right to compel people to the polls to create a more inclusive electoral system?) But together, these three values provide a benchmark of liberal democratic values to help craft the substance of the law. Straddling the realist and liberal camps, James Gardner succinctly explained recently that 'election law bridges the gap between our aspirations for, and the frequently messy reality of, our political lives'.[10]

What I wish to argue in this chapter is that there is another, less instrumental,[11] yet no less 'real' or even pragmatic way of thinking about the law of electoral politics. And that is to examine the ritual dimension of it all.[12] No-one would deny that the traditions of the opening of Parliament, for example, form obvious, public law rituals. But I want to make a much broader and, I hope, more interesting claim that there is an element of ritual all the way down. Ritual concerns the repeated patterns of everyday life, in this case of recurrent electoral activity. Law, whether it knows it or not, plays a role in opening up space for, constraining or guiding that ritual element. We should not be surprised, therefore, to find ritual manifest by and, in some cases embedded in, not just democratic practice, but throughout public law.

As a working definition, I borrow Murray Edelman's definition of ritual as any 'activity that involves its participants symbolically in a common enterprise, calling their attention to their relatedness and joint interests in a compelling way'.[13] To this we must add, however, the need for a ritual to be something

---

the idea that the electoral self-interest of parliamentary majorities requires supervision. John Hart Ely, *Democracy and Distrust: A Theory of Judicial Review* (Harvard University Press, 1980).

9   Compare Richard Pildes, 'Competitive, Deliberative and Rights-Oriented Democracy' (2004) 3 *Election Law Journal*, and Andrew Geddis, 'Three Conceptions of the Electoral Moment' (2003) 28 *Australian Journal of Legal Philosophy* 53. Of these, the liberty and equality 'visions' are most developed, albeit in tension. Some doubt that electoral campaigns, however well-regulated, can be deliberative. James A Gardner, *What are Campaigns For?: The Role of Persuasion in Electoral Law and Politics* (Oxford University Press, 2009).

10   James A Gardner, 'Election Law as Applied Democratic Theory' (2012) 56 *St Louis University Law Journal* 689.

11   Less instrumental in that ritual considers things such as elections as events in themselves, and not merely unavoidable steps in some broader governmental process.

12   I first sketched this in 'The Ritual and Aesthetic in Electoral Law' (2004) 32 *Federal Law Review* 425. The present essay is part of a larger book on 'Ritual and Rhythm in Electoral Systems' (Ashgate, 2015).

13   Murray Edelman, *The Symbolic Uses of Politics* (University of Illinois Press, 5th ed, 1985) 16.

patterned, repeated or rhythmic. Ritual, so understood, is intimately connected to common experiences (albeit ones that different people may respond to, intellectually and emotionally, in different ways). Rituals carry meanings, but they are not limited to occasions exhibiting grand themes like the sacred or the constitutive, which we find in ceremonial and liminal moments of creation or loss. Elections in a settled democracy are, simultaneously, both significant (re) constitutive moments and relatively routine acts of public participation and administration.

Rituals and rhythms—and their relationship with myths, symbols and aesthetics

As regularised events, elections have an inescapably ritual dimension. Elections are nothing if not public *events*, *experienced* by citizens and political actors alike. Ritual has classically been understood in semi-religious terms, particularly through notions such as rite and myth in the sense of legend. More secular understandings of ritual emphasise theatre and myth in terms of the symbolism of public life. Elements such as rite and theatre can certainly be identified in moments of solemn or high political behaviour, whether they be the formal dissolution of Parliament and issuing of electoral writs, or the gatherings at tally rooms and concession speeches that dominate election night. But ritual is not exhausted by these moments of political behaviour. The ritual that most intrigues me is a much more quotidian beast, such as the experiences at the polling station. But before we get to those everyday experiences, it is worth contrasting ritual with some key related concepts of myth, symbolics and aesthetics.

The religious or transcendent connotations of rite and ritual have been explored in both traditional anthropological literature and, more recently, in the notion of civil religion.[14] The original insight of civil religion was to reveal how public and political order can be imbued with transcendent meaning: politics as religion. A more recent focus, most obviously in the US, has been on the public aspect of religion and how its cleavages are written into political order: religion as politics.[15] Both the traditional anthropological approach, and the civil and public religion viewpoints draw our attention to a broader baggage often transported by ritual: the notion of myth.

---

14   With roots in Robert Bellah, 'Civil Religion in America' (1967) 96(1) *Dædalus* 1.
15   Compare Robert Withnow, *The Restructuring of American Religion* (Princeton University Press, 1988) ch 10, identifying a conservative and liberal civil religions and theologies.

Myth is carried by and replicated not just through explicit stories, but also in the more implicit practices we transmit across generations. Democracy revels in myth as much as any other system of government. (Indeed, to Claude Lévi-Strauss, the political ideology of contemporary liberal societies is of an order with the myth and religion of older societies).[16] There are stories of forgetting, especially in foundational myths. Australians are proud of their relatively rapid and egalitarian expansion of the vote in the 19th century. That expansion took late 19th century Australia, in a handful of decades, from a property-based franchise which countenanced multiple voting, through the evolution of one-man, one-vote, and onto adult suffrage with the enfranchisement of women around the time of federation. But that pride requires sublimation of the fact that most Indigenous Australians waited up to 60 years longer to gain this first order liberal right.[17] Similarly, does the average British or North American person today remember that women were denied the vote by law until 1918–20, barely one lifetime ago?[18]

Most democracies espouse their own particular, inflected legends of democracy, whether of loss, change or renewal. These legends extend beyond simple tales of movements demanding popular and local sovereignty, to include the role of the media and foreign affairs. Many Americans, for instance, believe that the broadcaster Walter Cronkite declared the Vietnam War unwinnable, channelling the fears of the zeitgeist, and thereby sealed the fate of the conflict. This is pure myth.[19] Australians, depending on whether they are social democrats or conservatives, invest the short-lived Whitlam government with either the status of Camelot made real, or as a warning of the limits of politics and governmental ambition. Each of those positions on the Whitlam government makes sense in itself, but is overstated relative to the administration's short-life (1972–75). Nonetheless, the government's dramatic undoing — it was controversially dismissed by the Queen's representative in Australia — fuses these conflicting narratives, of Camelot-lost and a failed government, into an even *larger* legend.

Myth generates meaning through the use of bold colours and big canvasses, by lionising or demonising particular key characters or major events. A ritual such as a presidential inauguration, or a leader claiming victory on election night, may recall these wider stories and histories. But whilst myth can colour the way we read and experience rituals, rituals are not the agents of myth. Rather, rituals tend to carry embedded meanings: meanings they emblemise or symbolise. An

---

16   Claude Lévi-Strauss, *Structural Anthropology* (Claire Jacobson trans, Basic Books, 1963) 306.
17   Adrian Brooks, '"A Paragon of Democratic Virtues?": The Development of the Commonwealth Franchise' (1993) 12 *University of Tasmania Law Review* 208.
18   Even then, British women did not enjoy equal suffrage with men until the *Representation of the People (Equal Franchise) Act 1928* (UK).
19   W Joseph Campbell, *Getting It Wrong: Ten of the Greatest Misreported Stories in American Journalism* (University of California Press, 2010) ch 5.

example of this is the way that polling routinely takes place in schools, whose significance we will examine shortly. The symbolic meanings inherent in rituals differ from myth, because ritual is less singular, and typically more routine. Ritual is the fabric of everyday life; myth is often cartoonish and perpetuated by a kind of history-for-beginners. The power of ritual lies both in its intimacy (of the lived experience of campaigns and voting) or in its repetition (the cycle of an election summonsed, its results declared, a new government or president commissioned).

There is another related concept, the aesthetic, which also requires a little explanation and exploration. Aesthetics is an ancient branch of thinking; traditionally it was a source of virtue. Legal aesthetics is a vibrant and broad ranging body of thought, which can cover everything from the relatively concrete — such as the architecture and design of Parliaments and court buildings — through to reflections on how different notions of time and space are inescapably embedded in understandings of, say, religious freedom.[20] Discussions of legal aesthetics, whether in public or private law, however, can be fraught. They can risk collapsing into formalism, in the sense of fetishising the formal neatness of legal structures or logic. They can even dissolve into a striving for a kind of beauty informed by poetic but mystical, even totalitarian, impulses.[21]

But we cannot think about ritual without a notion of the aesthetic in the sense of fit or harmony. This encapsulates both a concrete or sensory experience of fit, and also fit in the sense of proportionality. Sensory examples are not difficult to find, once one digs a little into the law. In election campaigns, for instance, we find concrete regulation in everything from local government strictures on the size and location of 'vote for me' posters, through to bans on displays, demonstrations and hubbub near polling booths. In the more abstract sense of proportionality, we find different political aesthetics implicit in different approaches to regulating election finance and preferred (or frowned upon) forms of campaigning. Compare, for instance, the American laissez-faire model of expenditure, with the British law banning all paid political broadcasts but granting airtime instead for substantial 'party political broadcasts'.[22]

Now, of course, these examples all inter-relate with the other theories for conceiving of electoral rules. Sometimes judges frown on limitations on the size

---

20   Benjamin L Berger, 'The Aesthetics of Religious Freedom' in Winifred Sullivan and Lori Beaman (eds), *Varieties of Religious Establishment* (Ashgate, 2013).

21   Consider D'Annunzio's constitution for the province of Carnaro, in which music was a core principle of the state. Of ten corporations (or sectors) one was reserved as a 'votive offering to the genius of the unknown' and represented by a public flame to the ideal of *Fatica senza Fatica* ('Work without Toil').

22   The UK is not alone: Israel and New Zealand have similar regimes. The UK goes further in erecting a year round limitation on paid political — nor merely electoral — broadcasts. Australia briefly borrowed the electorally puritan model before the High Court struck it down. See *ACTV v Commonwealth* (1992) 177 CLR 106.

or number of electoral posters on private property, by reasoning that liberty interests prevail over amenity.[23] The 'cordon sanitaire', established by the rule against campaigning near or inside polling booths,[24] creates an aesthetic experience of quiet order, a sense of deliberativeness as well as a potential repose for deliberation for any electors yet to decide how to direct their preferences. The valorising of the liberty of money in the US, as opposed to the more egalitarian British approach to political finance, overshadows aesthetic considerations such as the ideal forms of political speech. My point is not that aesthetic concerns are overt drivers of regulation, but that an aesthetic is involved in each issue and approach, even if only as a by-product. We cannot think about the ritual or experience of a campaign with streets festooned with election placards (or not), of voting in a hubbub (or in a quite ballot booth) or of campaigns flush with television advertisements (or starved of them), without considering the aesthetic element.

The rituals of election day and polling

Armed with an understanding of ritual as patterned actions and shared experiences, we can now turn to more practical questions. What of the actions that constitute elections, especially the central acts of casting and counting votes? How does law — broadly understood to include institutional practice and custom, as well as black-letter rules — set up the ground for ritual in electoral politics?

Let us take the act of voting, which we have come to take for granted. Les Murray finished his poem *My Ancestress and the Secret Ballot, 1848 and 1851* with the metaphor of the ballot booth becoming 'a closet of prayer'.[25] Not so much a command to the gods who govern us, but a hope sent forth in good conscience. Yet, 150 years after the emergence of the secret ballot, in his book *Voting Rites*, Ron Hirschbein lamented that voter turnout in the US had dwindled, relative to headier days. He blamed this only in part because voting 'no longer offers the illusion that it is instrumental (politically efficacious)'. The deeper problem, Hirschbein claims, is that 'electoral politics is bereft of expressive value: Casting a ballot no longer provides ritualistic gratification and hardy entertainment.'[26] Voting, Hirschbein lamented, had lost too much of its *affective*, as well as its

---

23 *Liberal Party of Australia (Western Australian Division) Inc v City of Armadale* [2013] WASC 27. Yet the national law forbids such activity as chalking electoral arguments on roads, or projecting slogans on buildings. *Commonwealth Electoral Act 1918* (Cth) s 334.

24 *Commonwealth Electoral Act 1918* (Cth) ss 335, 340–1. See also s 328.

25 Les Murray, *Subhuman Redneck Poems* (Duffy & Snellgrove, 1996). A copy of the poem also opens Mark McKenna's revisionist account of the ballot, 'Building a "Closet of Prayer" in the New World: The Story of the "Australian Ballot"' in Marian Sawer (ed), *Elections: Full, Free and Fair* (The Federation Press, 2001) 45.

26 Ron Hirschbein, *Voting Rites: The Devolution of American Politics* (Praeger, 1999) 2 (emphasis altered).

effective, dimensions. It had lost 'its former liturgical fullness [and] carnival spirit'.[27] Chronicling the history of election day in Philadelphia, Mark Brewin similarly highlights a loss of the 'public celebration' as the physical element is transformed into a ritual mediated by electronic communication systems.[28]

Jon Lawrence, another political historian, but in this case writing from a UK perspective, warns against simplistic or romantic historical comparisons, whilst admitting that it is easy to read 19th century UK hustings 'at one level ... as ritualised celebrations of Britain's unequal, hierarchical society'.[29] The historian's insight seems to be that everything has changed: legally, with the advent of the mass franchise, and technologically, with the bureaucratisation of modern life. Yet elections remain a time when the governing class — albeit now a professional political class rather than a class defined by inherited privilege[30] — temporarily faces a public humbling. The largesse of vote-buying is now done through public promises rather than private bribery,[31] and the heckling from the crowd is replaced by talk-back radio or television interviewers. But elections remain a demotic ritual.

Without any stretching or romanticism, we can still see election day as a unique communal event. Traditionalists might yearn for some transcendent 'liturgical fullness', but election day is not bereft without it. Some Australians are habituated into participating, less by intrinsic desire and more by legal compulsion — corralled into participating not, as Athenians were, by a cord dyed red, but by the vague threat of a $20 fine. Yet a communal ritual remains, even if some experience it as a political confessional whilst others feel it to be a public duty or chore.[32] The ritual is primarily built up in the patterned behaviour — what transpires in the internal reflections of different individuals is another matter. In this more everyday understanding of ritual, we only need to describe the scene of polling day in Australia to see its ritual dimensions. The local scouts and charities set up their sausage sizzles and cake stalls; the party activists wrap bunting along the school gates;[33] the elector quickens her pace as she dodges (or politely accepts) offers of 'how-to-vote cards', before entering

---

27 ibid 130.

28 Mark W Brewin, *Celebrating Democracy: The Mass-Mediated Ritual of Election Day* (Peter Lang, 2008) ch 9.

29 Jon Lawrence, *Electing our Masters: The Hustings in British Politics from Hogarth to Blair* (Oxford University Press, 2009) 6.

30 One might say a political class '*mostly* not defined by inherited privilege': the present UK Prime Minister and Deputy Prime Minister are Old Etonians; in the US, dynasties such as the Kennedys are superseded by the Bushes. But they are exceptions, not rules.

31 Graeme Orr, 'Dealing in Votes: Regulating Electoral Bribery' in Graeme Orr et al. (eds), *Realising Democracy: Electoral Law in Australia* (The Federation Press, 2003) 130.

32 Just as, to extend the religious metaphor, some Christians take communion as a sacrament, others out of unreflective habit.

33 But not too close. *Commonwealth Electoral Act 1918* (Cth) s 40 forbids such colour within six metres of the entrance to the sanctity of the polling booth. In two jurisdictions, Tasmania and the ACT, the aesthetic of repose extends wider, to a 100-metre cordon sanitaire around polling stations.

the calm of the polling station to retire to a booth and place pencil marks on the official ballot papers. All this, to varying degrees, is a product of law, whether black-letter or institutional policy choices.

Citizens thus gather — or rather they are summonsed by the law of compulsory participation that we call compulsory voting — on the one day every three or so years that our secular society comes together. This periodicity is laid down constitutionally: three years nationally, four years for most States and Territories.[34] They wait in line after running the gauntlet of how-to-vote cards, which are themselves a product of preferential voting laws.[35] They find themselves milling in the quiet of the polling booth itself, a place whose repose is protected by law.[36] Finally, they have their names marked off the roll, ballots completed by trusty pencil and consigned with a wish or curse to a secure ballot box. All of this, down to the pencil, is safeguarded by legal regulation.[37]

Certainly, it might be objected that what scouts and party volunteers do is not legally determined in any strong sense. But in a profound sense it is shaped and enabled by law. Imagine a society that moved to internet voting, as some have advocated for noble reasons relating to maximising formal participation. There would be no physical event, presumably no 'election day' as such, just a final time limit to lodge one's electoral choices electronically. Elections would become an even more private and transactionalised activity.[38] Something significant of a communal nature would be lost. Paradoxically, the more secular and market-oriented Western nations become, the more polling day stands out as the one-day when a society comes together.

Rituals and beliefs, of course, bubble up or are inherited from many sources. Those sources may co-mingle; they may also clash. The secular 'civil religion' of electoral democracy aims to bring citizens together for at least one occasion every several years. Yet its demands are sometimes incompatible with other belief systems and practices. Most obviously, Jehovah's Witnesses do not partake of the electoral ritual, because they honour only their God and not secular political institutions. Compulsory voting in Australia accommodates such conscientious objections, but only if they stem from a shared creed and not an idiosyncratic belief, however sincerely held.[39]

---

34 For example *Australian Constitution* ss 28, 32 (three-year cycle for national elections).

35 Except in Tasmanian elections, where they are banned. *Electoral Act 2004* (Tas) s 198.

36 *Commonwealth Electoral Act 1918* (Cth) ss 335, 340–1.

37 Of course the ritual differs if one votes by post, at home. It is more private and the nesting of envelopes within envelopes reflects a bureaucratic promise as to one's anonymity. The ritual differs in its ease and inflection, but it is still, palpably, a ritual.

38 Compare Heather Lardy, 'Modernising Elections: The Silent Premises of the Electoral Pilot Schemes' (2003) 1 *Public Law* 6 (critiquing moves to extend postal balloting).

39 *Douglas v Ninnes* (1976) 14 SASR 377 at 382–3.

Praises are often sung for the fact that Australian law has long mandated that election day be a Saturday. In comparison, general elections are held on a Thursday in the UK and a Tuesday in the US. Saturday elections expressed an egalitarian value, as working hours had been reduced to a half-day and, for most permanent employees, Saturday became a work-free day altogether. Voting in Australia is thus a more leisurely affair than in countries where workers have to duck into polling stations on their way to or from work. Voting on working days also leads, as we see in the US, to irresistible pressure to offer early voting to everyone, which detracts from the ritualistic purpose of having a polling day at all.

Yet weekend voting presents drawbacks, as many religions reserve Saturdays or Sundays for worship. The September date chosen for the 2013 Australian election coincided with Yom Kippur, the most sacred day in the Judaic calendar. Religious observance entitles electors to an early or postal vote, but the result was that Jewish Australians could participate in their religious ritual and the formal franchise, yet they could not partake fully in the democratic ritual. In contrast, the law (where terms are fixed) and leaders of all stripes (where election dates are open), avoid elections overlapping with the finals of the two major football codes.[40] The Prime Minister offered this half-apology: 'I do understand the significance of the day in question for the Jewish community. But there would be many of my Melbourne Jewish friends who would also understand the significance of AFL grand final day.'[41] So it is that two great mainstream competitive rituals, sporting finals and electoral politics, are accorded separate spotlights, but other cultural practices can be neglected.

And just where do we vote? Admittedly Australian law has little explicitly to say on the point — other than frowning on 'licensed premises'.[42] But what the law does *not* do is notable. It does not say, as it well might if it cared most for administrative ease, that electors are to front at electoral offices or other government buildings. If it did so, it would reinforce a statist element to the ritual of voting. Instead, it leaves the matter in the discretion of the electoral commissions. In the US the matter is dispersed, like much electoral administration, across county and even city levels. Underfunded officials compete to rent suitable spaces. One official in California told me of resorting to using a motorcycle dealership. A condition of hiring was that sales were to cease that day: to mingle the rituals of commerce and politics would be too much.

---

40   Australian Rules (AFL) and Rugby League.

41   Julia Gillard, quoted in Ben Packham, 'Julia Gillard sets September 14 Election Date', *The Australian* (online), 30 January 2013, http://www.theaustralian.com.au/national-affairs/gillard-sets-september-14-election-date/story-fn59niix-1226565039127.

42   *Commonwealth Electoral Act 1918* (Cth) s 205. In rural towns, the pub may be the only 'public' building. The issue was a particular concern a century ago, because alcohol was linked to vote-buying through 'treating' and because it was seen as unseemly for newly enfranchised women to have to vote in such a male domain.

But the proprietor also insisted that one voting compartment be set up close to a fancy bike, so that electors could enjoy using the voting machine whilst straddling a road machine!

In Australia, electoral commissions overwhelmingly choose public halls — and school halls more than religious halls, for reasons that are both obvious (church/state and inter-religious sensitivities) and less obvious but still profound. What else, besides compulsory voting, symbolises equal citizenship more than compulsory education? Just as we all wandered to school every day as children, so as adults we wander back to school halls every three years to vote.[43] A similar aesthetic, or sense of proportion between the civic nature of the ballot and the status of school halls, is explicitly written into New Zealand law.[44]

The secrecy of the ballot is another obviously important legal form, of significance not just to poets dreaming of 'a closet of prayer'. The secret ballot laws are echoed in the action of every elector who accepts all — or none — of the how-to-vote cards on offer, thereby disguising her voting intentions.[45] Those cards, distinctly Australian artefacts of last minute campaigning, have survived laws putting party labels on ballots.[46] This survival is partly because the law about casting a formal ballot under preferential voting in Australia is more complex than either the first-past-the-post or the party list systems used elsewhere. How-to-vote cards also survive because the larger parties believe it gives them an advantage, since they can mobilise sufficient supporters and money to afford this type of canvassing. Otherwise they could amend the law against any partisan material being posted in the polling station, and permit every candidate to have their how-to-vote card displayed prominently.

---

43 More developed in Graeme Orr, 'The Ritual and Aesthetic in Electoral Law' (2004) 32 *Federal Law Review* 438.
44 *Electoral Act 1993* (NZ) s 156.
45 How-to-vote cards are replicas of ballots, adorned with photos of aspiring MPs and their leader, showing electors how to direct preferences for that candidate or party.
46 *Commonwealth Electoral Act 1918* (Cth) s 214 (ballot labelling) and part XI (registration of parties) date to 1983.

Election night and the count: Rhythms and theatre

Consider also the debate about abandoning the tradition of a central 'tally room'. To reduce costs, budgetary minded electoral authorities now favour a purely dispersed, electronic method of disseminating election results. Australian politicians and journalists, however, have fought to keep the theatre of a tally room, as an official or central stage.[47] UK electoral administration, by contrast, is decentralised. But it generates something even more ritualistic in its local ceremonies for the public declaration of constituency results, which take place during the early hours of the morning as election night counts unfold. Counting to resolve the Westminster Parliament is relatively simple, since the law provides for first-past-the-post voting. And UK postal votes have to be received by the close of polling on election day.[48] As a result, even with hand-counting, votes can be conclusively tallied within several hours.

Candidates for Westminster are invited and expected to attend the public declaration of their race, in their community, as the returning officer (often a local mayor) intones the votes received. With different supporters mixing together, and Ministers rubbing shoulders with joke candidates, a captivating ritual of surprise, humiliation and triumph ensues.[49] In turn, the smaller constituencies vie to become the first in the nation to declare their result, in a kind of race within the race.[50] This may be done to gain passing notoriety for the district on a night of national attention, or simply out of pride in the efficiency of the count. The idea of a race to finish the count would make no sense in Australia. Here, the laws governing the formality of preferential voting are more complex, and any sense of *rushing* to a declaration would suggest anything but efficiency.

In any event, under Australian law, provisional votes have to be checked, and postal ballots can dribble in until 13 days after polling day.[51] As a result, there is no conclusive public moment; rather, provisional results are released and updated, race by race, over election night and cumulative swings are calculated by computer-assisted psephologists, as if studying seismological data of how much the (political) ground shifted. In very close elections, the fate of a

---

47   See, Joint Standing Committee on Electoral Matters, Parliament of Australia, *Inquiry into Certain Aspects of the Administration of the Australian Electoral Commission* (2007) ch 4.

48   The Electoral Commission (UK), 'Voting by Post', http://www.aboutmyvote.co.uk/how_do_i_vote/voting_by_post.aspx.

49   The cover of Lawrence's book (Jon Lawrence, *Electing our Masters: The Hustings in British Politics from Hogarth to Blair* (Oxford University Press, 2009)) illustrates this, with a photograph of Prime Minister Blair attending his Sedgfield electorate declaration in 2005, flanked by anti-Iraq-war candidates. One, a father of a dead soldier, is delivering a speech, the other is wearing a hat labelled 'BLIAR'.

50   Chris Mullin, *A View From the Foothills: The Diaries of Chris Mullin* (Profile Books, 2009).

51   For example, *Commonwealth Electoral Act 1918* (Cth) s 266.

government may hang in the balance for many days. In the US, to give a further contrast, a plethora of different voting technologies ensure a relatively quick count. Indeed, a shift to all electronic voting could in theory lead to election results being known instantaneously, at the flick of a switch or key.

This is what currently happens in Australian Senate elections. To cope with the legal complexity of Hare-Clark proportional representation, ballots are counted by computer.[52] However, computerised ballots are not cast by voters; paper ballots are converted to electronic format by data-entry operators after polling day. This process is painstaking, so Senate results become something of an afterthought. Cynics might say that this leisurely process mimics the Senate itself, with its six-year sinecures fixed in the Constitution. It certainly reinforces the constitutional position of the Australian Senate as a secondary house of review. In contrast, first-past-the-post voting in the US ensures that attention to Senate races ranks ahead of the House and second only to the presidential race. Yet, through all these different rhythms — dependent in large part on the different electoral laws, policies and technologies in place — one ritual is common: the election night party of the partisans.[53]

After the electoral deluge: Rites of inauguration

Earlier I explained that 'ritual' should not simply invoke the language of 'rites', however tempting the analogy may be. A 'rite' is a narrower concept associated usually with solemn (religious) tradition, typically bearing a clear relationship with a point of transition. Frederick Damon, an anthropologist who explored the phenomenon from an American electoral perspective, argued that US elections were seminal rites of passage, mirroring rites in societies more overtly driven by custom. In effect, he portrayed US presidential elections as installation rites featuring a particular set of rhythms.[54]

First, the candidates declare or announce themselves, separating or distinguishing themselves and entering a period of 'masquerade', which includes the primary season. Then comes a period of social abnormality: the general election campaign inverts the normal order of politics, which is compromise and give-and-take. This generates a form of extreme testing, a winner-takes-all battle, which culminates in the election. After the election outcome follows a prolonged period when the victor moves to heal wounds, prior to the most formal stage of the entire

---

52   Technically, Senate electors do not just select a party list, but rank all candidates.
53   Captured in Australia in David Williamson's 1971 play, *Don's Party* (which was released as a movie in 1976).
54   Frederick A Damon, 'What Good are Elections: An Anthropological Analysis of American Elections (2003) 1 *Taiwan Journal of Anthropology* 39, especially at 53–62. Damon, at 62–71, also analogises US two-party electoral politics to 'joking relations' (a custom of the Kaguru people of east Africa, where groups spar via mutual insults, to purify or rectify social tensions or problems).

ritualistic process, the ceremony of inauguration. It may be no coincidence that the latent healing period overlaps with the festive season (statute sets US elections for early November,[55] terms of office are set constitutionally).[56] The latter two stages — healing then inauguration — are obviously pronounced in the US presidential model. Although a partisan elected official, the President is also the head of state and hence meant to be a unifying figure for the republic.

Most famously, the President has to be sworn in and inaugurated in Washington DC by noon on the 20th day of January.[57] Originally this was 4 March, an emblematic date representing the day the US Constitution came into effect.[58] Of course, the several-month wait between election day and inauguration reflected pragmatics more than any deeper design: the electoral college had to formally gather, and transportation across a large country was not easy. But all this is to say that ritual may spring up irrespective of conscious intention. The extensive wait permits not just a rite of healing and transition, but a now elaborately planned day that mixes a focus on the meaning of a national union and the formation of government, with a touch of to-the-victor-goes-the-spoils. On a less exalted note, inauguration renews the beltway culture, as political backers and insiders come together to participate in forming the fledgling administration.

In contrast, in the UK and Australian models, the law keeps election campaigns relatively short. With no directly elected executive, and shorn of laws mandating primary elections, parliamentary elections are centred less on individual candidates and more on party-dominated responsible government. A new Prime Minister is moved through the caretaker period onto the swearing in of their ministry, before the Queen's representative, more quickly and quietly than would be countenanced in the US system.

However there are occasions where parliamentary, as opposed to party, government reasserts itself. This was obvious after the inconclusive, hung elections of 2010 in both Canberra and Westminster. In each case, ad hoc rituals of inauguration (some might say marriages of convenience) were played out. In the UK it was the fairly mannered announcement, less than a week from election day, of a Conservative-Liberal Democrat pact. This was formalised in an initial seven-page agreement, ritually adopted with a handshake on the steps of Number 10 Downing Street. In Australia, the process was more protracted, with a new ministry taking over three weeks to assemble, as both the caretaker

---

55   The first Tuesday after the first Monday in November, in even-numbered years (2 USC ss 1, 7 and 3 USC s 1).

56   See *United States Constitution*, 20th amendment. (Prior to this, they began on 4 March, symbolically the date the Constitution first took effect.)

57   ibid. Exceptionally, as happened to Barack Obama in 2013 when 20 January was a Sunday, the president may have to be sworn in on a Sunday, then inaugurated the next day. Although inauguration day is not a holiday, its separation from the Christian day of rest positions it as a civic celebration distinct from any religious connotations.

58   Not to be confused with US Constitution Day in September, marking the 1787 signing of the original document.

Prime Minister and Opposition Leader sought to woo six cross-benchers. Several agreements were concluded in series with different players, before the chaotic day of announcements by two-out-of-three rural independents that they would support the continuation of a Labor government. These ad hoc rites of incorporation worked less well than in the US: the administrations formed have lacked the sense of legitimacy that even President Bush Jr assumed, despite his election in 2000 lacking a nationwide vote majority and requiring an extraordinary court decision to confirm it.

Conclusion: The strands of democracy

All we do is marked by rhythms. From the office worker who takes her daily coffee a certain way in the same cafe, through to the act of voting, by pencil on secret ballot in a cardboard booth each three years, to the communal singing of the national anthem before a sporting contest. These are all rituals, albeit rituals of different orders of publicness or privateness, and with different levels of inherent meaning. The cafe is a public place and, in her particular choice of venue and bean, the coffee drinker may be quietly projecting something about herself. But she is essentially enjoying a solitary ritual. The public meanings of the quasi-enforced observance of the anthem, weaving nationalism and the bombastic glories and hopes of a sporting encounter, hardly need decoding. Ritual, defined as shared, patterned behaviour, is everywhere.

This essay has sought to argue for an attention to ritual, alongside related concepts such as myth and aesthetics, as central to any rounded understanding of electoral democracy as it is contoured by public law. The illustrations we have discussed are suggestive rather than comprehensive. The samples given here have been drawn from polling day and its aftermath, rather than say the process of inception of fresh elections or the campaign itself. The examples we have encountered have drawn on several common law systems, both parliamentary and executive.

In discerning differences, both across time and space, we can see that once we leave both the meta-narratives of liberal democracy (of liberty, equality and deliberation) and the hard-nosed 'realist' account of elite democracy, there is another world to explore. Exploring it requires tools beyond the rhetoric of liberal legal and political philosophy or the modelling of public choice theorists. It requires an eye for observation of routines and an ear for the poetry of the everyday. That is not meant to sound grandiose; quite the reverse. Electoral democracy and its legal and institutional ordering is just one strand of public life. But it is a strand connected and integral to many others, and it is a strand of many colours.

8. Performing Citizenship, Embodying Obedience

Anne Macduff[1]

Many of the great religious and political figures of history have been agitators, and human progress owes much to the efforts of these and the many who are unknown. As Wilde aptly pointed out in *The Soul of Man under Socialism*, 'Agitators are a set of interfering, meddling people, who come down to some perfectly contented class of the community and sow the seeds of discontent amongst them. That is the reason why agitators are so absolutely necessary. Without them, in our incomplete state, there would be no advance towards civilisation.'[2]

Introduction

In March 2003, an Australian citizen and a British citizen protested against Australia's invasion of Iraq. The two men painted 'NO WAR' in red capital letters on the iconic white sails of the Sydney Opera House. A NSW local court found both men guilty of malicious damage and ordered them to serve weekend detention. The media later reported that immigration officials detained the British citizen and considered cancelling his visa.[3]

Although protests like this one are controversial, they are an important display of active citizenship. Active citizenship is more than political participation within the existing framework of laws and institutions,[4] and includes critical protests that question the founding framework. Although philosophers differ about when unlawful acts are justified, even a relatively narrow view accepts that there are circumstances when non-violent acts of public civil disobedience are warranted.[5] The acts of civil disobedience of Mahatma Ghandi, Martin

---

1 anne.macduff@anu.edu.au.
2 *Neal v The Queen* (1982) 149 CLR 305, 316–7 (Murphy J) quoting Oscar Wilde, *The Soul of Man Under Socialism* (Andrade, unspecified) 6.
3 'Opera House Defaced in War Protest', *The Age* (Online), 18 March 2003, http://www.theage.com.au/articles/2003/03/18/1047749763708.html; 'No War Scrawl to Cost Doctor', *The Sydney Morning Herald* (Online), 26 March 2003, http://www.smh.com.au/articles/2003/04/16/1050172650756.html.
4 Sue Kenny, 'Non-Government Organisations and Contesting Active Citizenship' in Glenn Patmore (ed), *The Vocal Citizen* (Arena, 2004) 70.
5 Kent Greenawalt, 'Justifying Non-violent Disobedience' in Hugo Bedau (ed), *Civil Disobedience in Focus* (Routledge, 1991) 170.

Luther King Jr and Rosa Parkes enhanced their democracies. Their unlawful and public actions strongly criticised laws, government policies and decisions, and stimulated social change that led to more inclusive and democratic societies.

This chapter considers the extent to which active citizenship is currently supported by the Australian government. The Australian government has stated that it encourages active citizenship.[6] However, this chapter argues that the law conveys a very different message. In particular, recent changes to the *Australian Citizenship Act 2007* (Cth) (the 'ACA') have emphasised citizenship as obedience to the law.

The argument in this chapter unfolds in three sections. The first section argues that even though there is no definition of citizenship in the ACA, the government conveys meanings about Australian citizenship through the regulation of associated citizenship practices. The second section argues how recent changes to the legislative criteria of the ACA have led to an increasing significance being placed on the pledge of commitment. The third section analyses the meaning conveyed by the pledge of commitment by exploring its performative dimensions. It analyses the pledge as a speech act and a public ritual and argues that the citizenship pledge embodies obedience to the existing democratic structures. With no Australian Bill of Rights to protect political rights generally, this chapter concludes that the meaning of citizenship currently conveyed by the government undermines active citizenship and threatens the quality of political participation in Australian democracy.

Conveying the meaning of citizenship through law and practice

The meaning of Australian citizenship is conveyed by the practices associated with the ACA, rather than the text itself. The ACA does not define citizenship.[7] Nor does the legislation include a statement about the rights and responsibilities that must be complied with in order to become an Australian citizen.[8] Instead,

---

6   Senate Select Committee on Employment, Education and Training, Parliament of Australia, *Education for Active Citizenship Education in Australian Schools and Youth Organisations* (1989); Senate Select Committee on Employment, Education and Training, Parliament of Australia, *Education for Citizenship Revisited* (1991), Civics Expert Group, *Whereas the People: Civics and Citizenship Education* (Commonwealth of Australia, 1994) 6; Department of Education, Science and Training, Parliament of Australia, *Discovering Democracy Program* 'Civics and Citizenship Education', http://www1.curriculum.edu.au/ddunits/about/about.htm#about.

7   That is, a definition of citizenship is not included. There is an attempt to describe the meaning of citizenship through the preamble, which is discussed below.

8   Sir Ninian Stephen, 'Australian Citizenship: Past, Present and Future' (2000) 26(2) *Monash University Law Review* 333, 336; Joint Standing Committee on Migration, Parliament of Australia, *Australians All: Enhancing Citizenship* (1994) 85; Australian Citizenship Council, *Australian Citizenship for A New Century* (February 2000).

the ACA sets out the statutory basis upon which individuals acquire, lose and resume the legal status of citizenship. Scholars have therefore described the ACA as 'mechanical'[9] and a piece of 'legislative machinery'.[10] Yet characterising Australian citizenship legislation as machinery ignores the many different ways legislation conveys meaning about citizenship. Informed by critical legal studies, this section explores how official meanings of citizenship are generated through citizenship practices. In other words, this section explores the ways that the government promotes certain meanings of citizenship through the ACA by changing what people do and how they act. Two examples illustrate this point: the introduction of the legal status of citizenship in 1948, and the introduction of the preamble in 1993. Both these moments generated citizenship practices that conveyed a celebratory meaning of Australian citizenship. While a celebratory notion of citizenship is not necessarily inconsistent with protest and civil disobedience,[11] neither does it clearly accommodate them.

The legal status of citizenship

The legislation that first introduced the legal status of citizenship also generated the first Australian citizenship practices. The legal status of citizenship was introduced in Australia through the *Nationality and Citizenship Act 1948* (Cth) (the '1948 Act'). Prior to 1948, membership in the Australian community was recognised through British subject status.[12] Although the 1948 Act did not include a definition of citizenship, it did convey a meaning of citizenship by introducing two new citizenship practices. First, the legislation sought to change how a group of people described themselves. Second, it also sought to change aspects of the citizenship ceremony. How each of these citizenship practices conveyed a celebratory meaning of citizenship is described in more depth below.

The 1948 Act gave Australians a new way of describing themselves. In debating the bill, parliamentarian Mr Haylen stated that '[w]hen this Bill becomes law, an Australian may call himself an Australian because he holds Australian

---

9   Commonwealth, *Parliamentary Debates*, House of Representatives, 16 November 1993, 2904 (Phillip Ruddock).

10   Joint Standing Committee on Migration, Parliament of Australia, *Australians All: Enhancing Citizenship* (September 1994) 89. See also Sir Ninian Stephen, 'Australian Citizenship: Past, Present and Future' (2000) 26(2) *Monash University Law Review*; Margaret Thornton, 'The Legocentric Citizen' (1996) 21 *Australian Law Journal* 72.

11   Tristan Ewins, 'Citizenship Education in Australia: Beyond Consensus' in Glenn Patmore (ed), *The Vocal Citizen* (Arena, 2004) 100, 102.

12   Kim Rubenstein, *Australian Citizenship Law in Context* (Law Book, 2002) 9.

citizenship'.[13] It was explicitly hoped that this new way of describing oneself would create a distinct sense of national identity. In the second reading speech of the Bill, the former Minister for Immigration Mr Calwell noted that

> [t]o say that one is Australian is, of course, to indicate beyond all doubt that one is British; but to claim to be of the British race does not make it clear that one is Australian. The time has come for Australia and other dominions to recognize officially and legally their maturity as members of the British Commonwealth by the passage of separate citizenship laws.[14]

The 1948 Act changed the way that Australians described themselves in order to distinguish themselves from other British subjects. Using the term Australian citizen to describe oneself was also intended to evoke positive emotions. Mr Calwell stated in parliamentary debate that the 1948 Act would 'help him express his pride in citizenship of this great country'.[15] Mr Calwell further claimed that '[t]his Bill is more than a cold, legalistic formula. It is a warm, pulsating document that enshrines the love of country of every genuine Australian.'[16] The novelty of the use of legislation to capture an affective sense of Australian identity is highlighted by the parliamentarians who argued against the introduction of the 1948 Act. For instance, Mr Gullet asked: 'Does anyone feel any more Australian as the result of establishing an Australian nationality?'[17] Mr Ryan further doubted whether citizenship could be reduced to words at all, noting that '[t]he ties which bind the Empire cannot be defined in words; they are bonds of sympathy, blood and kinship'.[18] Yet the 1948 Act was passed and from that moment onwards, the term 'Australian citizen' has been used to describe membership in the Australian community.

Second, the 1948 Act introduced the requirement that applicants for Australian citizenship take a public oath of allegiance.[19] While taking an oath had been a requirement for naturalisation for some time,[20] before 1948 oaths were

---

13 Commonwealth, *Parliamentary Debates*, House of Representatives, 18 November 1948, 3248 (Leslie Haylen).
14 Commonwealth, *Parliamentary Debates*, House of Representatives, 30 September 1948, 1060 (Arthur Calwell).
15 ibid.
16 ibid 1066.
17 Commonwealth, *Parliamentary Debates*, House of Representatives, 19 November 1948, 3281 (Henry Gullet).
18 Commonwealth, *Parliamentary Debates*, House of Representatives, 19 November 1948, 3278 (Rupert Ryan).
19 *Nationality and Citizenship Act 1948* (Cth) s 41.
20 Conal Condren, *Argument and Authority in Early Modern England: The Presupposition of Oaths and Offices* (Cambridge University Press, 2006); Clive Parry *Nationality and Citizenship Laws of The Commonwealth and of The Republic of Ireland* (Stevens & Sons, 1957) 53, 65; *Naturalization Act 1870* (Imp) 35 & 36 Vict, c.39 s 9. For a history of oaths in Australia see Deidre McKeowan, 'Changes in the Australian Oath of Citizenship' (Parliamentary Research Note No 20, Parliamentary Library, Parliament of Australia, 2002).

made privately before a justice, judge or magistrate.[21] The 1948 Act gave the Minister powers to make arrangements that the oath could be made in public and 'accompanied by proceedings designed to impress upon applicants the importance of the occasion'. [22] Mr Calwell noted that

> [i]t is proposed that the oath be made in open court, where the Australian flag shall be prominently displayed and have pride of place ... The old system, under which a man's naturalization papers came to him through the mail, like his annual licence for his dog or his motor car, was inappropriate.[23]

Making the pledge in public gave applicants a sense that becoming an Australian citizen was a 'great and joyful decision'[24] and more than 'merely a piece of office routine'.[25] In 1954, the legislation clarified that the Minister could require that the oath be taken in public.[26]

Although the 1948 Act included no definition of citizenship, it is clear that Parliament intended that it was more than a piece of legislative machinery. The 1948 Act promoted the meaning of Australian citizenship by introducing two new citizenship practices: a new way of describing oneself, and a public demonstration of pride in acquiring citizenship. These two practices emphasise the meaning of citizenship as a public celebration of a newly created Australian national identity.

The preamble and the pledge

In 1993, the government amended the 1948 Act and generated new citizenship practices that altered and reinforced meanings about Australian citizenship. In 1993, the Keating government added a preamble to the 1948 Act by passing the *Australian Citizenship Amendment Act 1993* (Cth) (the '1993 Amendment Act').[27] The new preamble led to a change in citizenship practices relating to the oath. The oath was reworded to mirror the preamble and was called a pledge of commitment. The new pledge of commitment was more than a change in the machinery of the 1948 Act. It was a new practice that altered and reinforced a celebratory meaning of citizenship.

---

21 Commonwealth, *Parliamentary Debates*, House of Representatives, 30 September 1948, 1064 (Arthur Calwell).
22 *Nationality and Citizenship Act 1948* (Cth) s 41.
23 Commonwealth, *Parliamentary Debates*, House of Representatives, 30 September 1948, 1064–5 (Arthur Calwell).
24 ibid 1065.
25 ibid.
26 *Nationality and Citizenship Act 1953* (Cth) s 41.
27 *Australian Citizenship Act 1948* (Cth) preamble, as amended by *Australian Citizenship Amendment Act 1993* (Cth).

In 1992, amidst public concern about the need to promote a commitment to democratic rights and values,[28] former Senator Michael Tate commissioned well-known Australian poet Les Murray to craft the words of a new preamble to Australia's citizenship legislation.[29] The introduction of the preamble was designed to raise awareness of the importance of citizenship. In the parliamentary debates, Mr O'Keefe said: 'The act should also contain a preamble defining the meaning which the parliament and the people of Australia accord to citizenship. This is what the preamble will do.'[30] The words of the new preamble were:

> The Parliament recognises that Australian citizenship represents formal membership of the community of the Commonwealth of Australia, and Australian citizenship is a common bond, involving reciprocal rights and obligations, uniting all Australians, while respecting their diversity; and persons granted Australian citizenship enjoy these rights and undertake to accept these obligations
>
> (a) by pledging loyalty to Australia and its people; and
>
> (b) by sharing their democratic beliefs; and
>
> (c) by respecting their rights and liberties; and
>
> (d) by upholding and obeying the laws of Australia[31]

The words used in the preamble suggest that the government supported active participation in the Australian democracy. However, words such as 'democracy', 'freedom' and 'loyalty' can have many, varied meanings. During the debate of the 1993 amendment, some parliamentarians expressed dissatisfaction with the wording of the pledge, describing it as 'wishy-washy'[32] and argued that it should be a much stronger statement.[33]

Insight into the meaning of citizenship that the government sought to convey through the preamble can be gained by considering the words that were not included in the preamble. The initial draft of the preamble, written by Les Murray went as follows:

> Under God, from this time forward

---

28 Mark McKenna, 'First Words: A Brief History of Public Debate on a New Preamble to the Australian Constitution 1991–99' (Research Paper No 16, Parliamentary Library, Parliament of Australia, 2000).

29 Les Murray, *The Quality of Sprawl* (Duffy & Snellgrove, 1999) 16.

30 ibid 2000.

31 *Australian Citizenship Act 1948* (Cth) preamble, as amended by *Australian Citizenship Amendment Act 1993* (Cth), preamble.

32 Commonwealth, *Parliamentary Debates*, House of Representatives, 16 November 1993, 2989 (Alan Cadman).

33 Commonwealth, *Parliamentary Debates*, House of Representatives, 16 November 1993, 2924 (Warren Truss).

I am part of the Australian people

I share their democracy and their freedom, I obey their laws,

I will never despise their customs or their faith

And I expect Australia to be loyal to me.[34]

In the final version, the government did not include the words 'freedom' or 'customs and faith'. Les Murray later commented that these words referred to tolerance of diverse ways of life and religious affiliations.[35] Instead, the government inserted a new line which referred to 'respecting rights and liberties'. The government also deleted the last line of Les Murray's draft. Les Murray indicated that the last line referred to 'the voice of the sovereign citizen making promises and demands as of right vis-à-vis the nation and its servant — the government'.[36] This deletion suggests that the government intended to convey a meaning of citizenship that was more celebratory of existing structures of parliamentary sovereignty, than a meaning that called on citizens to actively seek to hold government accountable.

The impact of the new preamble was clearly symbolic. The meaning of citizenship conveyed through the preamble was not designed to alter any citizenship rights or obligations. For although preambles are legally part of an act,[37] the only impact of the preamble is on judges and decision-makers engaged in statutory interpretation. That is, where there are competing interpretations of another term in the Act, then the preamble might be referred to in order to decide which interpretation best achieves the purpose or purposes of the Act.[38]

However the preamble did impact on citizenship practices. Alongside the introduction of the preamble, the oath was reworded and renamed a 'pledge of commitment'. The words of the new pledge draw explicitly on the words of the preamble:

From this time forward [under God]

I pledge my loyalty to Australia and its people

Whose democratic rights and liberties I respect, and

Whose laws I will uphold and obey.[39]

---

34   ibid.
35   Murray, above n 29, 16.
36   ibid 17.
37   *Acts Interpretation Act 1901* (Cth) s 13(b).
38   *Acts Interpretation Act 1901* (Cth) s 15AA.
39   *Australian Citizenship Act 2007* (Cth) sch 1.

The 1993 Amendment Act created a new practice which required candidates for citizenship by grant (previously called naturalisation, now called conferral) to recite these words aloud before their citizenship took legal effect. The significance of the new wording was that the pledge was now made to 'Australia and its people'. Prior to 1993, the citizenship oath had been made to the British monarch.[40] The parliamentary debate surrounding the new pledge focused on whether it was more Australian to make a pledge of loyalty to historical English institutions including a foreign monarch, or to make a pledge of loyalty to Australia and 'its own symbols'.[41] The successful passage of the 1993 Amendment Act removed from the pledge any reference to the British monarch.

Although the words used in the pledge affirmed Australian independence from Britain, it missed an opportunity to convey active citizenship. Although the pledge includes words such as 'democratic beliefs', 'rights' and 'freedoms', these words of the pledge do not clearly convey active Australian citizenship. These characteristics are held by Australians in a passive tense. The future citizen-subject merely 'shares' their democratic beliefs with others. The future citizen-subject promises to 'respect' the rights and freedoms of others, without mentioning the positive obligation to realise and protect those rights and freedoms. The future citizen subject also obeys the law without a hint of critical or ethical concern. These words of the pledge might be contrasted with a proposed draft of the Australian constitutional preamble, which while 'celebrating unity', also was 'believing in freedom and equality, and embracing democracy'.[42] The words of the preamble emphasise the celebration of Australia's democratic institutions and its independence from Britain.

The introduction of the preamble triggered a change in the practice of the oath. The oath, now a pledge of commitment, requires candidates for citizenship to recite aloud a shortened form of the words contained in the new preamble. Both the preamble and the pledge, sought to convey citizenship as a public celebration of a newly created Australian national identity.

These two examples demonstrate that the ACA is not only a mechanistic set of rules about the acquisition, loss and resumption of citizenship status. Rather, the government uses citizenship legislation as a vehicle to generate citizenship practices which effectively convey particular meanings about Australian citizenship. The introduction of the legal status of citizenship in 1948 changed

---

40   Deidre McKeowan, 'Changes in the Australian Oath of Citizenship' (Parliamentary Research Note No 20, Parliamentary Library, Parliament of Australia, 2002).
41   Commonwealth, *Parliamentary Debates*, Senate, 29 September 1993, 1433 (Christopher Schacht). See also Commonwealth, *Parliamentary Debates*, House of Representatives, 17 November 1993, 2994 (Alan Cadman).
42   Non-Government Parties Preamble to the Australian Constitutional Referendum by Gareth Evans, Natasha Stott-Despoja and Bob Brown on 28th April 1999. Cited in Mark McKenna, Amelia Simpson and George Williams, 'With Hope in God, the Prime Minister and the Poet: Lessons from the 1999 Referendum on the Preamble' (2001) 24 (2) *University of New South Wales Law Journal* 401, 405.

the way that people described themselves and made the oath public. These practices sought to convey a celebratory notion of Australian citizenship. The introduction of the preamble in 1993 changed the wording of the oath. The government intended that this new practice more clearly convey a celebratory notion of independent Australian citizenship. The rest of this chapter examines the most recent reforms to Australian citizenship legislation and considers the extent to which these reforms have changed citizenship practices and altered the meaning of citizenship.

The meaning of citizenship and the increasing significance of the citizenship pledge

The Australian government has shown a renewed interest in Australian citizenship law and policy in the last two decades. There have been numerous government inquiries and reports,[43] leading to a number of legislative reforms to the citizenship eligibility criteria.[44] Some of these reforms have been controversial,[45] while others have passed without much comment.[46] This section outlines how two changes to the current ACA have led to the government placing increasing significance of the pledge of commitment. The two changes considered are the introduction of the citizenship test and the legal regulation of the citizenship ceremony.

43 Senate Select Committee on Employment, Education and Training, Parliament of Australia, *Education for Active Citizenship Education in Australian Schools and Youth Organisations* (1989); Senate Select Committee on Employment, Education and Training, Parliament of Australia, *Education for Citizenship Revisited* (1991), Joint Standing Committee on Migration, Parliament of Australia, *Australians All: Enhancing Australian Citizenship* (1994); Nick Bolkus, 'Ties that Bind: A 4-year plan for Australian citizenship' (Media release, 4 September 1995); Senate Legal and Constitutional Reference Committee, Parliament of Australia, *National Well-Being: A System of National Citizenship Indicators and Benchmarks* (1996); Civics Expert Group, *Whereas the People: Civics and Citizenship Education* (Commonwealth of Australia, 1994); Australian Citizenship Council 'Australian Citizenship for a New Century' (Report, Commonwealth of Australia, February 2000).
44 *Australian Citizenship Legislation Amendment Act 2002* (Cth); *Australian Citizenship Act 2007* (Cth); *Australian Citizenship (Transitionals and Consequentials) 2007* (Cth); *Australian Citizenship Amendment (Citizenship Testing) Act 2007* (Cth); *Australian Citizenship Amendment (Citizenship Test Review and Other Measures) Act 2009* (Cth); *Australian Citizenship Amendment (Defence Families) Act 2012* (Cth); *Australian Citizenship Amendment (Special Residence Requirements) Act 2013* (Cth).
45 Such as the citizenship testing criteria, and the length of time before a permanent resident can apply for citizenship. See Fardia Fozdar and Brian Spittles, 'The Australian Citizenship Test: Process and Rhetoric' (2009) 55(4) *Australian Journal of Politics and History* 496; John Tate, 'John Howard's "Nation" and Citizenship Test: Multiculturalism, Citizenship and Identity' (2009) 55(1) *Australian Journal of Politics and History* 97.
46 Julie Szego, 'I am, you are, we are…', *The Age* (online), 26 September 2006, http://www.theage.com.au/news/in-depth/i-am-you-are-we-are-/2006/09/24/1159036415375.html. Also note that the name of the Department of Immigration and Multicultural Affairs was change to the Department of Immigration and Citizenship in 2007.

The pledge and the citizenship test

In October 2007, the Australian federal Parliament introduced testing of all candidates for Australian citizenship by conferral. Following a subsequent review of the citizenship testing regime, an independent committee recommended that citizenship testing be kept, but that the knowledge required to pass the test should be more closely aligned with the citizenship pledge.[47] The Rudd government agreed and sought to make the pledge of commitment 'the centre-piece of the Australian citizenship testing'.[48] A brief explanation of the citizenship test and its purpose provides some useful background to explain the new significance of the pledge.

In 2007, Parliament introduced a citizenship testing regime with bi-partisan support.[49] Passing the citizenship test is now the only way that a candidate for citizenship by conferral can satisfy three eligibility criteria,[50] unless an exception applies.[51] The eligibility criteria satisfied by the test are: an understanding of the nature of the application, a basic understanding of English, and knowledge of Australia and the responsibilities and privileges of Australian citizenship.[52] Previously, officials interviewed candidates to determine whether they satisfied these criteria.[53] The purpose of the new written test format was to

> encourage prospective citizens to obtain the knowledge they need to support successful integration into Australian society. The citizenship test will provide them with the opportunity to demonstrate in an objective way that they have the required knowledge of Australia, including the responsibilities and privileges of citizenship, and a basic knowledge and comprehension of English.[54]

The government stated that the test created an incentive for candidates to gain the necessary knowledge to support their future participation in Australian society, and to provide a mechanism by which they could demonstrate this

---

47   Australian Test Review Committee, 'Moving Forward … Improving Pathways to Citizenship' (Report, August 2008) 3, 4.

48   Australian Government, 'Moving Forward … Improving Pathways to Citizenship' (Government Response to the Report by the Australian Citizenship Test Review Committee, November 2008) 2.

49   See Fardia Fozdar and Brian Spittles, above n 45. The introduction of citizenship testing in Australia is part of a wider international practice of introducing citizenship tests, particularly in Europe. However, other forms of integration tests have also been introduced such as requirements for courses, pledges etc. See Sara Goodman, 'Integration Requirements for Integration's Sake?: Identifying, Categorising and Comparing Civic Integration Policies' (2010) 35(5) *Journal of Ethnic and Migration Studies* 753.

50   *Australian Citizenship Act 2007* (Cth) as amended by *Australian Citizenship (Citizenship Testing) Act 2007* (Cth) s 23A.

51   ibid s 21(2A).

52   *Australian Citizenship Act 2007* (Cth) s 21(2)(d)–(f).

53   Senate Standing Committee on Legal and Constitutional Affairs, Parliament of Australia, *Australian Citizenship Amendment (Citizenship Testing) Bill* (2007) 11.

54   Commonwealth, *Parliamentary Debates*, House of Representatives, 30 May 2007, 4 (Kevin Andrews).

knowledge.[55] While the test's purpose might be simply stated, identifying the knowledge that was necessary was more difficult. The government's solution was a pragmatic one. The government developed a citizenship booklet and stated that the questions in the citizenship test would be based on that booklet.[56] When the first edition of the booklet was prepared in 2007 it included topics such as: responsibilities and privileges of Australian citizenship, Australian values, the Australian people today, Australia's name and symbols, a story of Australia, government in Australia, the Australian Constitution, levels of government, and elected representatives.[57]

The subsequent independent committee later found that the testing framework did 'not sit well with the legislative requirements'.[58] The committee recommended that the knowledge required in the citizenship test should be aligned with the pledge.[59] The Rudd government accepted this recommendation and revised the content of the booklet.[60] The information in the second edition of the citizenship testing booklet was split into 'testable' and 'non-testable' sections.[61] The testable section was further divided into sections which corresponded to different parts of the pledge. The restructure both reduced the volume of knowledge required and more clearly identified how the information related to the pledge of commitment. However, the content of the knowledge in the testable section of the second edition is largely the same as the first. The second edition continues to focus on knowledge of the symbols, history, and the basic institutions of Australian democracy. This suggests that aligning the citizenship test with the pledge was less about modifying the content of the citizenship test, and more about finding a more persuasive justification for the citizenship test. As a result, the pledge of commitment acquired a new and heightened symbolic importance.

The legal regulation of the pledge

The significance of the pledge was also enhanced by two changes to the legal regulation of the pledge. First, the ACA elevated the significance of making the pledge as a distinct and essential step towards acquiring citizenship. Second, the pledge was increasingly prescribed by law.

55   Australian Government, 'Much More Than Just a Ceremony' (Discussion paper, September 2006) 11–12.
56   Australian Government 'Becoming an Australian Citizen' (Booklet, Commonwealth of Australia, 2007).
57   ibid.
58   Australian Citizenship Test Review Committee, above n 47.
59   ibid 16.
60   Australian Government, 'Moving Forward … Improving Pathways to Citizenship' above n 48, 2–3.
61   Australian Government, *Australian Citizenship: Our Common Bond* (Citizenship Booklet, Commonwealth of Australia, 2009).

The Howard government elevated the significance of the pledge in the legislative reforms of 2007. Prior to 2007, the requirement to make the pledge was located separately from the other eligibility criteria, and was described as a condition to be satisfied before the grant of citizenship had legal effect.[62] The ACA elevated the legal importance of the pledge by making it clear that there were two essential steps in acquiring citizenship by conferral: the application for citizenship must be approved, and the applicant must take the pledge.[63] The legal status of citizenship would not be conferred without the applicant making the pledge.

The ACA also clarified that the Minister had powers to make arrangements for how the pledge was to be made.[64] Although the Minister had this power previously, this provision of the ACA was now used to pass regulations which explicitly provided that the Minister 'may notify additional arrangements for making a pledge, or conducting a ceremony, that are designed to impress upon applicants the responsibilities and privileges of Australian citizenship'.[65] Under this regulation, a new citizenship ceremonies code (the Code) was published in 2008, prescribing certain guidelines concerning how the ceremonies should be conducted. The Code included a number of existing practices such as: the ceremony itself must be conducted by a duly authorised officer,[66] national symbols must be displayed during citizenship ceremonies,[67] all of the citizenship candidates must take the pledge,[68] the Presiding Officer must attest that each applicant has recited the pledge before the applicants are formally recognised as citizens,[69] a Minister's message which must be read aloud,[70] and that citizenship ceremonies should be promoted by the media.[71]

Following the alignment of the pledge with the test, the Rudd government updated the Code in 2011. While nearly all of the arrangements for conducting citizenship ceremonies under the previous Code were kept, the new Code provided additional information about how to publicise the ceremony,[72] and suggested a stronger emphasis on compliance by stating that some community

---

62   *Australian Citizenship Act 2007* (Cth) s 15.
63   ibid s 20.
64   ibid s 27.
65   *Australian Citizenship Regulations* 2007 (Cth) reg 8.
66   *Australian Citizenship Act 2007* (Cth) s 27(3).
67   ibid s 25.
68   ibid s 20(b).
69   Commonwealth of Australia, *Australian Citizenship Ceremonies Code* (Booklet, 2008) 12.
70   ibid 17, *Australian Citizenship Regulations 2007* (Cth) reg 8(b), sch 1.
71   Commonwealth of Australia, *Australian Citizenship Ceremonies Code* (Booklet, 2008) 11.
72   ibid 19. For instance, ABC TV covered the citizenship ceremony on Australia Day 2012 and 2013. See Australian Broadcasting Commission, *National Flag and Raising and Citizenship Ceremony* Australia Day, http://www.abc.net.au/australiaday/ceremony.htm. Citizenship ceremonies are also publicised on the Australia Day website events. See for example Australian Day, *Citizenship* 'What's On', http://www.australiaday.com.au/whatson/citizenship.aspx.

organisations would be required to 'sign an agreement with the department on how ceremonies are to be conducted'.[73] Increasing the legal regulation of first the pledge, and then the citizenship ceremony, intensified the significance of the pledge of commitment.

The emerging significance of the pledge in 2007 suggests that a fresh examination of the pledge as a practice is warranted. This chapter now turns to consider to what extent the new practice conveys a meaning of active citizenship, including the extent to which it values protest, disagreement and even acts of civil disobedience.

Interpreting the citizenship pledge as a performance

This section examines the meaning of citizenship conveyed by the current practice of the pledge of commitment. This section applies the theoretical frameworks of John Austin and David Kertzer to analyse the meaning of citizenship conveyed by the pledge of commitment as a performance. First, John Austin's well known theory about speech acts demonstrates the importance of focusing on the meaning communicated through the performative dimensions of the verbal statements. Second, David Kertzer's work on political rituals identifies the wider social meaning that the performance of the pledge plays in national societies. This section concludes by arguing that the performance of the pledge is a symbolic act which asks the citizen by conferral to embody obedience to the law by submitting to the authority of the government.

Austin's theory of speech acts

Analysing the pledge as a speech act helps to understand the pledge as a performance, rather than just the words that are used in the statement. This is particularly important as although the ACA has been subject to critique, the critique typically focuses on the text of the ACA. Examining the performative dimension of the pledge offers new insights into the meaning of citizenship conveyed by the pledge.

Philosopher John Austin argues that verbal statements not only describe or report facts, they are also 'performative'. In his lecture series 'How To Do Things With Words', Austin argues that the statement 'I name this ship Queen Elizabeth — as uttered when smashing a bottle against the stem',[74] is to perform

---

73   Commonwealth of Australia, *Australian Citizenship Ceremonies Code* (Booklet, 2008) 7.
74   J.L Austin, *How To Do Things With words* (Oxford University Press, 1962) 5.

the naming of the ship.[75] Similarly, the statement 'I do', means 'I marry you'.[76] A performative utterance or speech act can be made up of either verbal or non-verbal cues, or a combination of both.

For an utterance to amount to a speech act, Austin states that the utterance must have certain features. Those features are:

> A.1 There must exist an accepted conventional procedure having a certain conventional effect, that includes the uttering of certain words by certain persons in certain circumstances, further

> A.2 The particular persons and circumstances in a given case must be appropriate for the invocation of the particular procedure invoked, and

> B.1 The procedure must be executed by all participants both correctly and,

> B.2 Completely, and

> C.1 Where if certain feelings are to be communicated or felt, they are communicated or so felt

> C.2 Must actually conduct themselves subsequently.[77]

The convention procedure mentioned in A.1 is the most complex part of the speech act, and deserves some further explanation. A convention procedure is the context in which the verbal utterance is made. Words can become performative when they are recognised by an audience as being part of a particular context. Recognition of the context will depend on a number of other factors, including the roles that the speaker and audience play, how authority is exercised, as well as the presence of other symbols and cultural practices that might accompany the performance.

A citizenship pledge is a speech act when it is made during a citizenship ceremony. The citizenship ceremony is recognisable in that it is accompanied by legally prescribed symbols, and follows a consistent and recognised order that is clearly prescribed by the citizenship ceremonies code. Authorised persons must ensure that the pledge is spoken by each candidate. The convention effect, if properly followed, is that a person at the end of the ceremony will have the formal legal status of Australian citizenship. The appropriate emotion generated during the ceremony is of dignified celebration and a sense of unity. If the candidates do not take the pledge, then the performance is incomplete and citizenship will not be conferred.

---

75   ibid 6.
76   ibid 5.
77   ibid 14–15.

Austin's theory of speech acts brings into clear focus the importance of examining the context in which the pledge is performed. David Kertzer's theory of political ritual provides an analytical framework to interpret the performance of the pledge.

Kertzer and political ritual

David Kertzer's work offers insights into the meaning and emotional affect communicated through the performance of the citizenship pledge. Kertzer identifies a number of characteristics of modern rituals: rituals are typically formal in the sense that they are ceremonial;[78] a ritual will follow standardised procedures so that the ceremony is recognisable to the audience;[79] and rituals use simultaneity in physical space to generate and spread an appropriate emotional response.[80] The emotional response to the ritual is important as this is what contrasts ritual with a habit or custom. Kertzer also notes that to generate an appropriate emotional response, rituals avoid specific language.[81] Instead, rituals use dramatization and symbols to generate a rich ambiguity, or 'multi-vocality'.[82] Ambiguity avoids the potential for disagreement or dissent between the individuals and the group about the content of the ritual, and instead permits the participants to focus on the embodied experience of the ritual.

Kertzer argues that many political organisations, clubs, associations and nations use membership rituals.[83] These rituals reassert the power and legitimacy of the organisation and make the organisation be 'seen' in certain ways.[84] He argues that, during membership rituals in nation states, oaths of allegiance and pledges are primarily used to build solidarity,[85] particularly when consensus is lacking.[86]

Understanding the Australian citizenship pledge as a membership ritual highlights how the performance creates an embodied experience for the candidate. Unity is enacted through the formal, simultaneous and public recitation of certain words. The words of the pledge are vague, and employ multi-vocality to enhance the sensation of physical and sonorous unity. In 2000, when the Australian Citizenship Council considered whether the wording of the pledge of commitment should be amended, it said:

---

78   David Kertzer, *Ritual, Politics, and Power* (Yale University Press, 1988) 9.
79   ibid.
80   ibid 40: 'emotion'; ibid 30: 'space'.
81   ibid 30.
82   ibid 11.
83   ibid 13.
84   ibid 15; ibid 24: making organisations visible in relation to rituals and power.
85   ibid 67.
86   ibid 153.

> The view was put to the Council that because the Preamble is drafted in fairly general terms, it may not be as relevant to some Australians (for example those born in Australia) as it is to others. Nonetheless, in the Council's view, it is precisely this lack of prescription which allows the Preamble to be relevant to all Australian Citizens — whether born in Australia or overseas …[87]

The ritualised pledge creates a unified community through simultaneous performance.[88] Indeed, the government has explicitly acknowledged that placing increasing significance on the pledge enhances national unity. For instance, the government has stated that '[t]he Pledge joins all Australians in a statement of unity'.[89] The sense of unity is amplified by the growing public nature of the ceremony, its increased promotion and media coverage.[90] Not only is the sense of unity experienced by the candidates making the pledge, but the experience is shared by the general public, who are witnessing the pledge.

However, the physical sensation of unity is not the only embodied experience that is reinforced by the performance of the pledge of commitment. The performance also embodies obedience and, in particular, obedience as submission to government authority. This dimension of the performed pledge of commitment potentially undermines active citizenship in Australia.

Performing citizenship, embodying obedience

This section explores the ways in which the performance of citizenship pledge embodies obedience. It then identifies how this performance is problematic for active citizenship and Australian democracy.

The performance of the pledge is the means through which candidates demonstrate with their bodies their willingness to submit to the laws of Australia. The way that the pledge must be made is formal and tightly prescribed through a matrix of the quasi legislative documents, including the citizenship ceremony codes. A candidate must follow the citizenship rules of the performance, otherwise the legal status of citizenship will not be conferred. The performance of the pledge has little room for individual agency. The only choice is whether or not the candidate makes the pledge under God.[91] Moreover, there are generally

---

87 Australian Citizenship Council, *Australian Citizenship for A New Century* (Report, February 2000) 81.
88 ibid 23.
89 Australian Government, above n 48, 2.
90 ibid 19. For instance, ABC TV covered the citizenship ceremony on Australia Day 2012 and 2013. See Australian Broadcasting Commission, *National Flag and Raising and Citizenship Ceremony* Australia Day, http://www.abc.net.au/australiaday/ceremony.htm. Citizenship ceremonies are also publicised on the Australia Day website events. See for example Australian Day, *Citizenship* 'What's On', http://www.australiaday.com.au/whatson/citizenship.aspx.
91 *Australian Citizenship Act 2007* (Cth) s 27(1) sch 1.

only limited exceptions to the requirement to make the pledge in order to become a citizen.[92] The migrant's acceptance into the Australian democratic collective is therefore generally contingent on the candidate performing the pledge. The candidate must signal with their bodies that they will obey the laws by physically submitting the legal requirements for this performance.

The pledge enacts obedience as a submission to the government as the sovereign authority. It is significant that the pledge is taken by an 'authorised officer',[93] who is a representative of the state. The candidate is further reminded that it is the state that has the authority to accept the pledge, as either the Minister or, in his or her absence, the Minister's speech, is clearly present. The performance of the pledge is marked by the symbols of the state, the flag, the anthem, and the picture of the Queen. These symbols remind the candidate of the authority of the government. So although the text of the pledge expresses loyalty to Australia and its people, the context of the ceremony reinforces that it is the state who holds ultimate authority.

It is also significant that only migrants are required to perform the pledge. The renewed emphasis on the pledge and its performance has followed a period in Australia of increased suspicion towards non-white migrants,[94] in particular, a suspicion that migrants do not integrate into Australian society and that certain cultural beliefs and practices threaten social cohesion and national unity.[95] This context reinforces the argument that enacting the pledge reasserts the existing social and political order. In discussion surrounding the introduction of the citizenship test, parliamentarian Alan Cadman hinted that the value of the pledge was to reinforce the message to migrant future citizens that they must not seek to change Australian society:

> I think the only way in which we can influence those who want to subvert or change Australia to their own form of dictatorship or dominance and who want to be separate from the bulk of Australians is to have them understand that most Australians really do know what this country stands for and do want to support it and see it prosper. They want to see their families, and the generations who follow, prosper in an open, free and democratic society. The only way in which that can be achieved is

---

92   Exceptions are set out for those who are under 16, who have a permanent or enduring physical or mental incapacity, if they were born to a former Australian citizens, born in Papua, or stateless. *Australian Citizenship Act 2007* (Cth) s 26(1).
93   *Australian Citizenship Act 2007* (Cth) s 27(3).
94   Ghassan Hage, *White Nation* (Routledge, 2000).
95   Robert Holton 'Immigration, Social Cohesion and National Identity' (Parliamentary Research Paper, Social Policy Group, Research Paper No 1, 1 September 1997).

through the Citizenship Act and by having the Citizenship Act as a basis of understanding: if somebody who has taken the oath seeks to corrupt or ignore [sic], they become answerable to the processes of law.[96]

Performing the pledge therefore ensures that the migrant promises that they will submit to the existing political system or society, and if they do not, they will become traitors and be legitimately punished by the law. Therefore the performance of the pledge not only involves obedience, but submission, and weakens the understanding of the future migrant citizen as an independent and active agent for political change.

The recent introduction of affirmation ceremonies has not changed the focus on the performance of the pledge as an act of submission by migrant future citizens. In 2006, the government introduced a new practice in citizenship ceremonies that invites the audience to repeat the pledge of commitment. However, this new practice does not alter the meaning of the pledge as primarily performed by the migrant. Participation in affirmation ceremonies is not compulsory and does not have any legal effect. The affirmation ceremony is conducted after the pledge of commitment made by the new citizen-migrants. These aspects suggest that the affirmation ceremonies draw their meaning from the migrant pledge and reinforce it, rather than conveying any new meaning about citizenship.

It should be noted that the rich multi-vocality of political rituals permits opportunities for the generation of meanings of citizenship other than those determined by officials or the organisation.[97] Kertzer identifies that some rituals can challenge the official symbolic meaning of membership rituals.[98] These include rituals of rebellion (disobedience), reversion (inverting the power relations for 'a day'), or revolution. However, state control over the present citizenship pledge in the Australian ceremony is tight. Opportunities for subversion and challenge within the ceremony itself are limited. Perhaps if alternative civic rituals investing citizenship with different meanings become more commonplace, alternative ways of expressing Australian citizenship might generate new meanings. At present, the opportunities to undermine the official meaning of citizenship as obedience and submission are limited.

The meaning of citizenship generated by the law and conveyed by citizenship practices has the potential to influence the degree and scope of critical political engagement in Australian democracy. There are at least two implications for Australian democracy of a meaning of citizenship that reinforces obedience and submission. First, the emphasis on citizenship as obedience may influence the interpretation of the ACA, and so may exclude some applications for

---

96   Commonwealth, *Parliamentary Debates*, House of Representatives, 21 June 2007, 58 (Alan Cadman).

97   David Kertzer, *Ritual, Politics, and Power* (Yale University Press, 1988) 12.

98   ibid 13.

Australian citizenship. Second, the emphasis on obedience and submission might discourage permanent residents from engaging in active citizenship in Australia, both before they become citizens and afterwards. These implications diminish the level of critical political engagement in Australian democracy.

First, the emphasis on citizenship as obedience has the potential to influence decisions about which applications are accepted or rejected. At present, 'good character' is one of the eligibility criteria for citizenship by conferral.[99] Criminal offences are a key consideration which may indicate that a person is not of good character, although mitigating factors are considered. Mitigating factors include assessing the seriousness of the offence, age when committed, length of time since commission of the offence, and whether or not the offence was a one-off occurrence.[100] Another factor relevant to character is whether the person has been involved in activities which show 'disregard for the law'.[101] With an emphasis on citizenship as obedience, this could lead to the rejection of candidates who have engaged in political protest and acts of civil disobedience, such as the British citizen who painted 'NO WAR' on the Opera House. Alternatively, an emphasis on obedience may influence the exercise of the Minister's residual discretion.[102] The policy guidelines that govern how the Minister may exercise his or her residual discretion are vague.[103] The explanatory memorandum suggests that the discretion could be exercised where 'a person incites hatred or religious intolerance'.[104] But the line between political action and religious intolerance is difficult to ascertain, and may operate to reinforce discriminatory stereotypes. For instance, the protests about the release of the film *Innocence of Muslims* in Sydney in 2012 were framed as acts of religious intolerance, rather than political protests.[105] Political agitators might therefore be excluded from Australian citizenship under the wide scope of the Minister's residual discretion. The performance of the pledge which conveys a meaning of citizenship that reinforces obedience and submission has the potential to influence how the ACA is applied, and exclude those who are active citizens.

---

99   *Australian Citizenship Act 2007* (Cth) s 21(2)(h).
100   Department of Immigration and Citizenship, *Australian Citizenship Instructions*, 1 July 2013, ch 10.5.2 'Good Character'. Note that the 'good character' guidelines for citizenship are different to the 'good character' guidelines for the purposes of the *Migration Act 1958* (Cth). At the time this chapter went to press, the Australian Citizenship and Other Legislation Amendment Bill 2014 was before the Parliament. If passed, it will clarify and extend the scope of the character provisions in the *Australian Citizenship Act 2007* (Cth).'.
101   ibid [10.2].
102   *Australian Citizenship Act 2007* (Cth) s 24.
103   Department of Immigration and Citizenship, *Australian Citizenship Instructions*, 1 July 2013, ch 5.27 'Decision Making'.
104   Explanatory Memorandum, Australian Citizenship Bill 2005 (Cth) 30.
105   Yoni Bashan, 'Arrests Made After Police Officers Injured at Anti-Islamic Film Protest in Sydney CBD' *The Daily Telegraph* (online), 16 September 2012, http://www.heraldsun.com.au/news/national/police-use-pepper-spray-on-anti-islamic-film-protesters-in-sydney-at-the-us-consulate/story-fndo317g-1226474744811.

Second, an emphasis on citizenship as obedience and submission may discourage the political engagement of migrants both before they become citizens, as well as afterwards.

Those seeking Australian citizenship might avoid acts of active citizenship prior to their application. A citizenship application might be rejected where a person has committed a crime, even when this crime was an expression of political activity. Engaging in active citizenship is therefore risky. However, contributions by non-citizens have been very valuable in shaping Australian democracy. For instance, Australian democracy might be entirely different if the Italian migrant Raphaello Carboni had been reluctant to participate in the events during and after the Eureka Stockade.[106]

The emphasis on submission to legal authority may also influence the behavior of candidates after they become citizens. Certainly, once a migrant-applicant becomes a citizen, then they are legally free to engage in Australian democracy as they choose and to benefit from the democratic freedoms that other Australian citizens have. However, apart from the government rhetoric about active citizenship, there is a general absence of critical practices that emphasise the importance of critical engagement with Australian democracy. There are only minimal protections of participation in politics, and no express federal legislative charter of liberal rights or tolerance.[107] This political environment creates inconsistent messages for new citizens about the extent to which they are encouraged to participate as active citizens, and to engage in protest action or even civil disobedience. Indeed, research suggests that Australian citizens by conferral are less likely to engage in political action than Australian citizens by birth.[108] While it is difficult to speculate the extent to which the meaning of citizenship as communicated through the performance of the pledge contributes to this result, it does suggest that any emphasis on citizenship as obedience and submission will only further undermine an already low level of political engagement.

Although only applicants for citizenship by conferral need to perform the pledge and embody obedience and submission, the practice has a far reaching impact on Australian democracy. Citizenship by conferral is a significant means of gaining membership in a country of high immigration such as Australia. Government statistics estimate that 26.8 per cent of the Australian population is born overseas, and it is likely that a large proportion of those born overseas acquire

---

106   Jennifer Lorch, 'Rafaello Carboni' *Australian Dictionary of Biography* (Melbourne University Press, 1968) http://adb.anu.edu.au/biography/carboni-raffaello-3163.
107   Donald Horne, 'A Constitution of Openness, Accessibility and Shared Discourse?' (2001) 24(3) *University of NSW Law Journal* 610, 616.
108   Antoine Bilodeau, 'Immigrants' Voice Through Protest Politics in Canada and Australia: Assessing the Impact of Pre-Migration Political Repression' (2008) 34 (6) *Journal of Ethnic and Migration Studies* 975.

Australian citizenship through citizenship by conferral.[109] A performance of citizenship that embodies obedience is problematic for Australian democracy because it undermines the critical agency of nearly a quarter of the population. Furthermore, the public performance of the pledge conveys a submissive understanding of citizenship to the wider public through the media and high profile events, which influences the understanding of citizenship in the Australian community more broadly.

Conclusion

This chapter argues that even though the rhetoric of the Australian government supports active citizenship, the meaning about citizenship conveyed by the law suggests otherwise. Through expanding the analysis to include an examination of citizenship practices in the ACA, this chapter explores the meaning of citizenship conveyed by the government. Although Australian citizenship practices have historically conveyed a celebratory meaning of citizenship, this chapter reveals how the recent government emphasis on the practice of the pledge of commitment has altered the meaning of citizenship. Using the theory of speech act and political ritual, it argues that the performance of the pledge conveys Australian citizenship as obedience and submission to the law and existing democratic structures. Without room made for disagreement and contestation, a robust notion of active citizenship is therefore undermined. The current Australian practice of making a pledge works against active citizenship in Australia, as well as undermining active political engagement in Australian democracy.

---

109 Commonwealth of Australia *Fact Sheet 15: Population Growth* June 2012, Department of Immigration and Citizenship, http://www.immi.gov.au/media/fact-sheets/15population.htm.

9. People You Might Know: Social Media in the Conflict Between Law and Democracy

Stephen Tully[1]

Twitter and other blogs, Facebook, emails, SMS messages, LinkedIn, Youtube and Flickr are ubiquitous forms of communication within modern society. The role of these tools in enabling individuals to express their political opinions, as well as whether and how social media should be regulated, have emerged as questions of considerable interest. However, the issue of locating social media within a possible conflict between regulation and democracy remains underexplored. Law is just one of the forces or 'regulators' that control and define systems such as the internet, the others being markets, architectures and norms.[2] Civil or political liberties within cyberspace will only be enhanced if these forces are democratic in nature.[3]

This chapter will assess two broad propositions: first, that social media has the potential to enhance democratic participation, and secondly, that legal restrictions can curtail this opportunity. These topics are significant because the influence of social media is frequently overstated and, in debates where democracy is at stake, the desirability of regulatory controls is typically overlooked. Part one defines social media and explores the premise that social media is conducive to enhanced democracy. It also identifies some of the risks and dangers of relying on this particular medium as a means of political participation. Part two will illustrate sources of and solutions to contests between law and democracy by reference to the human right to freedom of expression. Permissible limitations and restrictions on the exercise of that right can be identified from the paradigm of international human rights law. Those considerations will inform an analysis of a posited conflict between law and democracy. Particular attention is given to recent developments within the United States, Europe, China, and Australia. There is an observable trend towards greater government regulation of social media within each of these jurisdictions for national security, law enforcement and other reasons. Underlying themes to be addressed include notions of individual liberty, conditions of access to and participation in social media, the permissibility of restrictions within a democratic society, sound regulatory

---

1   srtully@gmail.com.

2   Lawrence Lessig, *Code and Other Laws of Cyberspace* (Basic Books, 1999).

3   Michael Best and Keegan Wade, 'Democratic and Anti-Democratic Regulators of the Internet: A Framework' (2006) http://mikeb.inta.gatech.edu/papers/democratic.best.wade.pdf.

development and ensuring government accountability. I contend that, in order to accommodate competing policy priorities, the adoption of regulatory measures inevitably but necessarily impairs the enjoyment of human rights and constrains the civic potential offered by social media.

Social media as a means of political participation

Social media may be defined as a group of internet-based applications which build on the ideological and technical foundations of Web 2.0, and allow the creation and exchange of user-generated content.[4] Social networking sites such as Facebook provide an online presence for users to share information, search for others and communicate. Blogs such as Twitter enable users to publish commentary and broadcast it publicly over the internet. Social media such as YouTube enables users to publish and share images, videos and music through the internet. Whatever the particular form, social media has several common characteristics. First, a capability to attract a wide audience. Second, content is created when one user communicates with another.[5]

Social media is fast becoming the preferred mode for education, employment, commerce and personal expression. Indeed, non-access and disconnection from the internet has been described as tantamount to 'non-existence'.[6] Social media may be employed for a range of purposes. For example, the capacity for social media to provide accurate and timely information makes it a useful tool for promoting human rights.[7] During the Kosovo conflict, for example, NATO states targeted Serb media outlets conveying government propaganda but not internet service providers. It was considered that '[f]ull and open access to the Internet can only help the Serbian people know the ugly truth about the atrocities and

---

4   Andreas Kaplan and Michael Haenlein, 'Users of the World, Unite!: The Challenges and Opportunities of Social Media' (2010) 53(1) *Business Horizons* 59, 61.

5   Content is 'user generated' if it is available to a select group on a publicly-accessible website or a social networking site, entails a minimum amount of creative effort, and is created outside of professional routines and practices: Organisation for Economic Cooperation and Development, *Participative Web and User-Created Content: Web 2.0, Wikis and Social Networking* (2007) 18.

6   Allen Hammond, 'The Telecommunications Act of 1996: Codifying the Digital Divide' (1997) 50 *Federal Communications Law Journal* 179, 185. See generally Jack Balkin, 'The Future of Free Expression in a Digital Age' (2009) 36 *Pepperdine Law Review* 427.

7   Jamie Metzl, 'Information Technology and Human Rights' (1996) 18 *Human Rights Quarterly* 705, 706.

crimes against humanity being perpetrated in Kosovo by the Milosevic regime'.[8] Human rights non-governmental organisations benefit from the internet with respect to information dissemination and ease of communication.[9]

The internet has also changed the social conditions of speech. The cultural and participatory features of the human right to freedom of expression are accentuated.[10] The United Nations (UN) Special Rapporteur on the promotion and protection of the right to freedom of opinion and expression, Mr Frank La Rue, has been mandated to provide his views on the advantages and challenges of new information and communication technologies, including the internet and mobile technologies.[11] He believes that the internet is 'inherently democratic' because it provides the public with access to information and enables individuals to actively participate in the process of communication.[12] In his view, the internet facilitates citizen participation in building democratic societies.[13] Marginalised or disadvantaged social sectors can also obtain information and participate in public debates concerning social, economic and political changes affecting their circumstances.[14]

But the relationship between social media and political participation is not so unequivocal. One view is that social media is the catalyst for political transformation — information is so widely accessible that individuals can formulate and express their own political opinions.[15] On this account, social media fosters popular participation and greater democratisation within states. Through the internet, '[i]ndividuals become less passive, and thus more engaged observers of social spaces that could potentially become subjects for political conversation; they become more engaged participants in the debates about their observations'.[16] Nevertheless, commentators are divided between those considering the internet to be a boon to democracy[17] and those believing it is a tool of oppression.[18]

---

8   James Rubin, US State Department spokesperson, quoted in David Briscoe, 'Kosovo-Propaganda War', Associated Press, 17 May 1999.
9   Peter Brophy and Edward Halpin, 'Through the Net to Freedom: Information, the Internet and Human Rights' (1999) 25 *Journal of Information Science* 351, 354.
10   Jack Balkin, 'Digital Speech and Democratic Culture: A Theory of Freedom of Expression for the Information Society' (2004) 79(1) *New York University Law Review* 3, 4.
11   Human Rights Council, Resolution 7/36 (2008) [4(f)].
12   Abid Hussain, Special Rapporteur, *Report on the Right to Freedom of Opinion and Expression*, UN Doc E/CN.4/1998/40 (28 January 1998) [45].
13   Frank La Rue, Special Rapporteur, *Report on the Promotion and Protection of the Right to Freedom of Opinion and Expression*, UN Doc A/HRC/17/27 (16 May 2011) [2], [19].
14   ibid [62].
15   Clay Shirky, 'The Political Power of Social Media' (2011) 90 *Foreign Affairs* 28, 28–9.
16   Yochai Benkler, *The Wealth of Networks: How Social Production Transforms Markets and Freedom* (Yale University Press, 2006) 11.
17   Dietram Scheufele and Matthew Nisbet, 'Being a Citizen Online: New Opportunities and Dead Ends' (2002) 7(3) *The Harvard International Journal of Press/Politics* 55.
18   Tyler Boas, 'The Dictator's Dilemma?: The Internet and US policy Toward Cuba' (2000) 23(3) *The Washington Quarterly*.

It is admittedly true that the internet can prove to be an effective mechanism for political activism, particularly when combined with traditional forms of communications media.[19] Social media facilitates activities as diverse as public education, fundraising, forming coalitions across geographical boundaries, distributing petitions or action alerts, and planning or coordinating events on a national, regional or international level. The internet and email, for example, has helped to organise consumer boycotts against multinational corporations and assist campaigns such as the adoption of selective purchasing legislation in Massachusetts against Myanmar.[20]

The role of social media during the so-called 'Arab Spring' has also attracted considerable comment.[21] In Egypt, for example, various groups used social media platforms, including Facebook and Twitter, to spread revolutionary messages and coordinate protests. Blogging became a source of information for political activists free from censorship or manipulation by the traditional state-controlled media. The government identified Facebook as a harmful application and officials joined Facebook groups to warn individuals not to strike. Mobile phones were banned in police stations to prevent the recording of YouTube videos.

Then, on 28 January 2011, then President Hosni Mubarak disconnected the internet for five days across the entire state. US President Obama indicated support for the right of Egyptians to the freedom of speech and to access information, observing that 'we've seen the incredible potential for technology to empower citizens and the dignity of those who stand up for a better future'.[22] US Secretary of State Clinton urged the Egyptian authorities 'not to prevent peaceful protests or block communications, including on social media sites'.[23] However, encouraging social media use as a means of facilitating human rights and a transition to a democratic political system runs up against the international

---

19   Dorothy Denning, 'Activism, Hacktivism, and Cyberterrorism: The Internet as a Tool for Influencing Foreign Policy' (1999) http://www.nautilus.org/info-policy/workshop/papers/denning.html.

20   Tiffany Danitz and Warren Strobel, 'Networking Dissent: Cyber Activists use the Internet to Promote Democracy in Burma' (US Institute of Peace, 2000). See generally Joel Reidenberg, 'Yahoo and Democracy on the Internet' (2002) 42 *Jurimetrics* 261.

21   Philip Howard et al., 'Opening Closed Regimes: What Was the Role of Social Media During the Arab Spring?' Project on Information Technology and Political Islam, Working Paper No. 2011(1), http://pitpi.org/?p= 1051; Zeynep Tufekci and Christopher Wilson, 'Social Media and the Decision to Participate in Political Protest: Observations from Tahrir Square' (2012) 62 *Journal of Communication* 363.

22   The White House, 'Remarks by the President on the Situation in Egypt' (Press Release, 1 February 2011) http://www.whitehouse.gov/the-press-office/2011/02/01/remarks-president-situationegypt.

23   Hillary Clinton, 'Remarks with Jordanian Foreign Minister Nasser Judeh after Their Meeting' (Press Release, 26 January 2011) http://www.state.gov/secretary/rm/2011/01/155388.htm.

legal norm prohibiting intervention within the internal affairs of a state.[24] Nevertheless, following 18 days of protest, Mubarak resigned from office and so ended 30 years of authoritarian rule.

Social media has had a comparable role in events within other states. In Tunisia, for example, video of protests were uploaded to Facebook. In 2001, written accounts, photographs, videos and other information from Syrian demonstrators were relayed around the world via social media by 20 Syrian exiles. But social media can also be used to coordinate destructive mayhem within democratic states as much as effect constructive political mobilisation within authoritarian ones. Blackberry's encrypted messenger service, for example, was blamed by UK Prime Minister David Cameron for coordinating British riots in August 2011. Twitter on the other hand was credited with organising cleanups.

The contrary view is that social media promotes weak political ties and low-risk activism (or 'slacktivism') because 'liking' something on Facebook, or retweeting a story, takes little effort but lulls protagonists into believing that they are acting meaningfully.[25] The vast quantity of information available through the internet can readily distract individuals from important political issues.[26]

It has also been suggested that the level of internet connectivity can predict the degree of democratic attainment.[27] In other words, the more enhanced the basic communications infrastructure of any given country then the more likely this will be conducive to the assertion and manifestation of liberties and rights for its citizens.[28] The important civic value of the internet is that 'those who have computers and internet communications find themselves better trained, better informed, and better able to participate in democracy'.[29] Internet usage was a more accurate predictor of democracy between 2001–2002 than 1992–2002, thereby suggesting that the internet has only recently come into its own as a positive force for democratisation.[30]

The experience of web-enabled open government illustrates the nature of individual behaviour and the challenges confronting agencies. The internet is opening up government agency methodologies to public scrutiny, prompting

---

24   But see Chatham House, 'The Principle of Non-Intervention in Contemporary International Law: Non-Interference in a State's Internal Affairs Used to be a Rule of International Law — is it Still?' (28 February 2007).

25   Malcolm Gladwell, 'Small Change', *New Yorker*, 4 October 2010, 42 http://www.newyorker.com/reporting/2010/10/04/101004fa-fact-gladwell.

26   Evgeny Morozov, *The Net Delusion* (Public Affairs, 2011) 81–2.

27   Christopher Kedzie, 'Communication and Democracy: Coincident Revolutions and the Emergent Dictator's Dilemma', Rand Document No RGSD-127, 1997, http://www.rand.org/publications/RGSD/RGSD127.

28   Audrey Selian, *IT's in Support of Human Rights, Democracy and Good Governance* (International Telecommunications Union, 2002).

29   Mark Cooper, 'Inequality in the Digital Society: Why the Digital Divide Deserves All the Attention It Gets' (2002) 20 *Cardozo Arts & Entertainment Law Journal* 73.

30   Michael Best and Keegan Wade, 'The Internet and Democracy: Global Catalyst or Democratic Dud?' (2009) 29(4) *Bulletin of Science, Technology & Society* 255.

greater transparency, making information more accessible and increasing public participation in agency decision-making.[31] For example, 'e-rulemaking' allows public comments to be submitted online through social media to formulate rules. However, individuals are exhibiting 'drive-by participation'.[32] Public participation can moreover delay agency action, overwhelm decision-makers and encourage agendas which meet the wishes of small, but vocal, interest groups.[33] Thus the law and Web 2.0 become 'very strange bedfellows. Law is authoritarian, hierarchical, and bounded; the Web is fluid, infinitely possibilistic, even anarchic.'[34]

One difficulty with social media is that participation is characterised by inequality.[35] There is intense participation by a small proportion of users who supply a large percentage of content. Ideally, individuals can collect factual information, voice their personal perspective, confront other points of view and rationally discuss issues.[36] However, the internet is also a powerful tool for spreading misinformation, propaganda and hateful messages. Drawing the line between robust debate which advances knowledge-creation and speech that harms civic deliberations is therefore challenging. Can these dangers and risks be adequately addressed by regulation?[37]

The second difficulty is that, while the number of internet users has increased exponentially, the internet's growth and corresponding benefits are unequally distributed. Is it satisfactory, then, that the opportunity for political participation is left to depend upon such rudimentary issues as technology, infrastructure or electricity access? The problem of relying upon the internet as a democratising tool is that there is no universal access. The 'digital divide' refers to the unequal distribution of information and communication technology between and within states.[38] In contrast to the 71.6 internet users per 100 inhabitants within developed states, there are only 21.1 internet users per 100 inhabitants in developing ones

---

31   Stephen Johnson, 'The Internet Changes Everything: Revolutionising Public Participation and Access to Government Information Through the Internet' (1998) 50 *Administrative Law Review* 277, 305–6.

32   Cynthia Farina, Paul Miller, Mary Newhart, Claire Cardie, Dan Cosley, Rebecca Vernon and the Cornell eRulemaking Initiative, 'Rulemaking in 140 Characters or Less: Social Networking and Public Participation in Rulemaking' (2011) 31 *Pace Law Review* 382, 445.

33   Jim Rossi, 'Participation Run Amok: The Costs of Mass Participation for Deliberative Agency Decisionmaking' (1997) 92 *Northwestern University Law Review* 173, 180.

34   Farina et al., 'Rulemaking in 140 Characters or Less: Social Networking and Public Participation in Rulemaking' (2011) 31 *Pace Law Review* 461.

35   ibid 453.

36   Jon Katz, 'Birth of a Digital Nation', *Wired*, April 1997, http://www.wired.com/wired/5.04/netizen.html.

37   Abid Hussain, Special Rapporteur, *Report on the Promotion and Protection of the Right to Freedom of Opinion and Expression*, UN Doc E/CN.4/2002/75 (30 January 2002) [69]–[70].

38   Peter Yu, 'Bridging the Digital Divide: Equality in the Information Age' (2002) 20 *Cardozo Arts and Entertainment Law Journal* 1, 2. See also Pippa Norris, *Digital Divide: Civic Engagement, Information Poverty and the Internet Worldwide* (Cambridge University Press, 2001).

and only 9.6 users per 100 inhabitants within Africa.[39] Digital divides also exist within states along wealth, gender, geographical and social lines. Internet access tends to be concentrated among socioeconomic elites, whereas individuals in rural areas confront obstacles including lack of technological availability, slower connection speeds and/or higher costs. Disadvantaged sectors, such as disabled persons or minority groups, often face barriers to accessing the internet in a way that is meaningful, relevant and useful to their daily lives.

The international community is only beginning to address these challenges. For example, the World Summit on the Information Society defined the digital divide in access-related statistics.[40] However, physical access — namely, possessing computers, user numbers, connection speeds and the underlying infrastructure — is only one dimension. By focusing upon access or enabling infrastructure, the question is posed: 'how do we increase the speed of connections?' This question should be reframed as how to encourage local communities to meaningfully participate.[41] Meaningful participation, however, may have to overcome yet another hurdle: regulation by governments.

Government regulation of social media as a democratic impediment

The leading developed states agree that the internet helps to promote democracy and the freedoms of opinion, expression, information, assembly and association.[42] Arbitrary or indiscriminate censorship or restrictions on internet access are said to be inconsistent with a state's international obligations and are unacceptable. They have accordingly committed themselves to encouraging internet use as a tool for advancing human rights and democratic participation. Importantly, however, implementing these objectives is qualified by respect for the rule of law.[43] Furthermore, as will be considered below, the promotion of social media use by governments has a Janus-like quality which reins in trends towards greater democratic participation.

---

39   International Telecommunication Union, *Key Global Telecom Indicators for the World Telecommunication Service Sector*, 21 October 2010.

40   World Summit on the Information Society, *The Digital Divide at a Glance* (International Telecommunications Union, 2005) http://www.iru.int/wsis/tunis/newsroom/stats.

41   Amir Ali, 'The Power of Social Media in Developing Nations: New Tools for Closing the Global Digital Divide and Beyond' (2010) 24 *Harvard Human Rights Journal* 185, 198.

42   Group of Eight Declaration, *Renewed Commitment for Freedom and Democracy*, G8 Summit, Deauville, 26–27 May 2011, [5] http://www.g20-g8.com/g8-g20/g8/english/live/news/renewedcommitment-for-freedom-and-democracy.1314.html.

43   ibid [11], [13], Section II [10].

It is clear from the previous discussion that the internet has a growing significance for the individual rights to freedom of opinion, expression and association as defined under international human rights law.[44] The right to freedom of expression, for example, can illustrate the conflict between law and democracy in the context of social media. This right includes the freedom to seek, receive and impart information and ideas of all kinds, irrespective of frontiers, through any media of an individual's choosing.[45]

More particularly, a direct link between freedom of expression through social media and political participation can be identified. The free exchange of information or ideas on matters relevant to the economic, social or political life of a state is crucial to, and inherent in the very nature of, a democratic country.[46] Freedom of expression including political debate is an essential foundation for a democratic society and a basic condition for individual self-fulfilment.[47] Freedom of expression, together with the right to take part in the public affairs of a state, 'implies that citizens, in particular through the media, should have wide access to information and the opportunity to disseminate information and opinions about the activities of elected bodies and their members'.[48] The UN Human Rights Committee has already made the point that excluding individuals from accessing the Press Gallery for reasons of parliamentary privilege, for example, violated the right to freedom of expression '[i]n view of the importance of access to information about the democratic process', notwithstanding the ability to report on proceedings through broadcasting services.[49]

So, what then is the nature of this conflict between law and democracy? The first part of this chapter indicated that the individual interest in free political expression does not always coincide — and indeed may clash — with governmental agendas. The appeal of an unhindered multimedia communication space appears at odds with exercising control in the broader public interest. What role if any does law have in either bridging or perpetuating that gulf?

---

44 *Universal Declaration of Human Rights*, UN GA Res 217A (III), UN GAOR, 3rd sess, 183rd plen mtg, UN Doc A/810 (10 December 1948) arts 19, 20; *International Covenant on Civil and Political Rights*, opened for signature 16 December 1966, 999 UNTS 171 (entered into force 23 March 1976) arts 19, 22; *European Convention on Human Rights and Fundamental Freedoms*, opened for signature 4 November 1950, 213 UNTS 221 (entry into force 3 September 1953) arts 10–11; *American Convention of Human Rights*, opened for signature 22 September 1969, 1144 UNTS 123 (entry into force 18 July 1978) arts 13, 16; *African Charter on Human and Peoples' Rights*, opened for signature 27 June 1981, 1520 UNTS 217 (entry into force 21 October 1986) arts 9–10.

45 *International Covenant on Civil and Political Rights*, opened for signature 16 December 1966, 999 UNTS 171 (entry into force 23 March 1976) art 19(2).

46 *Campbell v MGN Limited* [2004] UKHL 22, [148]–[149] (Baroness Hale).

47 *Lingens v Austria* [1986] 8 EHRR 407, [41]–[42].

48 Human Rights Committee, *Decision: Communication No 633/95*, UN Doc CCPR/C/ 65/D/633/1995 (5 May 1999) [13.4] ('*Gauthier v Canada*').

49 ibid [13.5].

First, the law provides boundaries on the measures which states are permitted to adopt. Using the right to freedom of expression to illustrate the point, any limitations on this right must satisfy a three-part, cumulative test:[50]

a) the limitation must be provided by law which is clear and accessible to everyone (that is, the principles of predictability and transparency);

b) the limitation must protect the rights or reputations of others, national security, public order, public health or morals[51] (the principle of legitimacy); and

c) the limitation must be necessary and the least restrictive means for achieving the purported aim (the principles of necessity and proportionality).

In addition, any legislative measure must be applied by a body which is independent of any political, commercial or other unwarranted influences in a manner that is neither arbitrary nor discriminatory, and having adequate safeguards against abuse, including the prospect of challenge and a remedy against any abusive application.[52]

International benchmarks such as these as a guide for national-level regulations are all well and good. But states are increasingly censoring online information by arbitrarily blocking or filtering content, criminalising legitimate expression, imposing intermediary liability,[53] disconnecting users from internet access[54] (for reasons including intellectual property rights protection)[55] and inadequately protecting data privacy. For example, 'timed' blocking prevents users from accessing the websites of opposition parties or independent or social media at key political moments such as elections, times of social unrest, or political

---

50   Frank La Rue, Special Rapporteur, *Report on the Promotion and Protection of the Right to Freedom of Opinion and Expression*, UN Doc A/HRC/17/27 (16 May 2011) [24].

51   *International Covenant on Civil and Political Rights*, opened for signature 16 December 1966, 999 UNTS 171 (entry into force 23 March 1976) art 19(3).

52   *Opinion and Expression*, UN Doc A/HRC/17/27 (16 May 2011) [24].

53   ibid [39], [40]. See, for example, *Law 5651 on the Prevention of Crime Committed in the Information Technology Domain 2007* (Turkey) grants authority to an administrative agency to issue orders to block websites for content hosted outside state borders. The *Computer Crimes Act 2007* (Thailand) imposes liability upon intermediaries which transmit or host third-party content as well as the authors themselves. States have instituted 'notice-and-takedown' regimes which protect intermediaries from liability provided they promptly remove unlawful material upon notification. See, for example, *Council Directive 2000/31/EC of 8 June 2000 on certain legal aspects of information society services, in particular electronic commerce, in the Internal Market* OJ L 178 (17 July 2000), 1–16, art 14; *Digital Millennium Copyright Act of 1998*, 112 Stat. 2860 (1998) s 512.

54   On a centralised 'on/off' control over Internet traffic, see 'Reaching for the Kill Switch', *The Economist*, 10 February 2011.

55   Legislation may disconnect users from the internet if they violate intellectual property rights, this occuring by way of a 'graduated response', that is, a series of increasing penalties which ultimately lead to suspending the internet service. See, for example, Conseil Constitutionnel, *Decision 2009–580, Act furthering the diffusion and protection of creation on the Internet*, 10 June 2010, http://www.conseil-constitutionnel.fr/conseilconstitutionnel/root/bank_mm/anglais/2009_580dc.pdf. See also *Digital Economy Act 2010* (UK) ss 3–16.

or historically-significant anniversaries. States restrict, control, manipulate or censor information disseminated through the internet either absent any legal basis, using broad and ambiguous laws without justification or in an unnecessary or disproportionate manner for achieving their intended aim. States are moreover introducing or modifying laws to increase their ability to monitor internet users' activities as well as the content of communications without sufficient guarantees against abuse. Government measures include a real-name identification system before users can post comments or upload content (which compromises anonymity) and restricting the use of encryption technology.[56]

Such steps might not at first glance appear conducive to democratic ideals. These regulatory measures are introduced for national security, counter-terrorism or public order reasons such as protecting an individual's reputation. Indeed, international agreements may require states Parties to criminalise certain activities committed over the internet.[57] Content which may legitimately be restricted includes child pornography, hate speech, defamation, direct and public incitement to genocide, advocating national, racial or religious hatred and incitement to discrimination, hostility or violence. These standards provide permissible grounds for states to regulate contrary to an individual's right to freedom of expression. States are moreover supporting the growth of information and communications technology to further their own specific ends including national development objectives.[58]

Within the international community China is frequently singled out for criticism. The government is encouraging expansion of the internet and putting more official information online.[59] Because political discussion occurs on bulletin boards and websites, the government has increased its efforts to monitor and control content. Sophisticated and extensive filtering systems block access to websites containing key terms such as 'democracy' and 'human rights'.[60] Politically-sensitive websites including foreign news services are shut down by authorities. Internet cafes are monitored or raided, and website operators are jailed for subversion or social crimes. The authorities also monitor and block

---

56   Frank La Rue, Special Rapporteur, *Report on the Promotion and Protection of the Right to Freedom of Opinion and Expression*, UN Doc A/HRC/17/27 (16 May 2011) [26], [30], [55].

57   *Convention on Cybercrime*, opened for signature 23 November 2001 (2001) ETS No 185 (entry into force 1 July 2004). The Convention entered into force for Australia on 1 March 2013: [2013] ATS 9.

58   *UN GA Res 55/2 on the Millennium Development Goals*, UN Doc A/RES/55/2 (18 September 2000) Target 8f; World Summit on the Information Society, *2003 Plan of Action*, WSIS-03/Geneva/DOC/5-E, Geneva, 12 December 2003, http://www.itu.int/wsis/docs/geneva/official/poa.html.

59   US State Department, Bureau of Democracy, Human Rights, and Labor, *Country Report on Human Rights Practices, China (including Hong Kong and Macau)*, 23 February 2001.

60   Reporters Sans Frontiers, *Enemies of the Internet*, March 2010, 8–12, http://en.rsf.org/IMG/pdf/Internet_enemies.pdf.

telephone conversations, fax transmissions, email and internet communications. An email filtration system for anti-government messages entering China has also been established.

These measures of political repression are effected by law. The Measures for Managing Internet Content Provision, for example, regulate who can own an internet business and what is published online. Internet content providers must retain files of posted communications including details of who has read it for 60 days. Internet service providers must record the time that users log on to the internet as well as telephone and account numbers, internet addresses and domain names. State Council Order Number 273 (1999) requires firms with encryption technology to register and provide the names, telephone numbers and email addresses of all persons using it. These efforts to block content and control internet use, however, has only had limited success because sophisticated users can bypass such measures, the number of internet sites has grown so rapidly, censorship regulations are applied inconsistently and enforcement efforts vary. In sum, the contest between government control through regulation and democratic participation, like numerous other contexts within China, is being played out through the use of social media tools.

But one need not limit scrutiny to China to observe comparable steps taken by other states. Indeed, tighter regulatory control over social media is not limited to authoritarian states. For example, the European Union has developed more effective legislation to counter terrorist websites than the US because the right to freedom of speech is upheld with less vigour.[61] European states must retain data generated or processed following a communication or use of a communication service.[62] Internet service providers must retain user identification, telephone numbers and IP addresses for both the sender and recipient of communications.

Around 45 other states restrict internet access by their citizens, typically by forcing individuals to subscribe to state-run internet service providers which filter out objectionable material.[63] The UN Human Rights Committee has also expressed concern that access to local and international sources of political commentary is blocked during election periods.[64] Government surveillance of human rights defenders or political opposition figures communicating via the internet and Facebook can occur in an arbitrary or covert manner.

---

61   Megan Healy, 'How the Legal Regimes of the European Union and the United States Approach Islamic Terrorist Web Sites: A Comparative Analysis' (2009–2010) 84 *Tulane Law Review* 165.
62   *Council Directive 2006/24 of 15 March 2006 on the retention of data generated or processed in connection with the provision of publicly available electronic communications services or of public communications networks and amending Directive 2002/58/EC* [2006] OJ L 105/54.
63   Reporters Sans Frontiers, *The Twenty Enemies of the Internet*, Press Release, 9 August 1999.
64   Human Rights Committee, *General Comment No 34: Article 19: Freedoms of opinion and expression*, UN Doc CCPR/C/GC/34 (12 September 2011) [37].

Non-governmental organisations in the human rights field are concerned that the threats to internet freedom are growing and becoming more diverse. In one study of 37 states, 15 blocked politically-relevant content.[65] Reports of internet filtering, content manipulation and imprisoning users have increased in recent years. For example, in Brazil, India, Indonesia, South Korea, Turkey and the UK, internet freedom is increasingly undermined by legal harassment, opaque censorship laws or expanding surveillance. In Venezuela, Azerbaijan, Jordan and Rwanda, politically-motivated internet controls are emerging, typically during election periods. Increasing censorship and user arrests occurred in Bahrain, Ethiopia and Tunisia following popular protests or contentious elections. Following the 2009 elections, Iran established a filtering system which can block websites nationwide within several hours. In Vietnam, four activists were imprisoned for using the internet to express pro-democratic views.[66] As is the case in China, however, resourceful citizens within these states continue to identify technical means with which to sidestep restrictions and employ internet-based platforms with a view to promoting greater participation.

The leading democratic states are by no means exceptional. Indeed, they have championed internet freedom for individuals located in other states — and to extend their governmental influence extraterritorially — whilst simultaneously introducing legislation which increases governmental surveillance and undermines the privacy of their own nationals.[67] For example, the US promotes internet freedom and encourages universal access. In 2010, Secretary of State Clinton advocated 'the freedom to connect — the idea that governments should not prevent people from connecting to the internet, to websites, or to each other'.[68] The State Department supported new tools which enabled citizens to exercise their right to freedom of expression by circumventing politically-motivated censorship.[69] It intends to put social media tools 'in the hands of people who will use them to advance democracy and human rights'.[70] However, the US is establishing links with foreign non-governmental actors with a view to furthering its own diplomatic objectives, including enhancing its ability to influence developments occurring within other states and skirt the norm of non-intervention in domestic affairs.[71]

---

65   Sanja Kelly and Sarah Cook, 'New Technologies, Innovative Repression: Growing Threats to Internet Freedom', in Freedom House, *Freedom on the Net 2011: A Global Assessment of Internet and Digital Media* (18 April 2011) http://www.freedomhouse.org/report/freedom-net/freedom-net-2011.

66   ibid 2–3.

67   See, for example, the *Cyber Intelligence Sharing and Protection Act of 2012* (US); *Cybersecurity Act of 2012* (US); *Strengthening and Enhancing Cybersecurity by Using Research, Education, Information, and Technology Act of 2012* (US).

68   Hillary Clinton, US Secretary of State, 'Remarks on Internet Freedom', Address at The Newseum Washington DC, 21 January 2010, http://www.state.gov/secretary/rm/2010/01/135519.htm.

69   ibid.

70   ibid.

71   Compare House of Commons, 'Transcript of Oral Evidence taken by the Foreign Affairs Committee, British Foreign Policy and the "Arab Spring": The Transition to Democracy', 18 April 2012, HC 1672-V.

The International Strategy for Cyberspace for the US notes that many states put arbitrary restrictions upon the free flow of information or apply restrictions to suppress dissent or opposition activity.[72] Individuals are encouraged to use digital media to express opinions, share information, monitor elections, expose corruption and organise social or political movements, and the US will denounce those who harass, unfairly arrest, threaten or commit violent acts against individuals who use this technology.[73] However, fidelity to the rule of law is simultaneously affirmed.[74] How this strategy proposes to reconcile these sometimes competing objectives is left unsaid.

Furthermore, the proposed *Global Online Freedom Act 2012* (US) intends to prevent US businesses from cooperating with governments who use the internet for censorship and repression.[75] 'Internet-restricting countries' would be designated for those governments who were directly or indirectly responsible for a systematic pattern involving 'substantial restrictions on Internet freedom'. By this means the lure of economic assistance displaces the free expression of political opinion in favour of the free availability of electronic information generally.

Here in Australia, around 69 per cent of the population has access to an internet connection at home and around 21 per cent access the internet from their mobile phone.[76] Access to online content is generally unhindered and Australians can openly criticise government policy. Australian law does not currently contemplate the mandatory blocking or filtering of websites, blogs, chat rooms or file-sharing platforms. However, material deemed by the Australian Communications and Media Authority (ACMA) to be 'prohibited content' may be subject to 'take-down' notices: the relevant internet service provider is notified by the ACMA that it is hosting offending content which must then be removed.[77] Online content which is categorised as 'Refused Classification' by the Classification Board is prohibited.[78] Australians are not subject to censorship provided content does not defame or qualify as a criminal offence (such as hate speech or racial vilification).[79] However, verified identification information must be provided to purchase any prepaid mobile telephone service, personal

---

72   US, International Strategy for Cyberspace, *Prosperity, Security and Openness in a Networked World* (2011) 21.

73   ibid 23–4.

74   ibid 5.

75   *Global Online Freedom Act of 2012* (US). For comment, see David Fidler, 'The Internet, Human Rights, and US Foreign Policy: The Global Online Freedom Act of 2012' (2012) 16(18) *ASIL Insight*.

76   Australian Communications and Media Authority, *Communications Report* 2010–11.

77   Sanja Kelly and Sarah Cook, 'New Technologies, Innovative Repression: Growing Threats to Internet Freedom', in Freedom House, *Freedom on the Net 2011: A Global Assessment of Internet and Digital Media* (18 April 2011) http://www.freedomhouse.org/report/freedom-net/freedom-net-2011, 33–5.

78   *Broadcasting Services Act 1992* (Cth).

79   See, for example, *Jones v Toben* [2002] FCA 1150; Re Lim, 'Cronulla Riot: Confiscation of Mobile Phones, Invasion of Privacy and the Curbing of Free Speech', *Act Now*, 15 March 2006, http://www.actnow.com.au/Opinion/Cronulla_riot.aspx; Les Kennedy, 'Man in Court over Cronulla Revenge SMS', *Sydney Morning Herald* (Sydney) 6 December 2006.

information is stored while the service remains active and this information can be accessed by law enforcement and emergency agencies upon presentation of a warrant.

As is evident within other states and reflecting global trends, there are emergent threats through regulation to online freedom in Australia. A proposed South Australian election law would have required any individual posting political comments on a blog or online before a local election to use their real name and address. The proposal was withdrawn following a public outcry.[80] Recent amendments to surveillance legislation, accompanied by proposals to implement censorship through directives to internet service providers, have raised concerns about privacy and freedom of expression. In 2010 draft legislation would have required internet service providers to filter illicit content (principally child pornography) and retain data on users' online activities. This proposed filtering system triggered a number of concerns, including over-blocking, censoring adult materials, 'scope creep' and impairing telecommunication access speeds.[81]

As has been observed in Egypt, the UK, the US and elsewhere, political participation can prompt destructive protests which have been organised online through social media tools. Twitter and other social media have cooperated with UK law enforcement in cases of obvious criminality such as rioting, tax avoidance and privacy violations.[82] Australian law enforcement agencies are currently empowered to search and seize computers, and compel internet service providers to intercept and store data from individuals suspected of criminal offences.[83] Internet service providers cannot ordinarily monitor or disclose the content of communications without customer consent.[84] However, intercepting telecommunications is a powerful and cost-effective tool for law enforcement

---

80   Nate Anderson, 'Internet Uprising Overturns Australian Censorship Law', *Ars Technica*, 2 February 2010, http://arstechnica.com/tech-policy/news/2010/02/internet-uprising-overturns-australian-censorship-law.ars; 'South Australian Government Gags Internet Debate', news.com.au, 2 February 2010, http://www.news.com.au/technology/south-australian-state-government-gags-internet-debate/story-e6frfro0-1225825750956.
81   Alana Maurushat and Renee Watt, 'Australia's Internet Filter Proposal in the International Context' (2009) 12(2) *Internet Law Bulletin* 18–25; David Vaile and Renee Watt, 'Inspecting the Despicable, Assessing the Unacceptable: Prohibited Packets and the Great Firewall of Canberra' (2009) *University of New South Wales Law Review Series* 35.
82   The Right Honourable Lord Justice Leveson, *Report of an Inquiry into the Culture, Practices and Ethics of the Press*, HC 780-I (29 November 2012) Vol 1 [3.14].
83   *Telecommunications (Interception and Access) Act 1979* (Cth). See also *Telecommunications Act 1997* (Cth) Pt 13.
84   ibid. Pt 2–1, s 7 prohibits disclosure of an interception or communication, and Pt 3–1, s 108 prohibits access to stored communications.

authorities and intelligence agencies to counter national security threats and investigate criminal offences.[85] The Australian Federal Police considers that it has a limited ability to lawfully intercept information.[86]

Increased resort to social media tools therefore highlights the familiar problem of regulatory lag. Australian internet service providers may soon be required to monitor, collect and store information pertaining to all users' communications. The Parliamentary Joint Committee on Intelligence and Security is considering the effectiveness and implications of proposals to ensure that law enforcement, intelligence and security agencies can meet the challenges of new and emerging technology upon their capabilities.[87] Software, ciphers and similar methodologies are being used by organised crime to impede detection by law enforcement authorities.[88] Australia's intelligence and law enforcement agencies face significant challenges in accessing communications and keeping pace with rapid telecommunications changes.[89] The legal framework also requires updating. For example, the *Telecommunications (Interception and Access) Act 1979* (Cth) assumes that interception can occur at a convenient point within a carrier's network. However, most contemporary communications networks can be accessed via multiple technologies from many locations and through more than one service provider. The Australian Parliament will shortly be asked how best to balance the protection of individual privacy against the ability of government agencies to access the information necessary to protect the community.[90]

Why then is regulation perceived as a threat to the democratic potential offered by social media, particularly if there are counterbalancing interests at stake? Social media empowers individuals by enabling free expression. Due to its low cost, decentralised nature and great reach, the internet is an important outlet for circulating independent opinions about state authorities and government policies. Many governments have developed an interest in controlling, monitoring

---

85   Anthony Blunn, *Report of the Review of the Regulation of Access to Communications* (2005) http://www. ag.gov.au/publications/pages/blunnreportofthereviewoftheregulationofaccesstocommunicationsAugust2005. aspx.

86   Australian Federal Police, *Response to the Public Discussion Paper: Connecting with Confidence: Optimising Australia's Digital Future* (2012) 4.

87   Parliamentary Joint Committee on Intelligence and Security, *Inquiry into Potential Reforms of National Security Legislation*, 2012, Terms of Reference [2].

88   The Australian Crime Commission, *Future of Organised Criminality in Australia 2020* (2009).

89   Attorney-General's Department, 'Equipping Australia against Emergent and Evolving Threats: A Discussion Paper to Accompany Consideration by the Parliamentary Joint Committee on Intelligence and Security of a Package of National Security Ideas Comprising Proposals for Telecommunications Interception Reform, Telecommunications Sector Security Reform and Australian Intelligence Community Legislation Reform' (2012) 3.

90   ibid 23. The former Opposition Spokesperson for Communications, Malcolm Turnbull, has called for 'more freedom [on the internet] rather than more regulation'. 'Turnbull Supports Freedom of Internet', *Sydney Morning Herald* (Sydney) 8–9 December 2012, 6.

and if necessary censoring digital media.[91] As indicated earlier in this chapter, the obvious benefits derived from social media use, including facilitating greater participation by individuals, are not without important qualifications. The desirability of imposing restrictions with a view to protecting privacy, reputations, intellectual property rights, national security or public order can readily be conceded. International human rights law provides only broad normative guidance to regulatory authorities on how respect for the right to freedom of expression is to be ensured and in any event expressly contemplates permissible limitations on its exercise. It ultimately appears that controlling social media can prove technically or politically difficult. Controlling public internet use might require governments to forgo the benefits of connection or expend political capital to block websites. The 'cute cat theory of digital activism' posits that governments cannot block political activity without also depriving access to other material, including pictures of cute cats.[92] Governments cannot shut down Facebook, for example, because doing so alienates individuals and might politicise those who lose access.

Social media tools, like other forms of communication, are susceptible to abuse. Its potential to enhance democratic participation should not be overstated. Caution is accordingly appropriate when promoting social media as an instrument for progressive political change.[93] The reality of unequal access and participation between individuals identified above, not to mention 'digital divides' between states and the technical challenges confronting government institutions, demands attention. More particularly, governments can subvert the utility of social media platforms by tracking and profiling dissidents, spreading propaganda and establishing false identities in cyberspace ('sock puppets') which poison popular trust. Social media can underpin repressive surveillance because data can provide information about a specific dissident and their connections. For example, during 2004 Yahoo provided information to China which helped to identify a dissident blogger, leading to his arrest and imprisonment arising from the content of his online expression.

Efforts to strike an appropriate balance between competing policy priorities in the use of social media, and not simply prioritising political participation, is an emergent regulatory development. Intergovernmental organisations composed of democratic states such as the Council of Europe have recognised that the internet enables people to access information, communicate and participate in

---

91   Ambeyi Ligabo, Special Rapporteur, *Report on the Promotion and Protection of the Right to Freedom of Opinion and Expression*, UN Doc A/HRC/7/14 (28 February 2008) [23].

92   Ethan Zuckerman, 'The Cute Cat Theory Talk at ETech', My Heart's in Accra, 8 March 2008, http://www.ethanzuckerman.com/blog/2008/03/08/the-cute-cat-theory-talk-at-etech/.

93   Sarah Joseph, 'Social Media, Political Change and Human Rights' (2012) 35 *Boston College International & Comparative Law Review* 145.

political deliberations.[94] Internet users should be empowered to exercise their fundamental rights and freedoms, make informed decisions and participate in the information society, including developing governance mechanisms and internet-related public policy.[95] However, the Council is also concerned that users tend to use a very limited number of dominant search engines whereby certain types of content or services may be unduly favoured. Those who are responsible for controlling the flow, content and accessibility of information over the internet ('gatekeepers') can either facilitate or hinder democratic deliberation and participation.[96] The Council is committed to protecting and promoting access, diversity, impartial treatment, security, transparency and media literacy.[97] Users should also be informed when personal data is used for profiling their behaviour.[98] One non-governmental organisation suggested strengthening the due process protections when blocking and filtering measures were requested by public authorities.[99]

Users of social media have a range of rights and freedoms which are not only limited to political participation. Nor is their interest in expressing opinions or information through a reliable, secure and safe mode of communication limited to social media. The Council of Europe recognises that social media services are human rights enablers and catalysts for democracy. Such services can enhance the participation of individuals in the political, social and cultural life of the state.[100] However, freedom of expression, privacy and human dignity can be threatened by social networking services which shelter discriminatory practices. States should co-operate with the private sector to help users understand the default settings of their profiles, inform users of the consequences of open access to their communications and ensure that users retain the right to limit data access.[101]

---

94   Council of Europe, *Recommendation CM/Rec(2011)8 of the Committee of Ministers to member states on the protection and promotion of the universality, integrity and openness of the Internet* (21 September 2011) [3].

95   Council of Europe, *Internet Governance Principles*, Conference entitled 'Internet Freedom: From Principles to Global Treaty Law', Strasbourg (18–19 April 2011) [4].

96   Emily Laidlaw, 'A Framework for Identifying Internet Information Gatekeepers' (2010) 24(3) *International Review of Law, Computers & Technology* 263.

97   Council of Europe, *Recommendation CM/Rec(2012)3 of the Committee of Ministers to member States on the protection of human rights with regard to search engines* (4 April 2012) [6].

98   Council of Europe, *Recommendation CM/Rec(2010)13 of the Committee of Ministers to member States on the protection of individuals with regard to automatic processing of personal data in the context of profiling* (23 November 2010).

99   Article 19, *Response to the Council of Europe Consultation on Search Engines and Social Networking Sites* (London, 2011).

100   Council of Europe, *Recommendation CM/Rec(2012)4 of the Committee of Ministers to member States on the protection of human rights with regard to social networking services* (4 April 2012) [2].

101   ibid [3]. See also Article 29 Data Protection Working Party, *Opinion 5/2009 on online social networking* (12 June 2009); 30th International Conference of Data Protection and Privacy Commissioners, *Resolution on Privacy Protection in Social Network Services*, Strasbourg (17 October 2008); International Working Group on Data Protection in Telecommunications, *Rome Memorandum*, Rome (3–4 March 2008).

Such solutions accompany proposals for global rules which ensure that the internet remains a democratic medium of expression.[102] The protections afforded to journalists, for example, could be extended to online authors.[103] Transparency, openness and accountability are the values to be promoted if political debates are to be enriched.[104] Individuals should be encouraged to participate in the ongoing dialogue on how social media tools are best regulated in the pursuit of democratic ideals. Ensuring that individuals are free to openly discuss the laws governing the conduct of their communities is moreover consistent with 'deliberative democracy'.[105]

Conclusions

Social media can mobilise populations for good or ill. It is conducive to democratisation insofar as this medium has the potential to enhance political participation by individuals. Social media facilitates enjoyment of the right to freedom of expression relatively unhindered by external controls and subject primarily to technological issues such as access and capability. The degree of political participation cannot be left to depend upon such technical aspects given the existence of 'digital divides'.

Although the utility of social media as a progressive political tool should not be overstated, governments can be made more accountable through this medium. Whereas social media is encouraging greater democratisation within authoritarian states, democratic states including Australia are moving towards tighter regulation. In this context what then is the nature of the conflict between legal restrictions imposed upon freedom of expression and democracy on the one hand, and the appropriate role of social media on the other? Efforts are observable within authoritarian and democratic states to regulate social media for legitimate purposes, such as addressing offensive content or for national security or law enforcement reasons. Governments are also seeking to match increasingly sophisticated communications networks with a more comprehensive surveillance and monitoring apparatus underpinned by law. Thus law inevitably has the potential to necessarily intrude into individual privacy, curtail the enjoyment of other human rights and suppress the democratic potential offered by social media. Stated at its highest, the use by governments of blocking

---

102   Ambeyi Ligabo, Special Rapporteur, *Report on the Promotion and Protection of the Right to Freedom of Opinion and Expression*, UN Doc A/HRC/4/27 (2 January 2007) [38].

103   Organisation for Security and Cooperation in Europe Representative on Freedom of the Media and Reporters without Borders, Joint Declaration, 21 June 2005.

104   Ambeyi Ligabo, Special Rapporteur, *Report on the Right to Freedom of Opinion and Expression*, UN Doc E/CN.4/2006/55 (17 December 2004) [79].

105   Robert Lukens, 'Discoursing on Democracy and the Law: A Deconstructive Analysis' (1997) 70 *Temple Law Review* 587.

or filtering technology violates the obligation of states to guarantee freedom of expression. This circumstance reflects the truism that the rule of law and technological determinism are engaged in a constant struggle for supremacy.[106] It is not a contest that will soon be resolved, if at all, and the context of social media presents no exception.

---

106   Joel Reidenberg, 'Technology and Internet Jurisdiction' (2005) 153 *University of Pennsylvania Law Review* 1951, 1973.

Notes on Contributors

Elisa Arcioni is a Senior Lecturer at the Sydney Law School. Prior to joining the Law School, Elisa was a Lecturer in Law at the University of Wollongong and an associate to the Honourable Justice Michael Kirby, High Court of Australia. Elisa teaches and researches in Australian public law. The focus of her current research is the concept of 'the people' in the Australian Constitution.

Joe Edwards is a Senior Lawyer at the Australian Government Solicitor, practising mainly in the areas of constitutional and administrative law. In 2013–2014, Joe was Counsel Assisting the Solicitor-General of the Commonwealth. He has also worked as an associate to a Justice of the Supreme Court of New South Wales. Joe graduated from the University of Sydney with a Bachelor of Arts and a Bachelor of Laws, and from New York University with a Master of Laws.

Anne Macduff is a lecturer at The Australia National University. Her academic interests relate to legal theory, social justice and law reform issues and legal education. She has explored critical race and gender theories and applied them to areas such as citizenship law, family law and migration and refugee law. She has also been active in researching the role of critical and reflective thinking in legal education, as well as continually developing her teaching and legal professional practice.

Niamh Lenagh-Maguire (BA/LLB (Hons, ANU) is an LLM candidate at the University of Melbourne.

Yee-Fui Ng is a Law Lecturer at RMIT University. She researches the interaction between constitutional/administrative law and politics. She has previously researched and taught at The Australian National University and Monash University. Yee-Fui has practised as a solicitor at top tier law firms in Melbourne, London and Canberra. In addition, she has worked as a Policy Adviser at the Department of the Prime Minister and Cabinet, a Senior Legal Adviser at the Victorian Department of Premier and Cabinet, as well as a Manager at the Victorian Department of Justice.

Graeme Orr is Professor of Law at the University of Queensland. He has written *The Law of Politics* (Federation Press 2010) and *Ritual and Rhythm in Electoral Systems: A Comparative Legal Approach* (Ashgate, 2015) and co-edited *Realising Democracy* (Federation Press, 2003) and *Electoral Democracy: Australian Prospects* (Melbourne University Press, 2011). Graeme is International Editor of the *Election Law Journal* and is completing a book with Ron Levy on *The Law of Deliberative Democracy* (Routledge, 2015).

Glenn Patmore is a Senior Lecturer in the Melbourne Law School and is a member of the Centre for Comparative Constitutional Studies at Melbourne University. His research interests include the law of democracy, constitutional law and republicanism. His book, *Choosing the Republic* (UNSW Press), was published in 2009, and was long-listed for the John Button prize for the best piece of Australian political writing of the year. He has also published two monographs, five books of collected essays, and numerous articles and book chapters.

Kim Rubenstein is Professor and Director of the Centre for International and Public Law, and a Public Policy Fellow at The Australian National University. A graduate of Melbourne and Harvard Universities, her research covers citizenship and nationality, and gender and the constitution. She is currently working on the second edition of her book, *Australian Citizenship Law in Context* (2002) and is the co-series editor of the Cambridge University six volume series, *Connecting International Law with Public Law*.

Stephen Tully is a barrister at Sixth Floor, St James' Hall Chambers in Sydney. He practises primarily in the area of administrative and government law and has an interest in several areas of public international law, including the practice of international law before national courts and the responsibility of corporations under international law. Most recently, Stephen edited *International Corporate Legal Responsibility* for Kluwer Law International (2012).

www.ingramcontent.com/pod-product-compliance
Lightning Source LLC
Chambersburg PA
CBHW041119280326
41928CB00061B/3441